T0372975

Praise for Joanne Harris

'So wise, so atmospheric, so beautifully written'
MARIAN KEYES

'I sobbed at the end because I couldn't bear to leave . . .
One of the world's finest storytellers'
JOANNA CANNON

'Haunting, obsessive and just a little nutty, like a freshly-
made praline'
ELISABETH LUARD

'Mouthwatering . . . your senses are left reeling'
OBSERVER

'Sheer pleasure from start to finish'
JAMES RUNCIE

'Sensuous and thought-provoking'
DAILY TELEGRAPH

'I devoured it in one go'
CHRISTOPHER FOWLER

'A place of magic and mysteries'
MONICA ALI

'A novel that shimmers with brilliance and truth'
KATE WILLIAMS

'Is this the best book ever written? Truly excellent'
LITERARY REVIEW

JOANNE HARRIS is an Anglo-French author, whose books include twenty novels, three cookbooks, and many short stories. Her work is extremely diverse, covering aspects of magic realism, suspense, historical fiction, mythology, and fantasy. In 2000, her 1999 novel Chocolat was adapted to the screen, starring Juliette Binoche and Johnny Depp. She is a fellow of the Royal Society of Literature, an honorary fellow of St Catharine's College, Cambridge, and in 2022 was awarded an OBE by the Queen.

JOANNE HARRIS

Vianne

ORION

First published in Great Britain in 2025 by Orion Fiction,
an imprint of The Orion Publishing Group Ltd.
Carmelite House, 50 Victoria Embankment
London EC4Y 0DZ

An Hachette UK Company

The authorised representative in the EEA is Hachette Ireland,
8 Castlecourt Centre, Castleknock Road, Castleknock, Dublin 15,
D15 XTP3, Republic of Ireland (email: info@hbgi.ie)

3 5 7 9 10 8 6 4 2

A CIP catalogue record for this book is
available from the British Library.

ISBN (Hardback) 9781 3987 1087 0
ISBN (Export Trade Paperback) 9781 3987 1088 7
ISBN (eBook) 9781 3987 1090 0
ISBN (Audio) 9781 3987 1091 7

Typeset by Born Group
Printed and bound in Great Britain by Clays Ltd, Elcograf S.p.A.

www.orionbooks.co.uk

This book contains references to infertility, miscarriage,
bereavement, homelessness, implicit racism and homophobia

To you.
Yes. You know who you are.

Bouillabaisse

I

22 July 1993

I scattered my mother's ashes in New York on the night of 4 July. I remember the scent of the harbour, and the warm wind over the sun-baked stone, and the sweet nostalgic trace in the air of pretzels, and doughboys, and garbage, and smoke, and the hot, sharp, dangerous scent of fireworks from the booming sky.

After that I was done with New York. That had been her dream, not mine. I spent our last dollars on a cheap flight to Marseille, and found myself three days later on a very different harbour front, looking out over the Mediterranean. The heat was the same, but there was a breeze, and a scent of salt and ozone coming from the water. I had the clothes I stood in and a single canvas travel bag, containing my papers, my wallet, a change of clothes, my mother's ring and the little toiletries kit they hand out in economy class. A battered pocket-sized map book of France and my mother's Tarot cards in their sandalwood box. I had barely five hundred francs, no family and nowhere to go. The name on my passport said Sylviane Rochas. Time for a change of scenery.

My mother and I have always kept largely to the cities. It's easier to disappear in a city, she used to say. Easier to be no

3

one. Easier to pass unseen. I never asked her why she longed so much for oblivion. But cities are crowded; impersonal; filled with people passing through. Cities are pockets to be picked; cheap hotels left without paying the bill; cheap food; second-hand clothes; no one asking questions. A child alone in a city provokes no curiosity unless she is clearly in distress. And I was a resourceful child who knew where to go; how to find things; how to source free food in markets; how to trade work for necessities. But now, for the first time, I was truly alone. My mother was gone, and so were her fears; the fear of staying too long in one place; of putting down roots; of the shadow. Of the shadow most of all – the Man in Black that pursued us. All gone now; all scattered into the breeze of the Hudson on that fourth of July. I was free.

Except it didn't feel that way. Total freedom sometimes feels like a kind of paralysis. So many choices. So many doors all clamouring to be opened. But with every choice we make, so many more must be put aside. Discarded futures, unknown friends; lives unlived and paths uncrossed. My mother had always been the one who had decided where to go. So many plans – and in the end, so little time to pursue them. And here was I at twenty-one, with nothing but choices ahead of me. I felt like something blown on the wind; disposable as litter.

That wind. Oh yes, I can feel it now. It changes its name as we always have: *Tramontane*; *Santa Ana*; *Sirocco*; *Levant*; *Ostria, Mistral*. I can feel it pulling me – to Italy, perhaps, or Spain; or along the coast to Montpellier, or inland, to Toulouse or Armagnac.

Which will it be, 'Viane, which will it be? Bordeaux, or Montpellier, or Nice? Rome, or Venice, or Milan? London, Oporto, Strasbourg, Berlin? But never a place we have been before. And never Paris. Never there.

4

I open the map book at random. Sometimes she used to do that, just to see what synchronicities might emerge. Spread before me, the pages reveal a section of the river Baïse, with a handful of little *bastides* clinging to it like leaves on a vine. It is a part of France that I do not know well, but to which I have returned at last, as if almost by instinct.

One of the bastides has a woman's name. *Vianne.* I like the sound of that. It's almost *my* name, but not quite; a name like a shoot growing out of a tree. A sign, perhaps, of things to come. A place of reinvention. It sounds like a good place to head for, at least until something better occurs. Yes, maybe I will head for Vianne, and find myself along the way.

For now, though, there are the questions of where to sleep tonight; what to eat; how to find my place in this city where I am a stranger. And there's something else, too. A kind of space inside me. Not grief – grief is not an absence. Grief is the weight of memories. The things you did together that you now must do alone. The knowledge that, even now, those memories are blurring like a chalked outline on a wall, and that soon – not today perhaps, but maybe next week, or next month, even next year – I will forget the shape of her face, the exact colour of her eyes.

I can see no trace of her when I look in the mirror. Only the shared things that come with a lifetime of companionship; the things that are etched on the body. Skin tanned by the same sun; the same laughter-lines around the eyes. We laughed a lot, my mother and I. I hope that my body remembers.

But there's a space. It *feels* like a space. Something waiting to be filled. A living potential, even in death; an echo of voices and laughter. If I were alone, I would read the cards to find out what the feeling means. *The cards know better than you do, 'Viane. Listen to what they have to say.* And now, at noon, by the water's edge, with the scent of diesel and salt and fried fish drifting over the harbour, it feels as if the answer is here, right here in the trembling air, waiting to reveal itself.

Looking up, I see a sky of perfect Virgin's-mantle blue, except for a double contrail, scratched against the summer sky. Its shape is almost like a rune, forking a path across the sky. It seems to point to the top of the hill that dominates the old quarter of the city; a hill topped by a blunt, square tower, like a fortress, crowned in gold. Sunlight heliographs from the tip. A cathedral? Where there is gold in a city like this, it always seems to belong to the Church. I know nothing about Marseille – though I will come to know it well – and so, for want of a better plan, I turn my face towards that gold splinter in the summer sky, and make my way up through the narrow streets, the many stumbling sets of stone steps, towards what I will soon come to know as Notre-Dame de la Garde, or to the locals, the Good Mother – *Bonne Mère*.

It feels like a long, long walk to the top. There must be a thousand steps to climb, linking the many cobbled streets. The cobbles are hot. I can feel them through the thin soles of my shoes. My legs ache, and suddenly I feel close to tears. I've felt that way a lot recently. I suppose it's only natural. My pregnancy is still in the very early stages, but I can already feel it. Something has changed. No nausea, but a sense of something building, like the edge of a storm cloud. I see serious trouble ahead. Not just because I am alone, or because I am too young, but because a child will anchor me. A child will force me to put down roots. I never learnt how to do that. She never allowed me to think that way. We were creatures of the air, nourished on light, on rainwater. The thought of responsibilities, of having *possessions* – even so much as a change of clothes – was dangerous. A precedent.

VIANNE

Stuff weighs you down, she used to say. *It makes you think you're special. It tells you that this piece of earth could be yours, instead of reminding you that we're insects on the skin of the world, dancing on a volcano.*

My mother talked like that a lot, especially in her last year, when the cancer had taken hold. We bought her medication from black-market sources in New York; strong opiates that dulled the pain, but which made her confused and volatile.

Why did I bring you? she used to say. *Why did I think you could save me?*

Of course, she wasn't herself at those times. But her changing moods had been a part of my earliest childhood. I remember the good days; the laughter, her delight at the smallest of things; and on her bad days, her growing fear of the thing that shadowed her. Later I came to understand. The Man in Black was a symbol of the future as well as the past. He was the reason we never stayed for more than a week or so anywhere; the reason she threw away my toys – the elephant, the old brown bear; Molfetta, dear Molfetta – whenever I got too attached.

He smells it on you, she used to say. *He knows when you begin to care. The only way to escape him is not to rely on anything, not to believe in anyone.*

I often wondered if that meant she would leave me behind some day. Some days I almost wanted her to. This is my secret shame, the fact that I sometimes *wanted* my mother to leave me behind. And now that I am soon to become a mother myself, I wonder if my child will ever think that of me, and dream of digging up the roots that I will have put down for her? Because I already know that this child will be the centre of my world. I feel that already, even though they are no more than a heartbeat. Just as I know that they will need a place to grow away from me.

7

That's what children do, 'Viane, my mother used to say to me. *They learn to grow away from you. Your job is to love them. Theirs is to escape from you. And you have to let them go, because that's what you owe to the universe.*

That was the lesson I had to learn, she told me, with Molfetta. Molfetta was a rabbit, the last and dearest of the toys of my early childhood. She was a kind of grubby pink, with a piece of ribbon around her neck, and I kept her with me for years. Even after I lost her, I whispered to her in the dark of innumerable motel rooms. I bathed her in the sinks of innumerable roadside cafés. She smelt of whatever passed for home in the furtive life we led, and when I was eight, my mother left her on a bench by a railway in Syracuse, to teach me not to get attached. *Because travelling light is easier.*

I don't know your name, I tell the child that is only a space in my future. *And yet I already know that, in time, you will leave me. Travelling light.* I try to banish the unhappy thought with a flick of the fingers. *Tsk-tsk, begone!* But the sadness endures. It always will. It's the price we must pay. It's a strangely adult thought for the girl I used to be; that girl who collected recipes and stolen menus from restaurants, and dreamed of meals she would never eat in places she would never stay. That girl who would creep back when my mother had fled without paying the bill in some cheap café, leaving the cash for the waitress to find in case she took the blame for our theft. I wonder how much of my mother remains now buried in my subconscious; how much of her has managed to cross over into this pregnancy. I wonder how much of my mother's debt to the world I will be expected to pay, so I can earn my happiness.

I promise, you'll keep your Molfetta, I tell the child inside me. *You'll keep her forever. We won't travel light. We'll weigh so heavy that the wind will blow right over us, into the hills.*

But my mother's voice is strong. *There is no gift without a loss. The world demands its balance. Be careful what you dream of, 'Viane. Be careful what you promise. Take what you can from the world, and move on before it knows what you've taken. Remember that, and you'll be safe. The Man in Black won't find you.*

The sun is hot. It burns my eyes. But looking up to the top of the Butte, I can see that the gleam of gold at the top of the tower is a statue of the Virgin Mary, holding the infant Christ in her arms. I don't know too much about churches. For many reasons, I don't attend. But this building – this basilica – has something attractive about it. Maybe it's the long cool slice of shadow that abuts it. Maybe it's the history ground into every cobblestone. Or maybe it's that mother, poised so high above the town, holding her child very tightly, in case the wind blows him from her arms.

Bonne Mère. Here in Marseille, it's a prayer, an oath, a profanity, an invocation. The Good Mother is here for all of us; in every part of our daily lives. She gives this orphan city hope; a memory of motherhood.

What makes a good mother, Maman? I don't know. No one sheltered me from the wind. Instead, you taught me to ride the storm, skimming the waters like a stone. Lose momentum, and you drown. Survival means never stop moving. I know what she would tell me now: that I should not try to keep this child. *A child is a stone around your heart. A child is a debt that must be repaid. Best give it back to the world,* she says, *before it changes who you are. Give it back to the universe before it drags you under.*

Too late, Maman. This child is mine. I cannot, will not give her away. It may be hard, I understand. It may mean difficult choices. But this is my decision, Maman; my first independent decision from you. It feels a little dangerous: almost like a

9

rejection of you, and of everything we were. But who was I really? And who am I now? These are all things that will take time to learn. But one thing I already know, Maman. I am no longer a satellite moving in your orbit. I am a mother. *Bonne Mère.* I hope I'll be a good one.

I reached the top of the hill at last. The door to the basilica stood open. Inside it was cool and smelt of incense and candle smoke. The ceiling was heavily gilded, and the arches were built in contrasting stones in dark-red and white, absurdly festive, like candy canes. The result was a bewildering harlequinade of colour and light, with sunlight reflecting the ceiling and with darker patches of shadow in the alcoves at each side.

A scatter of votive candles lights the entrance to the sanctum. I sit on a wooden bench by the door. Churches are cool in summer, and provide some shelter in winter. For a moment it feels good to sit there in the shadows, with no sound but the occasional soft shuffle of feet against the stones. I rest my aching head in my hands. It feels good to think of nothing. But gradually, I become aware that there's something beside me on the bench. It's some kind of fluffy toy, its fur worn to a peachy nap. In the semi-darkness, I cannot quite make out the colour, but there's a ribbon around its neck, and it seems somehow familiar, and when I lift it to my face, it smells of darkened rooms, and sweat, and hitch-hiking on dusty lanes, and fried food by the roadside, and the scent of library books. I know it's not, and yet I am sure that this is Molfetta, my childhood toy, veteran of so many roads, so many passing-places.

A sign. My mother saw omens everywhere. But why would Molfetta come back to me now? For a moment I feel the urge to slip her into my pocket. To have her as a touchstone. To whisper to her in the dark. And yet, perhaps there is a child looking for her somewhere. A child whose need is greater, and who needs to find a friend. And so I leave the toy behind on the bench for someone else. Someone who is lonely. And, with a flick of my fingers, I light an invisible votary at the feet of the Virgin of La Garde, and tell her, in the silent tongue that speaks more potently than words: *Hold onto your child, Bonne Mère. Make sure not to let him fall.*

And then I stand up, and leave the cool and dark of the basilica, and walk back out into the Marseille heat, where the dog days are just beginning.

2

Marseille is a city of extremes. Church and cobbles; gold and stone; food and famine; charity and the everyday cruelty of folk in a rush. It is the oldest city in France, dating back six hundred years before Christ, with all the human contradictions that entails.

Wealth comes from tourism, history, trade – and, of course, the Catholic Church, dominating the city in all its gold and gilding. Poverty lives in the *bidonvilles*, those shanty towns of corrugated iron and plastic containers, and plastic sheeting, and discarded doors. People here are both gaudily rude and unexpectedly warm and kind, much like the people we used to know when we lived in Naples. Poor people are like that sometimes; cold outside, warm inside. Maybe it's because the poor have to look after each other.

After leaving Notre-Dame de la Garde, I found an old-fashioned *bistrot* unsurprisingly called *La Bonne Mère* and ordered the set menu – *bouillabaisse*, with lots of bread, and a carafe of tap water. I realized I hadn't eaten anything since breakfast on the plane – a piece of fruit, a dry croissant, a cup of tepid coffee. The owner saw the way I ate and refilled my bowl without asking: the stew was rich with saffron and oil, and green anise, and orange. It's a cheap dish to make in Marseille: rockfish costs almost nothing. Mussels, too, are cheap, and squid, and the rock crabs that cost so much in elegant Paris restaurants are vermin here, good for nothing but stew. Food has a strange way of leaving home as a beggar and coming back a rich man, so the things we used to forage for free – wild greens, razor clams, wild garlic, herbs, shellfish, rock crabs, even snails – have been made into elegant dishes by chefs attempting to pique the jaded palates of those who lack nothing.

I still remember seeing the price of a dozen *escargots* on a menu in New York. How we laughed, my mother and I. *Those snails must have gold shells*, she said. *Who knew we were so fancy?* Grief hits me again. She's gone. No more laughing at menus. No more of her extravagant plans; no more of her fanciful stories.

'*Un p'tit pastis?*'

'No thanks, *monsieur*. I'm pregnant.' How strange, that I should need to tell my secret to this stranger. But secrets, too, are burdensome. Suddenly, I felt lighter. The bistrot owner, a stocky, stern-looking, grey-haired man in his fifties, gave me a smile.

'Congratulations. Here for a while? Maybe you're on holiday?'

I shook my head. 'Just passing through.'

I saw him look at my hands and note the absence of a wedding ring. 'Heading where?'

'I might follow the coast. I haven't lived by the sea for years. Or maybe I'll follow a river until I find a place to settle down.'

He frowned. His eyebrows were thick and forbidding, but underneath, his eyes were kind. 'You're very young to be alone. Do you have a place to stay?'

I thought of my five hundred francs, now reduced to three hundred and eighty-five. 'Do you know a good place? Clean? Not too expensive?'

He shrugged. 'Here in the centre, everything's twice as expensive as anywhere else. But out there, beyond the *14ème arrondissement*, the sleep-sellers will eat you alive.'

I know those sleep-sellers. I've met them before. Men in baseball caps and flares, with faces like the edge of a knife, and low, insinuating voices. Their hands are greasy from handling cash. Their eyes are like beads of frantic sweat. *Room for the night, miss? Room for the night?* And they lead you to a vertical slum, with cardboard homes on the landings, and shanty-buildings clinging to the roofs and balconies, where you will share a room with two other families, and where it stinks of urine and smoke, and where perhaps that night, or maybe the next, another man will drag you from your thin cocoon of sleep and throw you out into the rain because someone else paid a higher price for the space you occupied.

The bistrot owner brought me a cup of coffee with *navettes*, those little boat-shaped biscuits flavoured with orange blossom. 'I have a room above the bistrot that I sometimes let out to guests. A hundred and ninety. With breakfast. It's clean, and there's a lock on the door. I'm Louis Martin.'

'Vianne Rochas.' The name – not quite a lie – was out before I had time to think where it had come from.

'Unusual name. Is that short for something?'

'No.'

'Finish your coffee. I'll show you the room.'

It was a small and narrow room, high in the eaves of the building. From the south-facing window, I could see across the bay. A single bed with a yellow candlewick bedspread; a wardrobe. A basin. A porcelain jug. A pair of faded curtains with a floral pattern. It was good. It was perfect. I was aware that Louis had offered it to me because I was young, and pretty, and because I had said I was pregnant. But he was right: a woman alone is vulnerable in a place like this. Of course I had resources: skills I'd picked up on the road. But at some point in the next eight months, I would need to put down roots. I would need a home; a job. Somewhere permanent to stay. Right now, I had enough money for another night at the bistrot, and maybe another meal or two. After that, there was nothing left. Only the wind, the wall, and me.

'You can leave your things in there,' said Louis. 'They will be perfectly safe.'

I didn't have many possessions. My mother's box, with her Tarot cards. My toothbrush by the basin. My jacket in the wardrobe. I've always been good at making a place mine, for just a night or two. A handful of flowers in a vase. The pillows arranged how I like them. It's all just an illusion, I know – and yet, it makes it all seem less impersonal. As if there's a chance that I might one day find a place where I can say, *yes, this is home.*

I looked around the little room. Opened the tiny window to let in the scent of the ocean. I locked the door and put the key in the pocket of my canvas bag with my wallet and my mother's ring. The ring was gold; fourteen carats. A wedding ring, even though she was unmarried, because a woman alone, with a child, can sometimes attract attention. She'd bought it when I was a child, saying: *It's easier when people think you're married. Was* it easier? I thought. Should I keep it – *wear* it – so that people wouldn't judge me? But it wasn't judgement she feared. She was afraid to lose me. Perhaps someone had said something – suggested she was unfit to be a mother. Maybe even suggested that she was not my mother at all. I have a distant memory of a man in black – a priest – saying: *It's a sin, Jeanne. For the sake of the child, confess.* And afterwards, that night, she'd cried, and held me very close, and then, in the morning, we moved on, and she bought the ring from a pawnshop in Nantes, for the price of six nights at a hostel, and when I asked why, she told me: *This is how we go unseen. How we fool the Man in Black. Because he wants to take you, 'Viane. Because he's always hungry.*

I sold the ring. I found a place that offered cash for jewellery. A thin man with a jeweller's glass weighed the ring and gave me a price. Eight hundred and fifty francs, a little more than I'd hoped, but still not much. Enough to buy a few more nights, a few more meals. Enough for now. Of course, I thought, when my child is born, people will know that she has no father. But why should I care? Her father is gone. He was no one, nothing to me. Just a kind face and a bed when I was lost and grieving. I don't even remember his name – just the warmth of his brown skin and the scent of him, like smoke and sweat and cinnamon, and the way he slept with his arms around me for the rest of the night, and the way I fitted into his arms like a stone inside a peach.

I moved on after that one night. I've never needed longer. But for one night, I made him my own, just like those empty hotel rooms, and moved on into the world again as light as thistledown on the breeze.

Baggage only slows you down. Baggage, people, feelings. That was my mother's mantra, and it served us all these years, but now I needed to slow down. The space inside me told me that: the space that was the shape of a child, growing into the heart of me. I used some of my money to buy a pair of crocheted bootees from an old woman selling her work on the corner of Rue du Panier. They are shell-pink, and beautifully made, as intricate as antique lace. I shall carry them in the pocket of the canvas bag that has been my constant companion for all these years, so that by the time my daughter is born they will smell of the sea, and the lavender that I picked by the roadside in Puglia, and all the roads we trod, and the times the two of us laughed until we cried. By the time she is born, she will know. She will know *her*. She will know *me*.

'When's she due?' said the woman with the basket of crocheted things. She was old, eighty at least, brown-skinned, with bright little silvery flecks in her eyes and white hair under a shady straw hat. Her hands were like olive-roots, twisted and brown. In one she held a half-finished piece of work, a little white cap so intricate that fairies could have made it.

I told her. I noticed she did not question how I knew my child would be a daughter. The old woman smiled. 'A summer child.' Her voice was curiously accented, not with the harshness of Marseille, but with a bright, North African lilt. 'Summer children are filled with light. Here, take this.' She handed me a sachet, filled with scented herbs. 'Hang this in your wardrobe,' she said. 'In winter, your clothes will remember.'

I smiled and thanked her. With some of the rest of my cash, I bought underwear and some sandals. Then, in a tiny second-hand shop. I bought a white embroidered blouse, a silk scarf, a skirt with bells on the hem. An indulgence, I suppose, but the old woman of Rue du Panier had given me a sudden desire for my own things, in my own space.

In winter, your clothes will remember. I like that. I like even more the idea that perhaps I might still be here then. But I do not want Marseille for my child. My child will be born in a quiet place; a place in which she can thrive and grow.

17

Perhaps even that little *bastide*, by the side of the river. Still, that's for later, I told myself as I headed back to La Bonne Mère, where I slept without dreams and in comfort, and awoke to the sound of bells ringing from the summit of the Butte.

3

23 *July* 1993

It was half past eight when I went downstairs. A group of men – half a dozen of them, in sailcloth trousers, linen shirts and the flat caps of the region – were already sitting at the bar and at the two little tables that were set up outside on the street, drinking coffee and eating boiled eggs from a basket topped with a napkin. Flies were buzzing around the room: I saw that several were already caught on the long, yellow rolls of flypaper that hung from a rail above the bar. The radio was playing a pop song, something bright and American. Suddenly I missed New York, with its chrome, its diners, its talk, its greasy, enormous breakfasts; its pretzels by the roadside.

Everyone looked at me as I came down. It was silent. Uncomfortable. I greeted the men with a smile and a nod. Some nodded back; others stared.

'Breakfast's here, if you want it,' said Louis.

'Thank you.' I was hungry. There were eggs, and fresh baguette, and butter, and coffee, and apricot jam. I ate a lot of everything. We never take meals for granted, we who follow the wind. We welcome every meal as a gift; every night in a bed with blankets as a blessing.

'What's today?' said Louis. 'The beach? Sightseeing? Shopping? The Château d'If? The Canebière?'

I shrugged. 'I thought I'd walk a bit. Maybe get lost a little. I've always found that the best way to know a city is to get lost in it.'

A man with a narrow face and sharp eyes made a little, contemptuous sound. 'Only a tourist would say that.'

'Don't be a wet blanket, Emile.' Louis looked at me. 'You staying tonight?'

'If I can?'

'Of course. Lunch today is *pissaladière*, and a *crème caramel*. I make my own, so you know it's good.'

I finished my breakfast and picked up my bag. The regulars – all older men, with broad sunburnt faces and bright dark eyes – watched me with that mixture of curiosity and hostility I've seen so many times before. I smiled and drew a finger-sign across the palm of my left hand. *A pretty*, Maman would have called it. *A pretty opens up the air.* I flicked up a ripple of brightness, and saw the answering gleam in their eyes, as if I'd used a tiny prism to dance light onto their faces.

'Nice to meet you all, *messieurs*. I'm Vianne.'

'Haven't heard that name before,' said a man in a black beret. That's Rodolphe, a retired ex-primary teacher from Cassis. Married. Widowed. Three children. The dancing prism relays it to me in a series of rainbow images.

'You're not from here.' That was Emile: whip-thin, suspicious, angry. A painter and decorator by trade, anger shines out like a gas flame from the top of his bald head – anger, not at me, but the world, and at strangers in general. There's a secret sadness there, which the prism cannot relay. Something about a woman, maybe. Maybe something about a child.

Once more I smiled. 'No, not from here. I've lived in a lot of places.'

That close, suspicious look was for all the places that were not *this* place. I could feel him checking my clothes, my skin, my accent. Was my hair too curly, too dark? Was my skin the brown of the sun, or the brown of foreign shores? Once more I looked around the circle of sunburnt. I saw no active hostility there – except perhaps in the angry Emile – but for some people, anything new or different can be an attack. And I am *very* different and new, in ways that are not always visible. I felt it in New York, but here I feel it still more keenly. This circle of men is bound by time, and custom, and proximity. A very small circle, within which have played a number of dramas and comedies. I can feel their resistance to me, to the stranger from elsewhere, to the young woman in their space, with all her unknown quantities. And I can feel the need in them – the hope that someday, a stranger will come to change their lives forever.

You owe them nothing. My mother's voice. *No explanations, no concerns. No miracles. Not even a smile. Besides, these things are dangerous. Change summons the Man in Black. The more changes we make, the closer he gets.*

I banished the prism. My mother was right. These people were no business of mine. Other people's problems – their needs – were a distraction I could not afford.

I smiled. 'I'll see you at lunch,' I said. 'Have a pleasant day, *messieurs.*'

4

In a city like Marseille, people are always looking for work. People like me, unofficial residents, with no address or bank account. Homeless people, eking out a tiny living from occasional jobs. People sleeping in tents by night, and by day holding down a poorly paid job in an office or by the docks, ever fearful of being exposed to their colleagues as destitute. All of us looking for cash-in-hand employment; some of us immigrants; some living in the *bidonvilles*, those sprawling satellite cities of plastic and corrugated iron that stretch like octopus tentacles from the body of Marseille, to escape the *marchands de sommeil* and their promises of sleep.

I needed a job. Any job. Something to give me security. Maman and I did so many casual jobs over the years. Cleaning houses. Working tills. Waitressing in roadside cafés. Sometimes we picked fruit on farms, or gutted fish, painted houses, or walked dogs for ladies too rich to walk. Sometimes, when things were hard, we begged. More than once, my mother ran contraband over borders – a woman with a child is more likely to pass scrutiny. But as I reached adolescence, that stopped. I was glad. The money was good, and so were the forged documents that came with the job, but the risks were too high, and I hated the way she was in the weeks before our trips.

They'll take you away if I'm caught, she would say, frowning over her Tarot cards. *The Two of Cups. A good card. That's the kind of card we want. But here's the Chariot, reversed. That means trouble at Customs. Three of Swords. That means deceit. They'll try to cheat us of our cut. And Death. The Man in Black. A bad sign. It means he's catching up with us. One more run, then time to go.*

But now she was gone, and I was alone. Of course, I'd been alone before in the months before her death, when she was in no state to work. In New York, I'd worked for tips in a diner in Brooklyn, as well as cleaning a lady's house on a shady street in the Heights. Sometimes, I would wake in the night, and check to see if she was still breathing. Sometimes, I would leave early just to get away from her. Sometimes I prayed to the Man in Black, blasphemous prayers that revolted me. I was exhausted all the time. I was always empty inside.

Today, I thought, I will go out and search for opportunities. But my options are limited to those that do not need a paper trail. To *make* money, you *need* money, or at least, the trappings of it. A fixed address; a bank account; all the things we never had. *We are not respectable*, she used to say. She liked it that way. I am beginning to wonder whether I do. I am different. I do not need to reflect her. The thought of living in one place – for months, maybe for years – is like a reflection on water. A mirage, perhaps. A forlorn hope. And yet I feel it's possible.

I have not read the cards since New York. This makes me feel strange and untethered. All my life, I have followed them. Now, they are the only thing that links me to my mother. I feel I should have consulted them before heading out this morning. And yet it never occurred to me. It feels as if I am losing her. The thought is both liberating, and sad. I keep thinking about that village, Vianne. A tiny place on the river Baïse, a hundred kilometres north-west of Toulouse. *Goose-fat country*, she would have said, with all the contempt of the city-born for the regional backwaters. And yet the thought of it draws me, and not just because it shares my name. A little walled village on the Baïse, that offshoot of the great Garonne, with its orchards and vineyards and little farms and castles on the river. Maybe I will find myself there, after so many years of striving to be lost. And maybe that's where my child will be born, my daughter, my little stranger.

But first, I need work. I need money. I do not know if I could find work in Vianne. The trip would eat all my savings, leaving nothing in reserve. And it's easier to find work in Marseille, where no one asks questions. And so I spend all the morning visiting restaurants, asking for work. I've always enjoyed restaurants. The money is often cash in hand. Washing dishes; waitressing. Sometimes, the bonus of food snatched in haste, leftovers from someone's plate. My mother never cooked a meal. She saw food as a source of anxiety, not a source of pleasure. We lived off what was cheapest.

Secretly I collected menus, stolen from tables. Recipes, clipped from magazines, dishes I would never make. As we travelled, the dishes changed. I whispered their names like magic spells. Milan was *mondeghili*, served in a twist of paper, and *michette*, those puffy rolls that look like blowsy roses. Naples was *pasta alla Genovese*, and pizza with olives and anchovies, and Rome was artichokes in oil, and *cicoria*, with garlic and chilli, and twenty kinds of pasta. Berlin was *Currywurst* and beer, and blueberry pancakes, and sauerkraut. And New York was pieces of everything, brought over by generations of immigrants to remind themselves of home.

I look at the sun. I have no watch. The shadows show that it's long past noon. I try a café-restaurant in a courtyard, just off the Canebière. All syrupy with sunshine, with a crooked fig tree that casts its shade on the cobbles. I ask – perhaps for the twentieth time today – if there is an opening. Anything. Washing dishes. Waiting tables. Sweeping up.

The woman at the reception area is middle-aged; perhaps more polished than beautiful. I flash her a smile, but she only blinks. 'We don't engage our staff that way,' she says. 'We use an agency.'

It's the answer I have received all day, from every place I have approached. I know these agencies of old. They deal in desperation. Forty per cent of a person's wage goes to placate these monopolies. There are people eating at the shady terrasse, under the tree. The food must be good. The tables are full. The couple closest to me are sharing a bowl of *tapenade*. I realize now how hungry I am. I know that I have a meal waiting at La Bonne Mère, and run back towards Rue du Panier, getting lost several times on the way. By the time I arrive, the bistrot is empty, and Louis is wiping the tables. The outer door is shut, and the place looks dark and uninviting.

He gives me a look. 'Lunch is finished.'

'I'm sorry. I lost track of time.'

'Did you eat?' His voice is gruff.

I shake my head.

'I saved you a slice of pissaladière. I think it's better cold, anyway.'

The tart was good – sweet with onions and salty-rich with anchovies – and so was the little tomato salad that came with it, and the crème caramel to follow. The coffee came without my having to ask, once more with navettes on the side. Louis watched me eat with a look of oddly reluctant sympathy.

'This is really good,' I said. 'You say you make it all yourself?'

He nodded. 'My wife was a good cook. I still use all her recipes.'

His wife, he tells me, was Marguerite – Margot. She died nearly twenty years ago. She used to help him run the bistrot, and in cooking he respects her memory. I like that. I wish I had the same for myself. But I have never really *cooked* anything. Packet noodles. Boiled eggs. Toast. Things that can be prepared in haste in a hotel room, or a hostel, with only a kettle or gas fire. No pans. No cupboard. No ovens. No knives. No simple country recipes, handed down from my mother or my grandmother. I felt a sudden fierce desire for something beyond my mother's cards, my mother's incantations. To be, not the witch in the gingerbread house, but the harmless baker of gingerbread.

'Do you run the bistrot alone? No son or daughter to help you out?'

He gave me a look. 'We were never blessed.'

'*I* could help out, if you taught me,' I said. 'I'm a quick learner. And I need a job.'

Louis looked at me, surprised. I sensed his hesitation. I also sensed the grief in him, the memories he was keeping alive. Looking at myself through his eyes, I saw the young woman; her second-hand clothes. The promise of her. The *danger* of her.

I told him, very gently: 'Try me. You could use some help. I'm strong. I've worked in kitchens before. I'm not afraid of hard work. And if you taught me, I'd always be respectful of your wife's recipes.' And then I used my mother's trick; a pretty, in the palm of my hand, to shine a little light on his face; like the sun from a piece of mirror.

Louis has a fleeting smile that only comes out when his guard slips. It makes him softer, more vulnerable; it glances from his buried grief like the sun on a piece of mica. And in the reflections, I can see the fragments of her precious life. Marguerite at seventeen: carefree and girlish, giddy with dreams. Marguerite at twenty-three, after the first miscarriage, hoping next time would be different. Marguerite at thirty-five, those first silver hairs just beginning to show, twined in among her chestnut curls like filaments of angel hair – '*Heh.*' It is a percussive sound, as if the man is clearing his throat. I have already learnt that it can mean anything from approval to contempt. 'I suppose you *could* help with a few things. Shopping. Preparation. It wouldn't pay much. Food and board. I'm barely breaking even as it is.'

It was a start. I felt my heart beat a little faster. I nodded, sensing that a smile would feel too much like cajolery. 'That's good,' I said. 'When can I start?'

He gave me a look of suspicion. 'Not yet. We'll go to the market tomorrow.'

He goes to the market early, before the bistrot opens. The *Marché aux Poissons* opens as soon as the fishermen come in with their catch. For Louis, working on his own, it makes for a long and wearing day.

'Give me the list. I'll go,' I said.

'You don't know anyone,' he said. 'The traders will see you coming.'

'I'm used to market-traders,' I said. 'I promise, they won't short-change me. What are we making first?'

He made the dismissive sound again. 'You'll have to look at the recipes. Start with something simple enough for a complete beginner to try. But first, you need to get to know the kitchen. The utensils. The pans. The knives. The spoons. To understand a recipe you need far more than words on a page. You need to know how everything combines to make a recipe. So first, the kitchen.' He glared at me. 'Don't touch anything I don't tell you to.'

27

5

The kitchen of La Bonne Mère was tiny, cramped and
crammed with junk. An old-fashioned range, which must
have dated from sometime between the wars. A big, square
sink, all yellowed with time, and scarred with vicious scratches
and nicks. A dresser, which must once have been nice, with
stacks of cups and crockery. A big pestle and mortar in heavy,
dull ceramic. And there were pots and pans everywhere; some
dirty, some clean; some hanging from hooks on the walls, or
from the rack on the ceiling. Everything was chaos and grime;
the kind of ingrained, sepia grime that comes from decades of
fat-laden smoke. It gave everything in the tiny room a patina
like ancient bronze; and it smelt of sadness, and the ghosts of
summer days all gone to dust.

I forked a sign behind my back. *Tsk-tsk, begone!* My mother's
trick; to banish the ghosts.

Louis gave me a suspicious look. 'Did you say something?'

I shook my head.

'*Heh.* We'll start with the basics. Bouillabaisse. Everyone
knows that. You'll be using these utensils. This wooden
spoon. The mortar. The deep pot. And the *mouli.*' He handed

28

me the spoon; it was made from some kind of fine-grained wood, nibbled almost shapeless with time. It looked hand-made. I thought perhaps Louis himself had made it. People sometimes did, in those days. I wondered what it would be like to own such a thing. To use it. To know the history of every scratch, every burn mark, every scar. I ran my fingers gently along the well-worn wood.

'Never soak a wooden spoon,' said Louis. 'Just wipe it with a cloth. Otherwise the water gets into the wood and warps it.'

I nodded. I think I understand. He wants to keep her kitchen untouched. He wants to keep the marks of her hands on the kitchenware; the air she breathed; the fragments of her skin, her hair incorporated into the dust. He pulled down a big aluminium pot from the wall. Too large to be considered a pan, this too was old and blackened with age.

'Here's the pot we use,' he said. 'And then you'll have the *mouli*.' Louis indicated a large, chrome-plated utensil that looked as old and disreputable as the rest of the kitchen. A wooden handle, a series of discs, a metal sieve inside a pan the size of a washing-up bowl. 'We use this to sieve the fish bones out, and to purée the tomatoes.'

I touched the side of the *mouli*. It felt slightly greasy, as if he'd washed it in lukewarm water. I tried to imagine using it, turning the wooden handle. All these utensils are old, I thought. All of them have history. I wondered what it would be like to have history. To know the stories of everything – the tools, the pans, the recipes.

'Don't,' said Louis. 'Don't move things about. I need to know where everything is.'

I nodded. Yes, I understand. This kitchen is what's left of her. To him, the chaos is part of that, a darkness that must be maintained. It will be hard to work here. His grief is on everything like rust. I flashed him a little suggestion that maybe it would be nice to open the window, but he simply growled at me and opened a drawer in the dresser. There was a kind of bundle inside, tied with a grubby pink ribbon around a hand-stitched binder. As he opened it, I saw a series of handwritten pages, all in the same inelegant hand, some headed with what seemed to be quotations, some marked with coffee-cup rings, or wine, or grubby fingerprints. Louis, however, handled it with the reverence of a believer with a piece of the Cross.

'This was her cookbook. Don't touch it,' he said. 'These are all her recipes. I'll talk you through the recipes, but you mustn't change a thing. Not a thing, you understand?'

I nodded again. 'I understand.'

That sound again. '*Heh.* You'd better. Now. Bouillabaisse.'

His method of teaching is not unlike that of a master of martial arts, explaining the way of the sword to a pupil from the provinces. He lets me hold the wooden spoon. The rest, for the moment, is out of bounds. 'Just listen,' he says. 'And *feel* it. Cooking is feeling, not knowing.'

Margot's shapeless handwriting sprawled across the ragged page. *Bouillabaisse de Marseille*, it says. *One of Cyrano's favourites.*

Louis saw me noticing, and swept away the recipe. 'First, the aromatics. There's onion, garlic, fennel, thyme, saffron, cayenne and fresh orange rind. *Sauté* them all in olive oil, until the scents combine and begin to deepen. You still with me?'

I nodded.

'Fresh fennel, and some seeds, too. You'll need them both for this recipe.' He keeps his spices on a shelf by the side of the old black range. The fennel seeds are in a yellow tin that used to hold *Banania* drinking chocolate. The saffron is in a glass jar that once contained *Andros* cherry jam. He demonstrates how much I need; a big pinch of the fennel seeds; a little pinch of the saffron. He leaves the folder open, and once more I notice that odd little note, straggling down the side of the page.

One of Cyrano's favourites.

'Who's Cyrano?'

Louis dismissed the question with an impatient gesture. 'Never mind. Pay attention. Now for the tomato paste, and fresh tomatoes for sweetness. Go for the *Marmande* variety. It doesn't have as many seeds.' I must have looked a little blank. 'You do know what a Marmande is?'

'I'll learn,' I said. As a matter of fact, I was starting to feel a little overwhelmed. This was an *easy* recipe?

'Next, the fish,' Louis went on. 'You'll need a selection of rockfish. Conger eel, whiting, scorpionfish, sea bream, John Dory, red mullet. Get a selection. Get them cheap. See what they have most of. Buy the ugly ones. This is a soup for making the most of ugly fish, the fish that no one else can love.'

I nodded again. I had no idea what any of these fish looked like.

'Now add the fish in layers. You'll need to fillet the good ones, and keep the fillets for later. But heads and bones are good for this. Layer them all around the pot. Next, a baptism of white wine and a dash of pastis. Season everything as you go. Cover the fish with water and boil them till the fat comes out. This isn't a clear *bouillon* we're going for; we want it to look cloudy as sin. Then, cover the pot. Turn down the heat and let it simmer for an hour while you make the *rouille*. You'll need to blend garlic, egg yolk, cayenne and saffron with breadcrumbs in the mortar, and add olive oil, and pound it until it's all combined. You'll serve that with toasted slices of bread when the soup is finished.' He looked at me. 'Are you still with me?'

'Yes.'

'*Heh*. Now for the *mouli*. You'll use that to blend and separate the big bones and fish scales from your soup. Use the fine disc, and work it well – you'll need to use plenty of muscle. Then, you'll put your blended soup back into the big pot and poach the rest of the fish you kept by. Take them out as soon as they're cooked. You'll be serving them separately. You'll keep the soup warm on the range, and the fish in the warming-pan. Bring them out for people to help themselves. Serve the *rouille* in this flowered dish, next to the toasted bread slices. We usually get maybe half a dozen people in for the *plat du jour*: but everyone knows when it's gone, it's gone.'

Once more I nodded.

'Understood?'

'I'll get the hang of it. You'll see.'

It wasn't a lie – well, not quite. I *am* a very quick learner. The life I led with my mother meant I had to be adaptable. I have never been to school, although I have read a great deal – books bought from bargain bins, borrowed from libraries, found abandoned at bus stops and in railway stations. I can calculate the price of a basket of shopping in ten seconds flat. I speak four languages fluently, and can get by in several more. And I have so many maps in my head, so many passing-places, so many towns we loved, or fled, or sometimes settled in for a while, and I have absorbed so much history, so much culture on the way. But this is a new skill entirely. This is a different language. I cannot help but feel daunted at the many things I do not know, the instincts I have never learnt.

I try to imagine Marguerite working in this kitchen. I try to imagine her at my side, gently guiding my movements.

Louis' teaching style is abrupt. Hers would have been gentler. She would have laughed at his gruff ways. She would have opened the window. She would have sung to herself as she worked, heedless of who was listening. She would have been a good mother, although there are no signs in La Bonne Mère that any child was ever here. With Margot at my side, I can learn to be a different person. Someone who cooks, who listens, who cares; who does not hear the call of the wind, or follow when it changes.

6

24 *July* 1993

The *Marché aux Poissons* is by the old port, *Quai de la Fraternité*. A chaotic jumble of stands and stalls, some covered with umbrellas, some open to the morning sun. Some fishermen sell directly from their fishing boats; others from buckets and baskets and pots covered in layers of seaweed.

I'd expected something more organized. Labels, at least, with the names of the fish. But nothing here was labelled, and I knew hardly anything about fishing. I recognized oysters and lobsters, although I'd never eaten any myself, but what were those hideous spiny things, and the fish that was mostly head and teeth, and the sleek opalescent creatures with no eyes and feathery tentacles?

No one seemed to be queuing here. There were already plenty of customers in front of the stalls, all of them apparently certain of what they wanted. I lingered by a display of fish for long enough to provoke annoyance, both from a woman behind me and from the fishmonger himself, a man in a yellow waterproof and a sour expression.

'Are you buying fish, or what?'

'I – I need to make bouillabaisse.'

34

The woman behind me pushed to my side, and said: 'Six red mullet. Even size.'

The fishmonger reached over and took six fish from a pile. They were sleek and colourful, the shade of an autumn sunset, with eyes like glazed opals. I stood aside while the woman paid, holding my basket at arm's length. Then I repeated, a little more loudly: 'I have to make bouillabaisse. Louis sent me. From La Bonne Mère?'

The man looked up. 'Louis Martin?'

I nodded. 'He says I should get whiting, scorpionfish, John Dory—'

A woman from another stall said: 'Too fatty. Spiny lobsters. That's what you need. It'll make the broth nice and rich.'

Another said: 'Shellfish. Mussels. Crabs.'

Soon, everyone was shouting out the names of whatever they had on their stand, and I was there with my basket, feeling foolish and out of my depth, hearing their voices like clattering pans and suddenly wanting my mother so badly that I could almost cry –

'Don't listen to them. I know what you need.' The voice came from a stand to my left. Looking across, I saw an untidy-looking blondish man, aged between thirty or thirty-five, in cut-off jeans and a Hawaiian shirt, watching me from under the brim of a battered woven-straw hat. He picked up a piece of newspaper and rapidly selected fish from the display in front of him. 'Mullet. Rockfish. Sea hen. Wrasse. Eel. A couple of scorpionfish.' The man wrapped the fish in the paper and handed it to me with a smile. 'There. That should do it.' The smile broadened at my doubtful expression. 'Trust me. That's what you need for bouillabaisse.'

My mother used to say that a lot. *It's what you need* – while handing me one of her herbal charms. *Sandalwood, to sweeten your dreams. Rosemary, to remember. Trust me. It's what you need.*

I put the fish into my basket. 'Thank you. How much do I owe you?'

The man grinned. 'Oh, it's not my stall. I'm just waiting for my friend.' He indicated a battered grey VW van idling on the far side of the street. 'Hop in, won't you? We'll drop you off.'

I frowned at him and paid for the fish, remembering all the times I'd paid for something my mother had taken by stealth. Then I followed him to the van, lured by the thought of avoiding the long climb uphill to the bistrot. The passenger door made a terrible grating sound as I opened it. Another man was sitting at the wheel. Tall; mid-forties; short beard; greying hair tied carelessly back from a pleasant, expressive face.

'This is Mahmed,' said the man in the Hawaiian shirt. 'I'm Guy. You can sit in the middle.'

I climbed into the ancient van, which smelt of something unexpectedly sweet. A glass charm shaped like a round blue eye was hanging from the rear-view mirror. I used to have one of those, when Maman and I were travelling through Greece. A charm, to ward off the evil eye; a charm to make us invisible.

'Are you Greek?' I said to Guy, as he climbed in behind me.

'Not that I'm aware of. Are you?'

'I'm a little of everywhere.' That's what my mother taught me to say when people asked me where we were from. A little of everywhere, like seeds awaiting their season to flourish. Guy said something to Mahmed. Too low for me to understand, but I caught the name of La Bonne Mère, and saw something pass between them, a gleam that was warmer than friendship.

He turned back to me. 'And *your* name?'

'Vianne.'

'Like the bastide in Lot-et-Garonne?'

36

'Yes, like that,' I said, surprised. 'Have you ever been there?'

Guy smiled. 'I was born in Toulouse,' he said. 'But my grandfather lived up in Moncrabeau. I loved that part of the country. I wanted to live there forever. But most people want to move to the coast. Somewhere they can earn money.'

'And what do you do for money?'

He smiled. His eyes were a complicated shade of grey-green, like trees in winter sun. 'We're setting up a business. It's still a few months away from being completely up and running, but when it's finished, we'll be—'

'Golden,' said Mahmed, with the grin of someone who has heard this joke many times before.

'That's right. We'll both be golden,' said Guy. 'You'll see, o ye of little faith.'

'It's not my *faith* that's the problem,' said Mahmed. 'It's your sanity, my friend.'

Guy shook his head. 'It's the future.' He turned to me again, his eyes shining. 'See what I have to deal with?' he said. 'Scepticism and disrespect?'

Mahmed laughed. There was something good in that laughter; something I recognized, but had not felt since my mother fell ill. The inside of the van was warm, and I could smell the heat of it, mingled with that sweetness I could not quite identify; a sweetness like a childhood I only ever knew from books, a scent of vanilla and spices and cream, of bedclothes dried in the sunshine. And beneath it, a more complex scent of autumn leaves and petrichor, of forests that never see daylight, of sunken ships and pirate gold and fireworks and woodsmoke.

'What *is* that?' I said, looking back at the pile of boxes at the back of the van.

Guy smiled. 'What do you think?'

'I can't quite place what it is,' I said. 'But it smells almost familiar. Is it some kind of spice?'

'Not quite.' He paused, almost reverently. 'These are roasted *Porcelana* beans, from Peru; a subvariant of the *Criollo* bean, maybe the best – and the rarest – cacao beans in existence.'

'Cacao,' I said. 'You mean—?'

'Chocolate.'

7

I didn't have a sweet tooth as a child. My mother could never afford it. That didn't stop me being curious, though. I saw the advertisements. The displays. The names of sweets and chocolates. A packet of chocolate raisins. A cup of instant hot chocolate. The memory of a little bar of *Poulain* chocolate, handed to me by a stranger in a railway station; the Easter displays in the *confiseries*, with chocolate hens and ducks and fish nestled amongst gleaming bouquets of cellophane and ribbon.

I used to wonder who bought those things, those plump chocolate hens on their spun-sugar nests for the price of a room in an *auberge*; those little packets of toasted pralines for the price of a dozen loaves of bread. As a result, I'd never learnt to really appreciate chocolate. To me, it was an indulgence, not worth the time or the money. And then, when we were in America, the chocolate seemed so different, so greasy-sweet and tasteless that I never really wanted it—

Guy shot me a comical look of horror and indignation. 'What do you mean, *you don't like chocolate*?'

'It's not that I don't *like* it,' I said. 'But I was never used to it.'

39

'We're going to have to fix that,' said Guy. 'Come over to our place tomorrow, and I'll show you what we do.'

We were approaching La Bonne Mère. Mahmed stopped the van by the side of the kerb, the brakes squealing alarmingly, and as Guy helped me with my basket of fish he handed me a printed card with a name and a street address.

'A *confiserie*?'

'If only,' said Mahmed. 'We might have a chance with a *confiserie*. Right now, all we have is debts, no cow and a handful of magic beans.'

Guy shook his head. 'Don't listen to him. He's a cynic. Just be there tomorrow, and I'll show you around. Good luck with the bouillabaisse!'

And then, with a terrible tortured sound of metal and rubber, the old van made a U-turn and set off down the cobbled streets in defiance of the one-way sign, vanishing in a cloud of exhaust back towards the esplanade.

Louis was waiting by the door. Two of his regular customers were already at their tables. I recognized Emile, the painter-decorator with the narrow, angry face, now nursing a café-cognac and a buttered roll. 'I'm back!' I said to Louis. 'I think I managed to get everything.'

Louis frowned at the sight of my basket of fish. 'What about the tomatoes? The onions? The fennel?'

Damn. Between my hesitation over the fish and meeting Guy and Mahmed, I'd forgotten to detour via the vegetable market.

'I'll run to the *épicerie*,' I said. 'It won't take me a minute.'

Louis' frown deepened. 'The *épicerie* won't have the Marmande. You'll need to go to the market. That's going to eat up your cooking time. Who was that, in the old grey van?'

'Some friends,' I said. 'They gave me a lift.'

Louis made a sound of disapproval. 'Planning a meal takes serious thought. It's not going to work if you waste time hanging out with your friends.'

'I'm sorry,' I said. 'I won't be long.'

I left the fish in the pantry and ran with my basket to the vegetable market. Here the wares were labelled, and I managed to find the Marmande tomatoes, as well as the other ingredients; sweet onions; green fennel and fat bulbs of garlic as big as my fist. It was nine-forty when I got back, and Louis was looking sour and stressed.

'You should have started an hour ago,' he snapped, as I entered, tired and flushed. 'You'll need to hurry up if it's to be ready on time.'

I nodded and made for the kitchen. The utensils Louis had shown me were on the table, ready. The chopping-board. The pestle and mortar. The pans. The knives. The *mouli*. It all looked suddenly daunting, especially when I unwrapped the fish and saw the amount of cleaning and filleting and gutting I would have to do.

I took a breath. *It's only lunch. How hard can it really be?*

The hand-stitched binder of recipes – one could not quite call it a recipe *book* – was standing propped up on the shelf, showing the topmost recipe – *Bouillabaisse* – in Marguerite's earnest writing. Below it, I saw she had written a date: 19 July 1959, and a line of poetry:

> *Take joy in all flowers, fruits, even leaves*
> *That come from your own garden.*

So, Margot was a romantic. She makes the preparation of food into a kind of poetry; I cannot imagine *her* daunted by kitchen utensils, or ugly fish. She grew her garden; picked her herbs, took joy in them, one leaf at a time. I wonder what's left of

41

her garden now. A glance out of the window shows an over-grown patch of wilderness; a few old roses climbing the wall; a fruit tree; a thicket of rosemary. But Margot tended her garden then; grew leeks, and onions, and bay. Margot took joy in all of it, and brought that joy to her kitchen.

I took a deep and calming breath.

First, the aromatics.

Soon the kitchen was filled with the scent of freshly chopped fennel, garlic, herbs, orange peel, thyme, and aniseed. At least it *smelt* like food now. I felt a little better.

Next, the chopped tomatoes.

The Marmande tomatoes are beefy and large, with flesh that yields mostly texture, and few seeds. Their scent is deep and fruity, like damsons steeped in rich red wine. And maybe it is the thought of Margot working in her kitchen, or the scent of those aromatics, but now I am feeling more confident, wielding the utensils, first with care, and then with pleasure; aware that these things all have history, that they all have stories to tell.

So many ingredients to add; so many stages to process. Does Louis really consider this a *simple* dish? Or is this a test of character, to make sure I have the right attitude? He has deliberately not come into the kitchen to watch. 'I'll know when I taste the soup,' he told me. 'I don't need to watch a performance.'

And so I find myself singing as I stir the tomatoes into the pot; as I add the *Pernod*; as I fillet the fish. The sunlight enters through the small window over the sink; I have left it half-open to allow the steam to escape, and I can hear the sounds of the city – the traffic, the horns of delivery vans, the voices of passers-by, the calls of street-vendors, and the drone of an aeroplane overhead – a city sound that is somehow uniquely

Marseille, just as the sound of New York was uniquely New York, in spite of the many shared ingredients that make up the recipe.

Margot's voice is clear on the page; kinder than Louis', and gentle. *Now layer the fish for the broth base. Be kindest to the ugly ones.* I use a variety of fish, hoping that they are the right ones. Thanks to Guy, I know their names. Their flesh is still a mystery. Heads and bones remain for this dish; everything goes into the broth.

Glaze the pot and add water.

It's working: I can see it in the way the vapour rises. *Good.* And now I can almost see Margot's face in the little tendrils of steam; the face of a woman I barely know except through the words of this recipe.

I've always been able to do this. My mother had different names for it: *scrying, truesight, divination.* I thought of it simply as looking through the present into the future. Or in Margot's case—

The vapour from the pot has thickened as the broth boils. No subtle bouillon, this, but a murky confusion. Have I made a mistake? The broth is as opaque as my thoughts. Colours swirl in the vapour; a painted sign, with letters that I can partly make out – G. *Lacarrière, terie, Xocolatl* – but which make no sense to me. A battered grey van. A river, unimposing and brown, bracketed by wooden-framed houses, warped with age, that lean drunkenly into the slipstream of a handful of colourful narrowboats, with smoke coming out of the chimneys. And then—

There. There she is.

The breath catches in my throat like a fishbone. A little girl, maybe five or six, with candyfloss hair and a wistful smile. *Oh. My daughter. My summer child.* I know it just as I know the feel of my mother's Tarot cards in my hand. But the Tarot cards have never shown me anything as clear as this. My daughter, by this river, in this place I do not recognize, but which I already think of as home.

'Vianne? Are you listening to me?' It was Louis' voice from behind me, sharp now with annoyance. 'I *said* you need to hurry up, not go to sleep over the pot!'

I turned down the heat under the stew. 'I'm sorry. I must have—'

Louis shook his head. 'There's still too much for you to do. I will have to take over.'

'No, don't do that!' I protested. 'Let me do this. I know I can.'

He shrugged. 'I have a quiche on standby. I'll serve it with a salad if the soup isn't ready on time.'

There was no clock in the kitchen, and the last time I wore a watch was before my mother took us to New York. *There's time*, I told myself. *There's time.* I glanced at Margot's cookbook. *The rouille. You'll need the pestle and mortar for this.*

The pestle and mortar are larger than any I have seen before. A wedding present, perhaps, or maybe handed down from a relative. Garlic, egg yolk, and saffron. It smells both rich and harsh, like the accent here; a taste I have yet to acquire. Add breadcrumbs, cayenne and olive oil to make the paste. Good. It's working. Now to strain and thicken the soup. The *mouli* grins like an evil clown.

'How do I even assemble this?' The disc of the food mill is like the teeth of a circular saw: designed to crush and separate the larger bones and the scales, and to grind the smaller ones into something approaching the right texture. It wasn't easy: the *mouli* was old, and the hand-operated grinding mechanism was exhausting to use, apart from which, if I failed to keep the pressure consistent, then the milling disc had the habit of releasing and falling into the stew. By the time I had strained

44

and puréed the whole, the sun was no longer filtering through the window, and a kind of lull had fallen outside.

Lunchtime.

On the bright side, the broth looked good, and the rich scents of cooked fish and herbs and saffron and wine were deepening. I added the final layer of fish to poach in the broth, toasted the bread for the croûtons, transferred the lot to the soup tureen, added *rouille* to the toasted slices. Then, I covered the tureen, and carried it into the bistrot.

Nine faces turned to meet me. I saw Louis, Emile and Rodolphe, and some others, whose names I did not yet know. I saw their expressions, smiles and frowns. Used plates stacked up on the trolley. By the clock on the wall by the door I could see that it was one-forty-five.

Louis gave me a dark look. His colours were a gathering storm. I said: 'I used her recipe. I tried so hard to do every-thing right. But recipes are like children. You can't just put someone else in charge and expect them to behave themselves.'

For a moment I saw no change. I stood there, with the heavy tureen getting heavier with every second. Then he shrugged, and I thought his expression softened, just a little.

'Lunch is over, Vianne,' he said. 'But – if anyone wants to try the bouillabaisse, I won't charge extra.'

If anyone's curious. That was the point. Louis wasn't the only one I had to win over, and his regulars were less easy to read. There was Emile, watching me with a look that might have been satisfaction; and Rodolphe, pretending not to see, but gazing into his coffee cup; and a man whose name I did not know, feeding sugar to a dog at his feet. None of them seemed to be curious. None of them seemed to care that I was waiting, the tureen in my hands – and why should they? Who was I to them? A stranger, a woman who didn't belong, an intrusion on their routine—

And then I saw her sitting there, at a table by the door. It was the old woman from Rue du Panier, the one who had sold me the pink bootees. She had taken off her straw hat, but I recognized the snapping dark eyes beneath the halo of white hair, and the smile, both wistful and mischievous.

'You can do better than that,' she said. 'Come on, Vianne Rocher, don't tell me you're going to let a handful of old men intimidate you. This is your place – if you want it. But don't expect them to hand it to you.'

What did you call me? I wanted to say. But her words had struck a chord. She was right. *It's only lunch. I've been through so much worse than this.*

I took a breath and realized that I was trembling with anxiety and exhaustion. I raised my voice, and addressing the room, said: 'Well, I don't blame you for being suspicious. It's the first time I've made this recipe. In fact, unless you count making coffee, or adding hot water to instant noodles, it's the first time I've made *any* recipe. So try it. Taste it. Say what you think. But don't just leave me standing here.'

There was a silence, during which my heartbeat seemed to fill the world. All I could do was hold my breath and try to smile, and hope for an end to the silence.

Then—

'If it's free, I'll try it,' said Emile.

I felt all the breath in my body compress into a kind of ball in my chest. Suddenly, the room was too hot; the colours too bright; the smell of beer and coffee and smoke too strong for me to bear. I looked for the woman from Rue du Panier, but couldn't see her any more.

I put down the tureen. 'Thank you.'

And then I passed out cold on the dusty floor of La Bonne Mère.

8

24 *July 1993*

I awoke to the sound of voices, and the feel of a damp cloth on my face. 'It's all right,' said Louis. 'Just give her space!' I opened my eyes. 'You're going to be fine. You shouldn't have missed breakfast.'

'What about the bouillabaisse?'

The regulars were mostly standing around, looking both apprehensive and obscurely guilty, as men of a certain age often do when faced by women's weaknesses – except for Emile, who was still in his place, calmly eating bouillabaisse.

'Needed more pastis,' he said.

Louis turned and snapped at him: 'The last thing *you* need is more pastis.' He looked at me anxiously. 'Are you all right? Is it something to do with the baby?'

'I'm fine,' I said, sitting up on the bench. 'I overtired myself, that's all. What do you mean, it needs more pastis?' This was to Emile, who by now had finished his bowl of bouillabaisse and was eyeing the dish of toasted bread. I looked at Louis. 'I did everything just the way you showed me. I want to learn.'

Louis gave me one of his looks. He has reverted to his earlier position of watchful mistrust. I sense that my youth

47

is a problem; my pregnancy still more so. He wonders if I will change things. He wonders if I will break his heart. Not in any romantic way – all that ended with Marguerite – and yet I remind him of her, somehow. I trouble his composure.

Grief is love with nowhere to go. That's what my mother used to say. And there *is* love inside him. It's like a seam of something bright between two layers of bitter rock. But he has learnt to live with his grief. At least it is familiar. Love, on the other hand, is not. Love, and its dangerous sibling, Hope. I sense these things in Louis, and his resistance to their influence. I sense that, in spite of his kindness, he would rather I did not stay.

My mother would not have persisted. She was used to moving on. But there is something in me now – something like an anchor – that wants something more than the open road. It wants the constraint of being wanted. It wants the familiarity of its own utensils, burnished smooth; it wants the sounds of a place it knows inside-out, to the smallest detail. I flashed him a tiny, hopeful thought. It shone all around the dingy room like light shining through a moving prism.

I looked at him. '*You* try it,' I said. 'Try it. See if I went wrong.'

He shrugged, and picked up a spoon from the bar. Tried the broth; tried a piece of fish. Tried a sip of the broth again, and said: 'Next time, pissaladière.'

I hid my smile behind my hand. *Good.* For now, at least, I was in.

9

Sunday is the day that Louis goes to see Margot at Saint-Pierre. It is a grand old cemetery, replete with the tombs of the wealthy, but Marguerite isn't buried there. Instead, she rests in what they call *La Cathédrale du Silence*; a modern mausoleum not unlike the high-rise flats of the poorest neighbourhoods, in which the dead are stacked, ten thousand deep, in identical concrete alcoves overlooking the necropolis.

In this city, the dead have as many problems finding accommodation as the living; and this was the cheapest option. Of course, he doesn't own the plot: it's only rented for twenty-five years, and after that what's left of her will go into the *fosse commune*. He expresses this sentiment with deliberate brutality; although I can see the colours of his grief like a nimbus around him. But Louis is deliberate; the words – like these visits to the cemetery – are a form of penance. I sense it as he prepares to leave; the suit that he would have worn to church paired with well-polished shoes and the hat he only wears on Sundays. And I can see it in his walk; as if every step is on broken glass.

His schedule is almost immutable. He takes the nine-forty bus to Saint-Pierre in the 10ème arrondissement. He gets

49

off by the cemetery, and although he is not allowed to lay flowers by her concrete cell, instead he brings a single rose to the tomb of Edmond Rostand, author of *Cyrano de Bergerac*, which Marguerite considered to be the most romantic of love stories. This is her place, he tells himself, and not that concrete eyesore. Wouldn't anyone prefer the grave of a great French poet to a high-rise rental for the dead, cold and filled with strangers?

Of course Louis told me none of this. Instead, he left me with a list of jobs to do around the house, along with a curt instruction to rest. I rushed through the chores at speed, then went to look at Margot's recipes. I took care in handling the book; the pages were brittle as Bible-skin, and covered in footnotes and crossings-out. I tried to count the recipes – there must have been fifty pages or more, with many recipes from the Dordogne, from Monpazier to Bergerac. *Grandmother's Pescajoune. Simone's foie gras. Maman's candied walnut tart.* Many of these recipes have a family connection. All have a date, indicating when the page was added. And many have little side notes: *Make this up the day before: it tastes much better heated up! A recipe against sadness. Serve with a glass of good red, and a smile.*

I wonder how long it will take me to learn to make all of these dishes. A month, at least, assuming that I learn two recipes a day. *That's a long time to stay in one place. More than enough to get attached.* To my mother, attachment was death. *The Lovers,* the most dangerous of all the cards in the Tarot pack. *We have each other,* she would say. *That's already danger enough.* And so we moved on like shadows, from village to village, town to town. We slept together in the same bed. My friendships were as brief and bright as a handful of flowers picked by the road; lasting a couple of days at most; forgotten as soon as we moved on. By the time I started to notice boys,

I knew the rules. *Take what you need, but Love is too heavy to carry.* I wondered how she could reconcile that perspective with keeping me. But now, I'm free to write my own rules. I can stay as long as I choose, make friends as I choose, dream as I choose. Four walls, a job, a family – things I only know from books. And love; not like flowers picked by the road, but love like a tree that grows and bears fruit. Love that shines on the good days, and weathers the bad days like a storm. Love like a set of wooden spoons. *Love like Louis and Marguerite.*

I put back the bundle of recipes on the shelf in the kitchen. *One day I'll have my own recipes,* I told myself. *My own kitchen. One day perhaps, my own café, or a little shop of my own.* I can see these things in the smoke that rises from the harbourside. I can even see my child – slyly, from the tail of my eye. I sometimes feel as if I could reach out and take her in my arms. But there's no man in these dreams of mine; not even my daughter's father. Perhaps that's because I'm already complete in a way that Margot was not.

Recipes are like children, I thought, remembering the bouillabaisse. Maybe she felt that way, too. Perhaps she lives on in her recipes, the way others do in their children. Perhaps that's why she feels so close when I am in her kitchen. And perhaps it is my pregnancy that makes me aware of her presence.

The kitchen clock said half past one. I remembered my promise to Guy and Mahmed to visit their *chocolaterie.* I took the keys to the bistrot from the hook behind the door. Then, I locked up and made my way on foot, towards the address Guy had given me. *Xocolatl.* Allée du Pieu; no street number.

It took me a while to find it. The Vieux Quartier of Marseille is a warren of cobbled lanes, some almost too small for access, over which hang sheets and washing-lines, and little balconies crowded with flower pots and garden chairs and children's toys and votive figurines. And I'd expected a *chichi* place, like the chocolate shops in Rome and Milan. Instead I found a cul-de-sac, half-blocked with rubbish and packing-crates, where hung, above an unnumbered door, between a Chinese takeaway and a long-defunct print shop, a shaky, handwritten cardboard sign bearing the word: *XOCOLATL*.

The door was a dark and ancient green, chipped in many places to reveal the ghosts of businesses past. I couldn't imagine any of them to have been successful; the place had a sad look of neglect and decades-long dereliction. I knocked, and heard sounds of machinery; eventually the door opened a crack and I recognized Mahmed, wearing his hair in a messy bun, and wrapped in an apron that – judging by the stains – might have been worn to commit a particularly gruesome murder.

'Oh, it's you. Come in,' he said, opening the door wider. 'Guy's in the shop. I was cooking.'

'Cooking *what*?'

He looked down at his apron. 'Chocolate. What else?'

It didn't look like chocolate to me, and I said so. There was a scent, though: a dark, fruity, fermented scent, like someone's home-brewed wine gone wrong. I wondered if there was a still hidden away inside the building.

'I know it looks like blood,' said Mahmed. 'This is raw cacao liquor, bled from the fruit of the cacao tree. Bled at some cost, in fact, although Guy assures me that this is the only way to do it.'

I looked uncertainly at my surroundings. The place looked less like a shop, and more like a kind of shelter, in which crates and metal drums had been piled chaotically from floor to ceiling. A passage, lit by a naked bulb, led to a clearer space, and I followed behind Mahmed as the scent of fermentation grew, until I found myself in a room that looked like a kind of laboratory. Glass jars and demijohns against one wall; in the centre, a long metal table covered with something like almonds, but with a dry and dusty look that made me think they must be old.

'Cacao beans,' said Mahmed.

I picked one up and crushed it. It felt at the same time greasy and dry. But the scent it released was complex; dark and sweet and throaty. It made me think of ancient maps and places long-forgotten. Vanilla, from the scented isles. Saffron from Morocco. I thought back to that little bar of *Poulain* chocolate; as a child, I'd never asked myself what it was, or from what part of the world it had come. But there was history in that scent; history and a terrible age. And yet there was also childhood; a half-remembered sadness; a memory of different skies; a sweetness all but forgotten.

I looked up from the crushed bean in my hand to find Guy standing next to me, holding a cup of something. 'The Mayans and the Aztecs drank this thousands of years ago. Go on, taste it. Give it a try.'

It tasted bitter, like wormwood and sloes. He smiled at my expression. 'They called it *xocolatl*. The name means 'bitter water'.

'Oh.' I understood the shop sign now. 'Do you think people will understand the reference?'

He shrugged. 'Maybe they'll learn something.'

Mahmed's tone was censorious, but his eyes were warm and soft. 'Maybe they don't *want* to learn anything. Maybe all they really want is Easter eggs, and chocolate mice, and little boxes of pretty things to give their wives and girlfriends.'

Guy shrugged again. 'So what? They'll have them, too. You'll see, at our grand opening.'

'I'm saying there are easier ways,' said Mahmed, in the voice of a man who has said this many times before.

Guy grinned. 'Who wants easy?'

'*We* do,' said Mahmed, returning his smile. 'We both do. Easy, and very lucrative.'

I laughed. Mahmed joined in the laughter, and once again I saw in him that gleam of warm affection. 'I think you're in the wrong business, friend,' said Guy, then, turning to me again, took my arm. 'Come on,' he said. 'I'll show you how the magic works.'

IO

Like so many staples in the long history of humanity, chocolate is a thing that goes through many complex stages. Over
the next couple of hours or so, I saw the dried beans become
something else: saw them roasted, winnowed and ground;
peered into the conching machine that mixes the liquor
continuously and at a constant temperature, until it is smooth
and even. I even drizzled chocolate into the ceramic moulds,
which, cooling, would transform it into the kind of chocolate
I knew.

There is a kind of magic, says Guy, to this transformation.
He talks about it in a way that reminds me of my mother,
and more recently, of Margot. Not that my mother ever
cared for cooking or ingredients. But she understood the
process of changing base things into gold. She understood
magic, if magic means the transformation of the mundane
into something extraordinary. And she understood the power
of dreams, and narratives, and stories. Like her, Guy is filled
with stories about his favourite ingredient. Finally, by the time
I left, my head was ringing like a church tower. Don Juan
and Montezuma. Queen Catherine and Ixcacao. Popes and

priests and strange old gods with pointed heads and bloody hands. Temples ten times older than Rome. Golden urns, still bearing the dregs of bitter water from long ago, brewed with spices and served when France was still just a scatter of fiefdoms, bound together by forest and hills. *Food of the gods*, they called, it, *Theobroma Cacao*, and prized it more than common gold, and served the chocolate kings of old in cups of abalone and turtle shell.

How my childhood self would have loved the stories that he told me; stories that leaped and flashed in his eyes like pennies in a fountain. I fell in love a little that day – even though I could already see that nothing could happen between us – and even now, looking back, I feel the warmth of his passion, his smile a shining light along the way.

By the time I got back to La Bonne Mère, Louis was home from the cemetery. He glanced out from the kitchen, where he was making pastry.

'Where were you?'

'I was with a friend.'

'The same friend as the other day?'

I nodded, sensing displeasure.

'You need to watch yourself,' he said. 'A girl alone – a pregnant girl. You need to be on your guard. This is a city that eats girls like you.'

I wondered whether he understood that I had always been on my guard. I wondered if he understood that there were no other girls like me. I also wondered if he was always so brittle and disapproving when he had been to see Marguerite.

I dropped my bag onto the countertop and looked into the basin. 'What's that?'

'*Pâte brisée*,' said Louis. 'For tomorrow's *tarte Tatin*.'

'Will you let me help?'

He sighed. 'You can slice the apples. Use the smallest paring knife. And don't slice them too thinly. Otherwise they'll turn to mush.'

I nodded. 'Thank you, Louis.'

'And wash your hands first. What have you been doing?'

I looked down at my cacao-stained hands. 'My friend makes chocolate,' I said. 'He was showing me his shop.' In fact, I realized now that Guy hadn't shown me the shop at all: simply a series of dingy back rooms, in which the stages of winnowing, grinding, conching and tempering arose like islands from the sea. I still had very little idea of what the shop itself was like, although despite Mahmed's pessimism, Guy had assured me that it was progressing nicely. The grand opening had already been planned for 4 December, the Festival of Sainte Barbe, which marks the start of Christmas in Marseille.

Louis looked, if possible, even more disapproving. 'What did you say this man's name was?' he said.

'Guy.' I suddenly realized that Guy hadn't told me his surname. 'Guy, er—' I reached for the card with the address of the chocolaterie. 'Guy Lacarrière,' I told him. 'He works with his business partner, Mahmed.'

I've learnt that Louis has a repertoire of small and disapproving sounds. '*Heh*,' he said. 'Don't know the name. Where is it?'

I gave him the street name. 'Allée du Pieu.'

'I know it,' he said. 'It's a shithole. No one's going to buy chocolate there.'

I shrugged. 'I hope they will,' I said, and went back to my apples.

Ganache

I

31 July 1993

Over the course of the past week, I have learnt half a dozen new recipes. As I learn them, I write them down in a notebook I bought from the Tabac down the road. *Panisses*, those chickpea fritters sold by vendors on every street corner, and served with *harissa*, tomatoes, or roasted halloumi, or grilled sardines; navettes, the little orange-flower biscuits Louis serves with coffee; *fougasse*, that crispy Provençal bread, enriched with olive oil and herbs; *pieds paquets* in spicy tomato sauce; olive *tapenade* with salt lemon *confit*. It feels good to learn, and Louis admits that I may have an aptitude. He has grown warmer towards me. The customers are happy. I am even allowed officially to handle the book of recipes.

Each one has a story. This *tapenade* is the first thing she made, when she was only eight years old, in her grandmother's kitchen. This is her mother's *clafoutis*, made with the fat yellow cherries from the tree at the back of the garden. And these *pomponettes* are what she made for the guests on her wedding day; scented with orange blossom and sprinkled with nuts and sugar. *Orange is the scent of hope*, she writes in hasty handwriting. *A promise of something small and sweet. A vow, built from spun sugar and dreams, melting in the sunlight.*

I wonder if their marriage was as happy as Louis implies. I sensed it on my first day; I taste it in her recipes. There is a longing, a wistfulness there. I see it in the little notes scribbled in the margins, notes which are sometimes quotations from her favourite poet. *Laugh every day, so as not to weep. Fill your belly with laughter.* And there are stories in everything; stories Louis sometimes passes on. Every cup, every kitchen knife has a story to tell. This rolling-pin was his mother's. This wooden spoon he made for her, with wood that he bought from his first paid job, delivering newspapers on his way to school. His parents were poor. They taught him to work. Love was a lesson he learnt later on.

'This was a present to Margot on our anniversary.' He points to a painted plate on the wall. *Good Lord bless our happy home.* A chink has been knocked out of the side, as if by a piece of thrown crockery. In the vapour rising from a pan, I see her features pulled down like blinds. It was not always a happy home. His grief eclipses the memory. Thus we erase the bad times we endured with our loved ones. Soon my memories of Maman will be nothing but sunshine.

But I can almost hear her now; her murmured prayer, her sobbing. Next to her bed, there's a basket of *santons*, those little porcelain figurines they sometimes hide in the *Galette des Rois*. *Give me a child, Lord. Give me a child. Without that, what else is there?*

This afternoon, between cooking lunch and opening up for the evening, I went to call by Allée du Pieu. The chocolaterie is still under renovation, and although it looks better than it did – rotten beams replaced; a semblance of order around the front – it is still far from ready. Mahmed is in charge of all that: the plastering, the woodwork, the electrics, the plumbing of the stoneware sinks, the fitting of the counters.

Guy seems mostly oblivious to the work going on around him – at least until he notices plaster dust or smoke in the air, which he says will taint the precious cacao liquor in its bottles and demijohns piled up in the back rooms.

I found him today in the front space, the space that will become the shop, mixing cream and chocolate into an enamel bowl, while Mahmed, in the back room, was cleaning out the conching machine. The radio was playing very loudly, there was cacao dust everywhere, and the atmosphere, as always, was filled with chaotic energy.

'Throw me out if you're busy,' I said. 'I just dropped by to say hello.'

Guy grinned. 'Never too busy for you. In fact, you've come at an excellent time. I need a volunteer to taste one of my newest creations.' He gestured with his wooden spoon at the trolley behind him, on which were stacked metal trays of some kind of chocolate confection.

'I made these in a hurry,' he said. 'I had to make a batch of ganache because *somehow*, water got into the conching machine.' He raised his voice at this last part, making sure Mahmed could hear him.

'I can't help it if your machine hates chocolate!'

Guy grinned again. 'He hates that thing. I've told him he has to befriend it.'

I thought of the terrible *mouli*, and smiled. 'I sympathize with Mahmed,' I said. 'Louis' kitchen is a minefield, too.'

'Condensation's the killer,' said Guy. 'If it gets into the machine, the water will ruin the chocolate. You can sometimes salvage what's left by adding cream, but it doesn't keep. Which means now I have three hundred of *these* . . .' From the trolley, he picked up a chocolate, rolled in cacao powder. 'These are ganache truffles,' he said. 'The easiest chocolates to make. Even a child can make them. Even Mahmed could, probably.'

I took one. It smelt of darkness infused with gold; a scent that both drew and repelled me.

'I don't really like dark chocolate,' I said.

'Just try one. I made them myself, from bean to bar. Nothing artificial.'

I bit a piece from the chocolate. It was bitter and powdery, but there were other flavours there, struggling to be released.

'Rest it on your tongue for a while. Eyes closed. Mouth half open.'

I did as he said. The bitter scent started to intensify. It's odd; I didn't quite like it, and yet it was evocative. I can taste charcoal, and nutmeg, and salt, and olive, and strong wild honey. It makes me think of incense, and woodsmoke on a frosty night, and the scent of fallen leaves in the rain, and the memory of that night in the church, the warmth of the confessional.

I thought I didn't like chocolate. In fact, I never knew it. Those little squares of chocolate I'd had as a child were nothing like this.

'I know. It's different,' he said. 'It's eighty per cent cacao. It might taste a little bitter to you, but that's the nature of cacao: the stuff you get in shops here is really mostly sugar and palm oil and fat. But this is the soul of the cacao bean. This strength. This bitter potency. And in this form, it has a kick. It sharpens the mind. Gives energy.'

I put the rest of the chocolate aside. My mouth was furred with darkness.

He grinned. 'Don't you like it?'

'Not at all.'

'That's because you don't know it yet. Trust me, you'll get used to it. Here. Let me show you. You make one.'

In less than a week, recipes have become a part of my daily life. Margot's recipes, and now Guy's, each with their own mysteries. First he shows me the chocolate ganache – cream and butter and chocolate, melted together and left to chill – and then hand-rolled into a palm that is covered in cacao powder. And yes, he's right. It's easy. Easy, and somehow compelling.

'Try another. Take your time. Your palate will have adjusted by now.'

Once more, I try a truffle, resting it gently on my tongue. The cacao powder tastes earthy, somehow, like the dust of a distant land. And the centre is strangely bittersweet, but smooth as butter on the tongue. I don't know yet if I will ever like it. But it's interesting; it makes me want more.

Guy smiles. 'I told you, didn't I? I'm using *Forastero* beans right now. They're the most affordable. But once we're open, I'll be using the oldest, rarest varieties; the ones the Mayans and Incas used, deep in the Amazon basin.'

He makes it sound like travelling. I tell him so, and he smiles again. 'Perhaps it is,' he tells me. 'We don't just travel on roads and seas. We travel in stories and in dreams. Here. Try this. I made it.' He hands me a jar. A tiny handwritten label says *Xocolatl*, in brown ink. Inside is something that looks like dry soil, although it must be chocolate. He tells me: 'It's a condiment. You can put it in anything: stews, soups, coffee, even desserts – for an extra little kick. It isn't sweet; there's no sugar in there. Keep it. Tell me how it works. It's a *very* old recipe, from the time of the Chocolate Kings; handed down by Ixcacao, goddess of love and compassion.'

I take the jar of chocolate spice and bring it back to La Bonne Mère. I dare not use it in cooking here – Louis' orders were quite specific – but maybe I can use it in some other way. It feels meaningful as those pink bootees from the woman on Rue du Panier; as if somehow, together, they might reveal a glimpse of the future.

2

Only two weeks into my stay, I already have more possessions than I did when we were travelling. Colourful clothes bought from charity shops; the baby bootees and the scented sachet. The notebook in which I am writing Margot's recipes, one by one. Not much in the way of things, and yet I know what she would have said. *Too much baggage slows you down.* And yet today, I want to go slow. I want to be a tree; grow roots.

Roots, routes. Such similar words, and yet such different meanings. That contradiction has always been there. The urge to stay. The urge to run. Maybe my child will change all that. I look at the little pink bootees from the old woman on Rue du Panier. Already, the scent from the herb sachet has given them a memory: lavender, geranium; the scents of early summertime. My sense of smell has become more acute since the start of my pregnancy. Now I can smell the city in layers, emerging from the morning mists. First, the soft, salt scent of the sea; the fish market at the old docks; the sun-warmed streets, the bakeries. Then the flower market; filled with scented carnation, mimosa, gardenia and damask rose. Then the long climb up the hill to Bonne Mère, and the frankincense, and under that, the sweat of grief and guilt and worship. I wonder if that other child recovered her pink rabbit, or whether her mother, like mine, made her leave it by the road.

Tsk-tsk, begone. I banish the thought. It is the very simplest of spells. Even a child can use it. Children feel anxiety very keenly; as a child I learnt to banish those bad thoughts, those fears with a sound and a gesture. It has become a reflex since then; a simple means of grounding myself. Magic is mostly the belief that we can change ourselves, the world, our fate and other people. My mother liked to surround herself with rituals to remind her of this. I carry on those traditions now for comfort, as well as in memory of her.

My own child has lain very small and silent since the bouillabaisse. I feel her, like the ceramic bean baked into the crust of a galette des rois. She lives, but is not lively: awaiting the change of the seasons. *A summer child*, the old lady said. *Summer children are filled with light.* But my child will be born in March. A windswept, change-of-the-seasons child; sunny one day, in darkness the next. I feel that in her; that fugitive gleam, like sunlight on the ocean. And in my dreams I see her; always at five or six years old. Her hair is a tumbled candyfloss cloud. Her name comes in endless variants of my mother's name, Jeanne: Anne, Annette, Jeannette, Johanne, Jolène, Annie – *Anouk.*

Yes, that's it. *Anouk.* It's right. It binds us. Names are powerful things. In names, we build our identity. It occurs to me that I have changed my name. When the time comes, will she change hers? It seems an odd source of anxiety. This sense that I will lose her before I even have her. But my mother was just the same; always running, always afraid that somehow, someone would take me away. I promise myself

I will not be like that. I will find myself in my place. My child – *my Anouk* – will grow up safe, surrounded by familiar things. Not here, perhaps, but this will be my stepping-stone to safety.

Children are hope in a lifetime of woe, writes Margot in her recipe book. Above it, there's a recipe for green almond biscuits with apricot jam, and a series of fat, splashy stains that might have been tears, or just water. Like my mother's Tarot cards, Margot's recipes are a means of processing her experiences; of establishing some control – even some power – over her world. Maybe this is why I feel so different nowadays, so calm. Maybe by cooking her recipes, I too am beginning to change.

Louis, too, has mellowed with time, and no longer sees me as an intruder. I have full access to everything now: I am even allowed to choose my own cooking pots and utensils. I take this as a sign of trust. Even his customers have begun to see me as more than someone just passing through. I know them now: there's Rodolphe, who has a bad hip and a passion for model ships. Tonton and his dog, Galipette, who share the love–hate relationship most often seen in old couples. Then there's Emile, and his friend Henriot, and Monsieur Georges, an ex-schoolmaster whose pupils – in their sixties now – still find it hard to use his first name without the additional mark of respect. Then there's Amadou, from Tangiers, and Hélène from the flower shop down the road, who loves pocket romances, and often comes in with her friend, Marinette, who arrived in Marseille from Paris during the war under somewhat mysterious circumstances.

I don't know their stories, and yet I am starting to know most of their favourites: Emile likes anything that is free, but especially my bouillabaisse; and Henriot loves my crispy *panisses*; while Monsieur Georges loves seafood, and hates anything with cabbage; and Marinette has a sweet tooth, and always wants more of my peach *Tatin*, while Amadou says my *galettes-merguez* are as good as anything he tasted back home.

Not that it's always perfect. There have been some misadventures: a clafoutis that stuck to the pan; an over-ambitious cheese soufflé. No one learns without making mistakes. Even magic sometimes goes wrong. But it feels good, to see these folk satisfied: to see their plates come back empty. None of them are quite friends, of course, and yet these are the faces I see every day; the threads of an emerging tapestry that might one day become my life.

I have not seen the old woman from the end of Rue du Panier since the day of the bouillabaisse. I would have liked to have thanked her for her encouraging words that day, but she has not been in the bistrot since then, and I have not seen her selling her work in any of the markets. I have dreamed of her though: in the chocolaterie, sitting in a rocking-chair, with a baby on each arm. One was wearing pink crocheted bootees; the other blue. Otherwise, they were identical.

Choose carefully, Vianne Rocher, she said. *Only daughters follow the wind.* And in my dream I felt a chill, and understood that this was a choice: on the one side, my Anouk, and a wind that would never stop blowing; on the other, a little boy who would never hear its call. And in my dream I knew that this was the price of putting down roots: that the wind would steal the child of my heart and replace her with a changeling.

Tsk-tsk, begone. They're only dreams. No one is going to steal my child. No sly wind will blow us away. And yet I still feel uneasy; perhaps because I am happy here. Happiness, my mother said, can never be a constant. The only constant thing is Change, the wind that drives our destiny.

I finally read the cards last night. Perhaps I'm feeling guilty, somehow. The scent of the wooden box is like a memory from another world; the cards familiar as my palm, almost shuffling themselves. I use the pattern my mother preferred and try to make my mind go blank. The Lovers. It should be a good card, but my mother always mistrusted it. Next comes the Hermit; a man by a cave, carrying a lantern. Next, comes the falling Tower, reversed; meaning disruption and turbulence. The Six of Swords, a card that means grief, alongside the Fool, which means carelessness, and the Four of Cups, reversed, a card of mistrust and uncertainty. And finally, comes Change, the card we always associated with the wind, a card of places left behind; of hopeful plans abandoned.

This is a dark combination, Maman; suggesting secrets, uneasy plans, bad decisions, careless love. And yet there is no sign of danger on the horizon. Quite the opposite; I feel a quiet domesticity, a calm I've never felt before. Margot's cookbook tells me that life can sometimes be calm and loving; that life can be filled with flavours and scents; that a dream can be small and sweet, and rooted in security.

Nothing has to change, she says, under a recipe for navettes. *The tide comes in and goes back out. The seasons keep on changing. And yet some things can stay the same. Little things. A kiss. A touch. A dream. A love. A recipe.* Sometimes, when I'm cooking, I feel as if she's in the room beside me. Like my mother's cards, I suppose; except that the cards tell me to run, and the recipes tell me I am home. I put my mother's cards away. Recipes are easier.

Guy's chocolate spice is hidden away at the back of the spice shelf in the kitchen. I have not yet tried to use it, remembering Louis' stern warnings about changing Margot's recipes, but it draws me somehow; the scent of it, the age of its long

71

tradition. Stories are filled with magic, and this spice has so many stories to tell. Like any art, it longs to be used; longs to cast its seeds on the wind. But so far, the only chocolate I have introduced to La Bonne Mère are the chocolate truffles I made with Guy, rolled in cacao powder.

'What's this?' said Louis, as I brought them in with the coffee after lunch.

'Just something I'm trying,' I told him.

'We have navettes with coffee,' said Louis. 'We always have. Why change it now?'

'It's just an experiment,' I said. 'I like learning to make new things.'

Emile tasted a truffle, and pulled a face. 'Too bitter,' was his verdict.

But Tonton and Monsieur Georges seemed to enjoy the experiment, and Marinette, who purports to be more sophisticated than the rest, took three. 'These are very good,' she said. 'Let the girl experiment. It's nice to have something new for a change. Reminds me of *La Bonne Praline*, a chocolaterie I knew in Paris.'

'*Heh*,' said Louis. 'All right. I suppose. But don't go adding anything new, or *experimenting* with my recipes.'

I promised I wouldn't. And yet, that jar of spice calls to me from its high shelf, dreaming of other places. It's a magic my mother would probably have recognized; a magic like the wind, that calls to us when the seasons turn. And somehow I am certain that whoever I am meant to become, this new ingredient will somehow be part of that transformation.

3

8 August 1993

On Sundays I have the day to myself as Louis goes to the cemetery. I tend to use this time to see Guy and Mahmed at Allée du Pieu, where, over the past few days, they have been teaching me more about chocolate.

As I have learnt since I came to Marseille, everything has a story. Every recipe has a kind of transformation inside it. First come the roasted cacao beans, like so many moth cocoons awaiting rebirth. Next, the removal of the skin, and the separation of the two halves of the bean from the tiny connecting piece that Guy calls the embryo. This has to be done by hand, he says; that's why the process takes so long. That embryo is what makes raw cacao taste so bitter. That's why the finished chocolate will be richer and more complex. This is a job that Mahmed hates, and as he frequently points out, the end result is entirely disproportionate to the amount of time and effort expended.

But Guy is quixotic. He insists. To him, the process is everything. He tells me this as he shows me the next stage: the cracking and crushing and winnowing of the beans to make cacao nibs. He has a small machine for this, about the

73

size of an oven, which delivers the nibs at the end of a steel funnel. Next comes the grinding and conching; a lengthy, deliberate process which allows the cocoa butter to melt and break down into a smooth paste. At this point, Guy adds the sugar, milk powder and extra cocoa butter to the paste, then allows the chocolate to cool and set; then leaves it to rest for a couple of weeks to allow the flavours to deepen.

This is *couverture* chocolate, he says. It isn't ready to use yet, though: first, it must be tempered, to bring it from its dull, friable consistency to a smooth shine and a good, sharp snap. Some *chocolatiers* use machines for this, but Guy, of course, likes to do it by hand, in the kitchen, using a big copper pan and a sugar thermometer. It all seems rather daunting at first; but no more than Louis' terrible *mouli*. Guy promises to teach me. And the lovely summer days sail by in cooking, and in laughter, and the wind is steady from the south, and everything is simple.

Be careful, says my mother's voice in my mind. *Beware of this feeling of permanence. Our kind do not put down roots. We do not follow recipes. There is a reason for this, 'Viane. Or have you forgotten that, too?*

I push my mother's warning back into the box of Tarot cards. Let her stay there, I tell myself. That voice is just the part of me that feels afraid of happiness. But that was your fear, Maman, not mine. These doubts are just the fragments of the little girl I used to be. I am re-inventing myself, writing my own story; changing my name to fit the course that I have chosen for myself. The old woman called me *Vianne Rocher*. Not Rochas, but *Rocher*, like the chocolate. This seems meaningful, somehow. As if that village on the Baïse and the chocolaterie on Allée du Pieu might both be part of my future. And before I settle anywhere, I need to learn how be Vianne. How to live my own life instead of the one she chose for me.

4

14 August 1993

Another week at La Bonne Mère, and I have learnt to make six more dishes: pan-fried trout in butter sauce; seafood tempura with *aioli*; Margot's grandmother's *crème brûlée* with spiced apricot compote; Margot's mother's *pot-au-feu*, with beans and new potatoes, and Guy's chocolate ganache cake, which I presented (rather anxiously) at lunch yesterday, alongside a more traditional lemon tart from Margot's book of recipes. Louis looked dubiously at the cake, but Emile took two pieces, and Marinette swore it was almost as good as the ones in the pâtisserie window.

'Your friend Lacarrière teach you this?' said Louis, who had still not tried the cake.

I nodded. 'He's teaching me how to make chocolates.'

Louis shrugged. 'Well, if you enjoy it—'

I take this as permission. And yet he's oddly reluctant to try my chocolate recipes. And although Louis has permitted me to do some cleaning around the place, the kitchen still belongs to Margot and keeps her memory alive. I understand his reluctance to change, having recently lost someone dear to me, and yet after years of mourning her, doesn't he deserve happiness?

75

Doesn't he deserve to love? It suddenly occurs to me that this is what the cards were trying to tell me that night. Not a warning, but a *direction* – a means of giving me a goal. This is how I become Vianne: this is how I escape the past. Not by running away, but by helping this man who has helped me.

The Lovers. That must be Louis and Margot, flanked by the Six of Sorrows. The Hermit: that's Louis as he is now, surly and withdrawn. The Four of Cups; La Bonne Mère, bonded in grief like a creature in amber. And Change – that must be me, I think. Change, like the dance of the seasons. Change, like the turn of a friendly card; as simple as a passing cloud: as bittersweet as chocolate.

'I'll bring you some more coffee,' I said, and went into the kitchen. The little jar of chocolate spice was there, on a shelf, with the spices. The label read: *Xocolatl.* Of course, that's the name of the chocolate shop, but I sense it means something more to Guy. The word for *chocolate* is the same in every language in the world, he says, with a few spelling variants: and every variant comes from this, the Nahuatl name, brought back by the Spanish invaders. There's power in these things, I know; power in the stories. And there's power in desire; power in the passion of dreams.

I opened the jar. Guy's xocolatl smells of the ground after a short, hot fall of rain; of spices ground by hand in the dirt; of perfumes known to me only from stories. Here was vanilla, silphium, cardamom, ginger, and saffron. Here was cassia, star anise, fennel, mace and turmeric. But here too were stories of the great chocolate kings: Montezuma, Moctezuma, Itzcoatl, and Tizoc. My newly enhanced sense of smell could sense all this and more in the jar; carefully, I took a pinch and added it to the pot of coffee. Then I poured a cup of the brew, and took it out into the bar.

'Try this.'

Louis looked at his cup suspiciously.

I smiled. 'Just try it. I made a new blend.'

He shrugged and picked up the little cup. Drank his coffee slowly.

'Do you like it?'

He gave a shrug. 'It's coffee.' But he finished it, and I saw that his colours had shifted from sullen green to sunny rose-gold, and thought to myself: *it works, it works*, and hid my smile behind my hand.

And this morning, at breakfast, I added a pinch of xocolatl to the foam in Louis' *café-crème*, and a pinch to Emile's *café noir*, and to the pot of hot chocolate I made to go with the croissants, and the scent was so beguiling that half my regulars tried a cup, and some came back for a second.

'Hot chocolate at breakfast,' said Emile with a sneer that somehow combined greed with contempt. 'What are we now, children?'

I smiled at him. 'I tried something new. Maybe you could do the same.'

Emile shrugged. 'I'll try it, for free.'

It's easy, when you know what to do. Guy showed me the recipe. Milk, in a copper-bottomed pan. A scoop of grated chocolate. A generous pinch of the chocolate spice. All served in tiny espresso cups and flanked with fresh pastries and butter.

'On the house, Emile,' I said.

I saw Louis' eyebrow shoot up. I said, too low for Emile to hear: 'Trust me. It's just an experiment. Let's see if there's a demand.'

5

Today is 15 August, the Day of Sainte Marie, *Bonne Mère*, the Virgin of Notre-Dame de la Garde. The bistrot is closed for the day, and Louis has gone to take flowers to Margot, via the tomb of Edmond Rostand. Tonight, in the harbour, there will be fireworks. Maman always loved fireworks. She always said that at the end, she wanted to go up like a rocket. Perhaps that's why I've always found them a little sad: so much life and colour, for what? For just a few moments of wonder? For a little fleeting light? We will have much more than this, Anouk. In Vianne we will have a place of our own: a kitchen with many utensils. You will have toys, I promise you: a Molfetta that never gets left behind. And stories. So many stories, to show you where you came from.

Also today, at Allée du Pieu, Guy taught me how to make chestnut pralines. First the ganache; two parts chocolate to one part cream. To make the truffle smoother, add a little salted butter. Heat the cream in a copper pan; add the grated chocolate. It's just another recipe, easier than most of Margot's, and I soon find myself enjoying the unfamiliar implements; the little copper pan; the whisk; the big ceramic mixing bowl.

Add the chestnuts, roughly chopped, and maybe a little *kahlua*.
Roll the pralines into even-sized balls, then dip them in melted
chocolate, and leave to cool on a lined tray.

'Will you be there for the fireworks tonight? There'll be
dancing, and music, and wine. I'll get you home by midnight.'

I wasn't going to accept. But I found myself nodding
anyway. Maybe because of the chocolate. Maybe just because
he said *home*.

'Louis doesn't approve of me staying out at night,' I said.

'Louis doesn't seem to approve of very much,' said Guy.
'Why is he your problem?'

Good question. Of course, he isn't. And yet, he gave me
a room of my own when I had nothing, and no one. And
he introduced me to Margot – Margot, whose words, whose
recipes have brought about so many changes in me. I owe
him – I owe *her* – a debt. The world is a garden, not a mine.
We tend it so that we can grow.

'Anything could happen to a girl like you, out there, alone', he'd
said, when I left earlier.

'I won't be alone.'

'You know what I mean.'

I have to beware of that concern. Beware of the kindness
of others. For a while, their protectiveness can seem like love,
like security. But as my mother used to say, it soon turns into
ownership. We stay on the road because we do not want to
change ourselves for others. And yet, others *can* change me.
I can see that already. Louis has his hand on my heart. And
Guy, with his stories of Aztec kings, and Mahmed's gentle
gruffness. Most of all, though, Margot feels almost like a part
of myself. A presence like my mother's, kept pressed between
the pages. It makes me feel almost guilty, that this woman
means so much to me.

The Old Port smells of gunpowder, and cigarette smoke, and hot fried dough, and the sweat and the pleasure of the crowd, and the dust of the old streets underfoot. I breathe it in, almost like magic, layer by layer. Here, a stall selling candyfloss; there, the smell of beer and *Gitanes*. Perfume from a girl walking by, her young man's arm around her shoulders. Fried fish; hot dogs; aniseed; candle smoke from the lantern parade; petrol; powdered sugar; the not-quite-wholesome scent of the sea.

Inside me, baby Anouk lies low. She cannot be any larger than one of Guy's cacao beans – and yet I feel her moods somehow. She does not like the smoke, the noise. I would like to tell her that the noise is the price we have to pay for the way the faces in the crowd light up. Blue, green, pink, white. *Ahhhhhh*. The rockets open like umbrellas onto the harbour, the Butte, the sea. Bonne Mère is watching, too. She never misses a party.

Marseille's saint is gregarious, coming down from her place on the Butte to join in the celebrations. Her effigy parades along the lamplit streets of the Old Port, decorated with flowers, her painted plaster face smiling.

As I watch, I am conscious of Guy's scrutiny of my movements. He is wearing a Hawaiian shirt with a pattern of flowers and surfboards. I am a mystery to him: so young, so alone, so free of constraint. He wonders whether I am real; if I will melt away in the night. In a moment he will ask. I know he will. They all do; these men so fixed on their personal course that they assume I want that, too. I want to tell him that I am not the mystery he thinks I am. There's no romance in drifting. And that's how I've felt for most of life, like thistledown on a summer breeze, waiting for something to anchor me, to make me feel as if I belong. My mother did that, for a while. I lived in her giant shadow. We were

VIANNE

such friends that I often forgot that a mother is not an equal.
I won't forget that with Anouk. I cannot afford to befriend
her. A child is not forever; she will one day find her own
space in the world, and if I rely on her too much, as my
mother relied on me, then in the end I too will be left like a
broken compass, spinning helplessly in search of a north that
no longer stands true.

Red. White. Blue. Ahhhhh. New York smelt of pretzels and
beer. Here the scent is fiercer, somehow, like a wild awakening.

The fireworks have reached a climax. A bouquet of sea
anemones blossoms over the Old Port. A final, deafening
spray of applause. Then a lull, during which we can already
feel the slow dispersal of the crowd, the eventual dismantling
of the stalls, the long, slow journey of the Good Mother back
through the narrow cobbled streets towards the old basilica.
These moments always make me sad. So much organization,
so much energy, so much shared experience, and all for this.
It always ends. My mother tried to explain to me that nothing
lasts forever. But she never left a piece of her heart every
time she said goodbye. She was too busy looking forward to
the next adventure.

'Are you crying?'

I never cry. 'I'm just a little tired, that's all. I ought to get back.'

'I'll walk you home.'

Of course he will. They always do, these men who want to
protect me. And yet he is not like the others. He will not fall
in love with me. I sensed that from the start, as I knew that I
would never feel more for him than friendship. Maybe that's
why I like him so much; because he presents no threat to me.
And yet I wonder what it's like, to be in love. To belong to
someone. To walk hand-in-hand up the cobbled street with
the father of my child to a home we made together.

81

It sounds like a pretty picture, and yet the thought of it suddenly chilled me. 'I'm fine on my own. I don't need looking after,' I said.

Guy raised an eyebrow.

'I'm sorry,' I said. 'I didn't—'

'Don't apologize. But for the record, I never thought you needed a man's protection.'

I gave a sigh of relief. *Good.* He is not like the men I've known; the one-night lovers, the would-be protectors, the ones we shook from our clothing like burrs every time we had to move on. And yet he does want *something* of me; I can see it in the smoke drifting from the harbourside. I don't know what it is yet; but it smells of vanilla, and cardamom, and cacao beans roasting.

'I'll be perfectly safe,' I said.

He smiled. 'I'll walk you anyway.'

6

It was past twelve by the time I got home. That word again, so right, so *wrong*, with all those layers of wrongness. The light was still on in the bar, throwing a lattice of light and shade onto the moonstruck cobbles. Louis was sitting by the door, bundled into his winter coat although the summer night was still warm. He looked up sharply as I came in, and I saw a shift in his colours – a lurch from the grey-green of anxiety to a sudden dull burnt-orange.

'It's late,' he said. 'Where were you, *heh?*'

'I went to watch the fireworks.'

He made that sharp, percussive sound he often makes when he is displeased. 'I told you. It isn't safe at night. Especially for a girl in your position.'

He means my pregnancy, of course. He still thinks I am an innocent. I want to tell him that I have been to places he wouldn't imagine; that I have been a stowaway; a thief; an undesirable; a fugitive. I also want to tell him that my safety is none of his business; that I have survived too long on my own to be in need of a protector.

Instead, I said: 'I'll make some tea. It always helps when I need to relax.'

He made the sound again, but I was already making for the kitchen. There was a shelf of herbal teas, but I have always made my own, according to requirements. My mother was no cook, but she knew about herbs and their properties. *Valerian, to aid restful sleep. Rose petals, for sweetness. Silver leaves, to enhance the taste, and a handful of good fresh mint.* And now, a pinch of Guy's chocolate spice completes the soothing decoction:

'Come on, Louis. It will help you sleep.'

He drank the tea in silence, and I thought he seemed less troubled. 'Were you with Lacarrière again?' he said, putting down his empty cup.

I nodded.

'Is it serious?'

'Not in the way you mean. We're friends.'

'Just friends.' His voice was a growl, but I thought his eyes were kinder. 'Don't think I'm trying to interfere, but you're here under my roof, and I—'

'I'm fine, Louis.' I smiled at him. 'I've been looking after myself for a long time.'

'*Heh.*'

I poured another cup of tea. The vapour rose like meadow mist. My skill, my mother always said, was see, not only what people *are*, but what they *need*: and there is such a need in Louis, as yet unacknowledged, to love and protect.

But I am not his daughter, nor can I feed that hunger. Instead, I scratched a little sign on the side of the teacup; the sun rune, *Sól*, for comfort, and sweet dreams through the night. My mother's voice at the back of my mind whispers that this is dangerous. We should not form attachments. It makes it harder to move on. And yet, what harm can there be in spreading a little sweetness? After all, I'm not staying long. Just till the wind changes.

7

23 August 1993

I have now been at La Bonne Mère for exactly a month. It somehow seems longer than that; perhaps because of how much I am learning. Four weeks ago, I had no idea of how to follow a recipe; now I have almost forty different dishes under my belt, and I am gaining in confidence. Much of this is due to Margot; her presence permeates everything. I know her kitchen utensils, her books, her photographs, her ornaments. I have even been reading the works of her favourite poet – Edmond Rostand, a son of Marseille, a swashbuckler and romantic. I understand why she likes him: Margot, too, was a dreamer. I see it in her recipes, and in the notes in the margins of her favourite books.

Yesterday was a Sunday, and I used the opportunity to explore, in Louis' absence, the little patch of garden at the back of the bistrot. It must have been quite pretty once: climbing roses on the wall; fruit trees wreathed with mistletoe; the relics of what must have been a vegetable patch and an alley of herbs, with spears of rosemary and sage beneath the vaulting brambles.

I've always loved gardens. I know all the herbs. As a child, I used to plant acorns and beans in the places we stayed, hoping I could watch them grow. I liked to think of all those trees growing by the side of the road; growing because I planted them. Margot's garden was overgrown, but most of the debris was old growth; underneath there might be a chance to salvage something. With an old trowel and a gardening knife, I dug out the weeds, cut the brambles and turned over the impoverished soil, allowing the plants and herbs their space. It was oddly rewarding work; I thought I could almost hear the sigh of relief from a half-dead rose bush as I freed it from the net of bramble that imprisoned it. This is my garden now, I thought. This is where I will pick the herbs that I will use in Margot's recipes. And every time I pick a leaf, or a sprig, or a root, or a flower, I will think of her, and smile, and know that she is close by. I tugged at a curtain of ivy and saw that here too there had been flowers once; yellow nasturtiums on pale, leggy stems; a couple of late poppies; ragged shreds of rosemary reaching for the sunlight. And a single, yellow rose; almost leafless, but one small bloom shedding its petal-pale heart on the ground. A metal tag on the stem of the rose reads: *Cyrano de Bergerac.*

Margot must have planted this. A rose named after her hero. There is a copy of Rostand's play in a back room of La Bonne Mère. I read it one night when I couldn't sleep: the tale of a man – a brilliant man, a hero, a famous swordsman – who believing himself to be unlovable, helps his friend win the heart of the woman with whom he himself has been secretly in love for years, by means of a series of letters, in which Cyrano confesses his love, using his friend's identity. That copy must have belonged to Margot: some passages have been underlined, and there are notes in her handwriting, little phrases like the notes hidden among her recipes:

We call our children. Sometimes they come.
A child is a promise made to the world.

And saddest of all: *Some seeds never grow.* All of this in Margot's hand, a hand that I can almost see: brown and calloused with just one ring — a wedding-band — on the finger. I picked the single yellow rose and lifted it to my face; it was sweet, sweet as summer spices.

'Did Louis ask you to do that?'

The voice pulled me out of my reverie. Looking up, I saw Emile, watching me from over the wall, his narrow face suspicious.

'Emile.' I felt that sense of unease I often feel when he is around. Emile does not like me. He never has, since that very first day in July when I came down to breakfast. It's written in his colours, and in the sour way he looks at me. And his appetite for my cooking never extends to thanking me, or even acknowledging my work. Now his colours were muddled and resentful, although I could not see what there was to resent in my clearing the garden a little.

'Did Louis ask you?' he said again, dark eyes oil-drop bright beneath the visor of his beret. 'Because if he didn't—' He lit a *Gitane*. Took a long drag of the bitter smoke. Then went on in a different tone: 'You've really settled in here, haven't you?' he said. 'You mind the bar, you cook the meals — what else do you mean to take over?'

That was rather blunt for Emile, whose normal repertoire extends largely to looks, shrugs and sounds of derision. But in Louis' absence he has become bolder, like a hungry rat that perceives the opportunity to attack.

I said; 'I'm only here to help out. I'm not taking over anything.'

He raised an eyebrow. 'Could've fooled me. You've got your feet under the table, girl. Bit old for you, though, isn't he?'

I was so surprised, I laughed. 'I think you've got the wrong idea.'

He flicked the butt of his cigarette into the thicket of a climbing rose. 'You'd be better off staying at Allée du Pieu with your other friends. I've seen you, walking down there on Sundays, when Louis isn't there. Does he know how much time you spend hanging around that shithole? Does he know just how friendly you've got with those men in the chocolate shop?'

'I don't see what that has to do with you, or him, or anyone. But I don't see a reason why Louis would disapprove of my friends.'

Emile made a derisive sound. 'Try getting him to go there, then,' he said in his thin, unpleasant voice. 'Try getting him inside that place. There's a million things you don't know, girl, and this is only one of them.' And at that, he lit another *Gitane* and sauntered off down Rue du Panier, whistling between his teeth, like a rattlesnake in the skin of a man.

8

The end of August signals a change in the pace of this city. The tourists vanish overnight; the summer sinks into rapid decay. It's warm right into September, but now the heat is different. An urban heat, in spite of the sea that shelters and sustains us; a dusty heat, filled with petrol and grit and the promise of seasonal rains to come.

The wind is changing. Time to move on.

My mother's voice is hard to ignore. But I am not finished with Marseille. I still have things to learn here, not least, the rest of Margot's recipes. And then there's Louis, to whom I owe a debt as yet unpaid.

But first, something simpler: *ratatouille*. So simple in concept, ratatouille exists in many variants. Like a folk song, it has crossed continents, and found its way into a hundred different traditions. Marguerite's recipe calls for tomatoes, sweet red peppers, aubergines, onions, garlic, all combined with bay and seasonings, and a good splash of olive oil. Served with grilled red mullet, it makes a simple, wholesome dish, a dish that comes with a line of verse from Margot's favourite poet: *The greatest love can only grow beside a dream of equal size.* Food is love in Margot's world: simple, warm and constant.

As for myself, I am almost two thirds of the way through her book of recipes. I can make *madeleines*, *brioche*, pieds paquets, pomponettes, *leblebi*, chickpea stew with *merguez*, Marseille-style pizza, aioli, navettes, and *fiadoni*, the Corsican cheesecake so beloved by Louis' regulars. I know the difference between pâte brisée and *pâte feuilletée*, fougasse and pissaladière. I know how to fillet rockfish; how to keep the heads for stock; how to stir red saffron through rice to make the most luscious risotto. Cooking has become a joy, an unexpected talent. Domestic magic is humbler, perhaps, than my mother's glamours and tricks, and yet it makes a difference.

And then there are Guy's recipes, introduced from time to time under cover of trying out something new in the kitchen. His hot chocolate, especially, has proved a great success with many of our customers, although Louis yet has to taste it. Nothing replaces coffee, of course; but I have begun to add a pinch of xocolatl to every cup of coffee I make, and several of our regulars have begun to enjoy a small shot of *chocolat noir* alongside their usual breakfast. It has made rather a difference to our breakfast menu. Alongside the usual breakfast – eggs, coffee, fresh baguette – we also now serve hot chocolate, *pain au chocolat*, pomponettes, croissants and a selection of fresh fruit, which gives the meal a more festive look, and has even begun to attract a larger, more varied clientèle. La Bonne Mère is thriving again, after many years of neglect. Louis himself has begun to show signs of an Indian summer: the other day, at suppertime, I even caught him laughing. So why do I feel that my debt to him is no closer to being repaid than it was the day I arrived? And why is it that, in this sunshine, I feel the chill of autumn?

9

3 September 1993

At Allée du Pieu, the chocolaterie is still nowhere near completion. Guy assures me that everything is going according to plan, but Mahmed is unconvinced, and showing signs of anxiety. He is the one in charge of the company's finances, while Guy develops the product and the creative side of the business. It is an arrangement that suits the temperament of both; but I have become aware that Mahmed does not always share Guy's optimism.

First, the location is not ideal. Allée du Pieu is a back street, off the tourist trail by a mile, and sharing what little space it has with a takeaway, Happy Noodles: a tiny place; a kitchen, two tables, a counter and a stuttering neon sign. The family live above the shop: a mother, two girls and a grandmother, all of them Hong Kong Chinese. The girls speak good French, and often work behind the counter at weekends. The rest of the time the mother works there, while the grandmother works in the kitchen. The food is cheap and warming, and there are often queues there on a Friday or Saturday night. But all of this generates cooking smells, and litter, and noise, and empty drums of cooking oil stacked up in the alleyway, and morning deliveries that block the street and cause disruption, all of which Mahmed disapproves.

'The tourists will come when we're open,' says Guy, with the certainty of one who has seen neither numbers nor bills. 'We'll come to an arrangement with the Li family. They might even help us attract customers.'

'I didn't think rats ate chocolate.'

'Mahmed. You're better than that,' said Guy. 'Besides, you'll see. Word will get out. Some of the best-kept secrets in this city are in little streets just like this one.'

Mahmed shakes his head. 'It's all very well being an artist,' he says. 'But artists end up starving.'

Guy grins from a mask of cacao dust. 'Then let them eat chocolate,' he says, and pops a truffle into his mouth. 'Have a little faith, my friend. Give it six months. I promise you, in a year we'll be the Chocolate Kings of Marseille.'

Mahmed grins in spite of himself. There's a warmth in him when he talks to Guy, which comes out in spite of his caution. 'Kings of the back alleys,' he says. 'Kings of the open sewers.' He shakes his head ruefully. 'How will we get the kind of customers we want to come all the way to this part of town? Even assuming we're ready by then—'

'We'll be ready,' Guy tells him. 'They'll come.'

'How do you know?'

'Just trust me.'

I envy them their friendship. As a child, I never had friends. But over the past few weeks I have come to count them both as such; Mahmed for his dry sense of humour and his loyalty to Guy; Guy for his flamboyance and his passion for chocolate. But in spite of Louis' suspicions, I have no urge to take the relationship further, as if romance might draw a terminal line beneath our emerging friendship.

Louis finds this hard to understand. To him, a woman cannot be friends with a man without some ulterior motive. There has to be something more, he says; I am an attractive woman. I try to explain that Guy and Mahmed are an unbreakable unit; bound together by one man's dream to run a boutique chocolaterie.

'You ought to come and meet them,' I say. 'You'll understand when you talk to them.'

Up to now, he has always refused. It's a long walk back, he says, up all those steps from the Vieux Quartier. Besides, he has a bistrot to run; there's always something pressing to do. He doesn't like meeting new people; he never knows what to say to them. And besides which, he doesn't like chocolate; it's overpriced and sickly stuff, fit only for tourists and grandmothers.

I think back to what Emile said, that day in the garden. *Try getting him to go there, then. Try getting him inside that place.* Why was Emile so sure of this? What was it about Allée du Pieu — or chocolate — that Louis so disliked? I decided on a different approach. Today, after breakfast, before making lunch, I suggested a walk to the Old Port, to check out the daily markets and pick up some fresh vegetables. Louis agreed, and on the way back, with my basket of garlic and celery, I guided him towards Allée du Pieu, keeping a flow of merry conversation on the way.

'I just want to call in quickly somewhere. You don't mind a detour, do you, Louis?'

The alley was right at the foot of the Butte, and over the fifteen minutes or so that it took us to walk there from the Old Port, conversation between us had waned to a heavy silence. Perhaps the heat of the sun, I thought, or the little flights of stone steps that led into the Vieux Quartier; the washing-lines of sheets strung between the little cast-iron balconies, or the litter that had accumulated in the gutters and under the grates.

'So this is your detour,' he said, as we went down the dozen broken steps that led to the back end of Allée du Pieu. 'I told you. It's a shithole. No one can run a business here. People have tried. It never works.'

I had to admit to myself that the alley was not at its best that day. There must have been a delivery, and the passageway was half blocked by boxes, bags and pallets. Happy Noodles was open, and there was a strong scent of frying oil, and garlic, roast pork, and spices. Several drums of used cooking oil stood at the back of the takeaway, ready to be disposed of. And next to the disused print shop, there was Xocolatl: with its cardboard sign, and blank windows, and peeling paintwork, and the litter of empty boxes, cacao dust, building materials left in a heap outside the boarded-up window. Louis looked at it all in silence.

Finally he said: 'This is the place? Your chocolate shop?'

I said: 'It's a work in progress. Come inside and look around.'

I think perhaps I still believed that I could make him see what I saw. The magic hidden behind the mundane. The romance and the mystery. We went in through the back door, and found Guy in the storeroom, checking a delivery, which had arrived from Columbia. Sold as top-grade, hand-peeled beans, Guy had discovered that these had been heat-treated, and were therefore unsuitable for his process. As a result, he barely noticed when Mahmed ushered us inside, but launched into a tirade of abuse at the inferior product, as well as against the dealer himself, who according to Guy, deserved the treatment Aztecs gave to their captured enemies.

'That bandit. Call these Grade A beans? This is shit. *Expensive* shit. Fucking *exorbitant*, useless shit!' He crushed a handful

94

of the beans, releasing a powerful scent of cacao and a great deal of powdery dust, which fell from his fist onto the floor. 'What am I meant to do with this? Use it as fertilizer?'

Mahmed cleared his throat. 'Guy.'

Guy turned mid-sentence, and saw the three of us standing there. His Hawaiian shirt – a garish print of pineapples and hula girls – was half-unbuttoned, and his hair was a shock of porcupine spikes. He looked both demented and hilarious. 'You see what this crazy job does to me?' he said, holding out cacao-stained hands. 'I used to be reasonably civilized. Now I'm planning murder. Or would, if Columbia wasn't halfway across the planet. Now all I can hope for is some kind of long-distance voodoo.'

'Voodoo?' Louis looked blank.

I put my hand on his arm. He looked off-balance and out of place, looking at the stained and half-painted walls of the shop as if to find meaning there.

I said; 'Louis, this is Guy. My friend. And here's Mahmed, his partner—'

'In crime. And you must be Louis Martin,' said Guy. 'Vianne's told us all about you.'

Louis said nothing for a while, but took in the jumble of boxes and sacks, the pulverized cacao beans on the floor, the patches of smoke shooting up the walls. 'I used to know this place,' he said. 'It doesn't look like it's improved.'

'Give it time,' said Guy. 'It needs work. But when we have our grand opening, it's going to be something special. People are going to know our name. Let me show you the conching room. It's where the magic happens.'

'Magic?' said Louis.

'Oh yes.' Guy grinned. 'Chocolate is ancient magic. Brought from the sky by the Mayan gods as a gift to humanity. Valued higher than gold, and used in the most occult of rituals. Stolen by the conquistadors; it brought down two popes, divided the Church; crossed to every continent. And now it's here. Right here in Marseille, working its magic on everything.'

Louis made a hard sound in his throat. '*Heh*. Well, thanks for the offer. But I have a bistrot to open tonight, and it's a long climb up the Butte.'

'But Louis, you haven't seen——' I said.

'I've seen enough,' said Louis in a voice that was very nearly a growl. 'You brought me here. I've seen it. I don't need to see any more. And now we need to get back home. Things to get ready for tonight.'

We made the return climb in silence. Louis, it seems, does not like my friends. He does not like their neighbourhood. He especially dislikes Allée du Pieu; I see it in his colours, although I cannot discover what it is that he so despises. And Guy's talk of magic – of *rituals* – makes him deeply uncomfortable, although he has no love for the Church, or feelings of superstition.

'How do you know Allée du Pieu?' I said at last, as we arrived home. 'How did you know the chocolate shop?'

'It wasn't a chocolate shop then,' he said.

'What was it?'

'Some kind of backstreet herbalist. There was a fire. It gutted the place. Should have burnt it to the ground.'

His sullenness did not abate as we planned the next day's menu. None of my suggestions seemed to be to his liking. Not *cassoulet*, a winter dish, too rich for these late-summer days. Not salad again, the regulars need something more than rabbit food. Not mussels – out of season now that September has begun; or mackerel – the last lot I bought had been nothing but bones. We finally agreed on *soupe au pistou* with a side of garlic bread, and an apple *bourdon* for dessert.

'Be sure to choose the right apples,' said Louis. '*Reine de Reinette,* or *Golden.* Anything else will turn to mush as soon as the pastry starts cooking. And take more care with the *pâte brisée*: last time it was overcooked.'

10

The *soupe au pistou* was not a success. Emile, especially, complained, saying that soup was an old woman's meal, and that men needed proper nourishment.

'You'll need to know that, if you ever want to find a man yourself,' he said, as I brought him his second helping of dessert. 'A pretty face is one thing, but a generous hand in the kitchen, *well*—' He paused to inspect his apple *bourdon*. 'What's this stuff on top of it?'

'Toasted brown sugar and cinnamon, just to give the apple some spice.'

'Hm. Not bad. I guess it'll do.' Emile never makes compliments. To him, to finish is praise enough; anything else is indulgence. But Louis did not take dessert today, and once more refused my hot chocolate, saying: 'I have to watch my weight. You'll turn me into a pig at this rate.'

Of course, this has nothing to do with his weight. Something happened in Allée du Pieu; something that has to do with my friends, and with the chocolaterie. His silent disapproval feels like a piece of barbed-wire thread, twisted into a ball of wool. It's nothing to do with the chocolate, either; it's something to do with that herbalist's, and the fire that gutted the building. I have tried to find out more, but no one seems to know very much. Simply that Allée du Pieu is bad news, and that no business succeeds there.

I read the cards again tonight. I drew those seven cards again, but in a different order. Change. Flanked with the Hermit, it seems to relate to Louis, a man embedded in grief, slowly emerging into the light. The Fool, with his perpetual smile, reminds me of Guy — an innocent, buoyed with plans and optimism. And the Six of Swords, like the Tower, means grief: the grief of my mother's death, perhaps, or maybe something yet to come, something still more ruinous.

I wish I could see her. I miss her so much. *Help me. Help me understand.*

The box still smells of sandalwood and the dust of a thousand spices. Lavender, to bring restful sleep; St John's Wort, to banish care; ginger, to ease troubled blood; chamomile, for joint aches. My mother knew their names, their medicinal applications. I wonder what she would have made of Guy's xocolatl. Magic, I have learnt, is as simple or as complicated as you make it. We all long for the power to change our world, our lives, and sometimes even ourselves, which is why transformation plays such a part in stories of magic. Straw into gold, water into wine, a life of drudgery into a life of happiness and prosperity. Perhaps that's why we so often seek some kind of magic to bring it about. A magic wand. A religion. But magic isn't really about changing frogs into princes. Sometimes, all you need to bring about the change you need is to see the world in a different way — to show the world a new face — a new name. That's why the words for *magic* are so often linked with qualities that we see in other people. *Charm. Glamour. Charisma.* And, far from needing a magic wand, we already *have* the potential to change; it's just that we don't always dare to. That's why we invest objects and rituals with significance – a set of Tarot cards, a spell, a special spoon, a wafer – not because those things are magical in themselves, but as an aid to focus.

Focus, Vianne. Try to see.

But I see nothing in her cards, except her disapproval. Magic is *our* gift, she says, not to be wasted on others. I have allowed myself to become attached – to Louis, to Guy, to Mahmed, and most especially, to Margot – a mistake she would never have permitted. As a result, her Tarot cards are lifeless beneath my fingers. Outside, the voice of the turning tide is like the sound of a sharpened blade.

The wind is changing. Time to move on. The cards, like you, are frozen. Stay too long in one place, Vianne, and soon you'll be rooted to the spot; helpless as a flightless bird; a gift to any predator.

It's the voice that has been with me all my life. But that's the voice of *her* fear, not mine. A fear that kept us on the move for eighteen years, across continents. A fear that I refuse to pass on to my Anouk, when she is born. There is no Man in Black any more; the wind has no power over us. And if the cards refuse to speak, then I shall find my truth elsewhere. In a handwritten cookbook, perhaps, or in a jar of chocolate.

Be careful, 'Viane. My mother's voice on the night wind sounds like the lonely cry of an owl. *Don't do this. It's dangerous. Stop, while you still have a choice. Fixing other people's lives only leaves you broken.*

But I don't think that's true, Maman. We can mend each other. A kindness is never wasted, nor a word of comfort lost. And I think I know where to find them now; the answers I am looking for. Not in the cards, but in a kinder, more domestic magic. Barefoot in the kitchen, I pull the cookbook from the shelf. I open the book at a random page; trying to focus; trying to *see*.

I I

Magic has no rules. Sometimes it comes from the vapour in a pan; or reflections in a pool; or words whispered on the wind. Sometimes it comes from an accidental combination of elements: a spread of cards; a handful of runes; the juxtaposition of objects. And sometimes we can call magic from the very humblest of places; words at random in a book. A novel, a grimoire, a bible, perhaps. Maybe even a cookbook.

I consult the binder of recipes as I would a deck of cards. First, I draw her bouillabaisse, the very first recipe I learnt. A good and warming recipe, made with love and industry. Next comes a dish of *foie gras* with prunes; a dish from the regional south-west that I would never think to make; a memory of childhood, perhaps, from her years in Bergerac. Then comes a dish of chestnuts with beans; of boar stuffed with wild cherries. These land recipes are no good to Louis. Coastal Marseille is not the place to make this very regional food. But Margot still keeps them, and here too I hear her voice.

Straining to read in the moonlight, I find something else in the recipe book, tucked into the binding. I pull it out, unfold it. It looks like a loose page of recipes. But unlike the rest of Margot's book, it is closely written; cramped; the writing almost too small to make out.

Spice to ease a restless heart: Take cardamom, cinnamon; vanilla, star anise, chilli. Burn a eucalyptus leaf to dispel worries and unquiet thoughts. For true love: Light a red candle at midnight on Midsummer's Eve. Add the heart of a pomegranate, a feather from the breast of a dove. Say his name three times, with love, and love will surely come to you.

And as I read, I understand that these are not recipes, but *spells*. A spell to summon courage: *A pinch of Dragon's Blood, dissolved in a cup of water.* Another one, for making friends – *pink candle, lavender and nutmeg, lit at moonrise with the prayer* Come, friend, *and a meditation on Isis.* And here, most poignantly, a spell to welcome a child into the world and to give it a safe delivery: *Burn a white candle with sandalwood; holy water; cup of wine. Broken bread at the threshold of the home and the bedroom. Scatter salt around the house to ward off evil spirits. Sing a gentle lullaby to make the child feel welcome.*

So, our Margot is a witch. Not in the way my mother was, but in a hopeful, eager way that feels almost heartbreaking. Here's her spell for a broken heart – scattered seeds, blue candle, meditation to Bonne Mère in her incarnation as the Mother. And under that, a note to herself: *Some men are afraid to be loved; even more afraid to love. Cyrano would have understood.*

Cyrano de Bergerac. The man who loved in secret. What is she trying to tell me here? What did she hope to conjure with these hedge-witch spells and enchantments?

Turning over the close-written sheet, I find a list of names on the back. *Raphaël. Loïc. Alexian. François. Henriot. Jean-Louis. Pierre-Emile. Bienheureux.* And finally, *Edmond,* underlined, alongside a little drawing of church bells and a cradle.

Sing a gentle lullaby to make the child feel welcome.

And now I think I understand the secret sadness in her. Poor Margot, who would have been such a good mother, given the chance. Poor Margot, who turned to spells and potions when prayer failed.

And now, in the moonlight, I see her, standing by the kitchen door; hair tied loosely from her face, eyes filled with reflections. She looks so real, so present that I could almost touch her. She reaches out a hand, and I see that she is holding a tiny pair of knitted bootees, just like the ones I bought from the old lady on Rue du Panier, except that these are not pink, but blue – blue as the Virgin's mantle.

Edmond. His name is Edmond, she says, and her voice is so close that she might be standing directly behind me. *Vianne, his name is Edmond. Vianne. Find him. Find him. Bring him home.*

What does this mean? Did she have a child? If so, Louis has never mentioned it. And yet, the drawing, the baby bootees – and perhaps most importantly, his name – all suggest that maybe she did. Who was Edmond? Was he real? Or was he a lonely woman's dream, a conjuration by moonlight?

But Margot has already gone. Her scent – a smudge of lavender – still lingers in the gilded air. But the words on the page are real, and the spell to call a child into the world. And now, as I think of my own child – my Anouk, who feels so *real* – I wonder, with a pang of unease, if she too might just be a dream?

12

18 September 1993

September in Marseille is warm; with only the hint of a change in the air to mark the turning seasons. The scorching heat of August is gone, but the softness of the wind remains, and the colours of the sea and sky have acquired a new depth and sweetness. Life in the bistrot has sweetened, too. The walk to the market; the cooking; the weekly visits to Allée du Pieu. The daily pot of hot chocolate, today with a dash of coconut milk and a scatter of toasted sesame seeds. Plus a new ingredient from the time of the Chocolate Kings; *Chillies and raw cacao; cinnamon, vanilla, saffron, nutmeg, allspice. Handed down by Ixcacao, goddess of love and compassion.*

Yes, I have taken to adding Guy's chocolate spice to some of my simpler recipes. A sprinkling on the top of a tart, to bring out the flavours of the fruit. A spoonful in my hot chocolate, to make the vapours eloquent. I use it to add extra warmth to a dish of vanilla rice; sweetness to a *tapenade*; depth to a soup or casserole. I like to think Margot would approve; recipes are living things, passed on to living people.

The change is very subtle; and yet I see it in our customers; in the way they speak to me now, in the shift in their colours.

People call me by name now, instead of just saying *mademoiselle*, and comment on the menu, and compliment my progress. Louis, too, has softened somehow, although he still scorns my hot chocolate: but I can see the change in him, and I know that the magic is working.

The only exception is Emile, whose sour face and sharp comments remain apparently unaffected by my domestic magic. The xocolatl spice must be missing something, or maybe it's simply Emile who is missing some essential ingredient. But today, Emile was running late: Louis had gone to call at the bank, and for the first time, I was alone to deal with lunch, and the customers.

Until today, I hadn't realized how proprietary Emile is where La Bonne Mère is concerned. Perhaps it's his lifelong friendship with Louis, or the fact that he practically lives here, but in the absence of both of them, the atmosphere was different; as if a window had opened, letting in the fresh air.

'What's on the menu today, Vianne?' That's Monsieur Georges, with his old friend Tonton, who always brings his elderly dog into the bistrot at lunchtime. I already know what he'll order. Two *plats du jour*, a bottle of red, and a piece of cold sausage for Galipette, whose trembling muzzle is already raised hopefully towards me.

I'd made some grilled sardines today, served on a bed of spiced *taboulé*. An easy recipe to make, which leaves me plenty of time to talk.

'You're a better cook than Louis,' said Tonton, through a mouthful of fish. 'Those grilled sardines—' He kissed his teeth, and Galipette looked up expectantly. 'What did you add to them? White wine? Rosemary?'

I smiled. 'They're fresh this morning. How about a little dessert? I have *tarte au citron*, and fresh navettes—'

Tonton made a sound in his throat, indicating approval. 'Yes, and some of your chocolate. I'm starting to get used to it.'

These old men never say thank you. A nod is their only acknowledgement. But I have begun to interpret their guttural sounds, their gestures. And in Louis' absence they talk to me more freely than when he is around.

I brought the chocolate, served with a pinch of xocolatl, as always. 'Did Louis never make chocolate? Not even when Margot was alive?'

Tonton glanced towards the bar, as if to reassure himself that neither Louis nor Emile was there. Then he shook his head. 'Not that I recall, no.'

'But you do remember her?' I said.

He nodded. 'Of course. Everyone does.'

I drew a little sign in the air. A pretty, inviting confidences. 'What was she like?'

He shrugged. 'Margot?' He looked around once more, as if to check that no one was listening. But apart from Monsieur Georges, who was sitting opposite him at the table, no one was paying attention. 'Everyone was sweet on Margot,' he told me, as I brought the dessert. 'She was the heart of La Bonne Mère.'

Monsieur Georges nodded. 'That she was. She had a shine.'

I poured two cups of chocolate from the silver pot on the bar. The vapour lingered in the air like the tail of a mythical bird. 'She must have been young when she died,' I said. 'What happened?'

'Didn't he tell you?'

I shook my head.

'She was pregnant,' said Tonton at last. 'There were complications. Louis was never the same after that. A tragedy for everyone.'

I teased out the tale from the rising steam, more eloquent than their comments. And of course, I already knew from Margot herself; from the little notes scrawled in her recipe book; the lingering signs of her presence, more meaningful than words. 'She so badly wanted a child. Went on trying long after the doctors told her she never would. That was Margot – she never gave up. Even when Louis wanted her to.' It was a miracle, they'd said. To be pregnant at forty-one; to finally carry a child to term after so many miscarriages. She'd spent six months hardly daring to move; had given up all but the lightest work. Her doctor was cautious, but positive; and Louis, having long since given up on the idea of children, was helping Emile repaint the guest room of La Bonne Mère, and furnishing it in readiness.

'Some people believe in miracles,' said Tonton, sipping his chocolate. 'Margot did. She believed in them all. She prayed to Mary and all the saints. She always kept their feast days. But she had a whole drawer full of charms that she bought from that woman on Allée du Pieu—'

'Allée du Pieu?'

'The place is long gone. It used to sell incense, and Tarot cards, and copper bracelets for rheumatism, and blue beads to ward off the evil eye, and silver charms for whatever the heart thinks it needs to be happy. With Margot, it was a baby. The woman said she could help her. Louis didn't like it, but she kept going there anyway.'

Some kind of backstreet herbalist. That would explain the folded sheet of spells at the back of her cookery book. The lists of arcane ingredients: white sandalwood, dragon's blood, root of John the Conqueror. The little incantations, the rhymes. And it explains his mistrust of Allée du Pieu, of Guy's glib talk of magic. Magic is desire made real by will and perseverance.

And Margot wanted a child so much – enough to follow any path, pursue any hope of achieving her dream. But everything has to be paid for. The world demands its balance. And everything that is taken must one day be returned.

Monsieur Georges went on: 'Perhaps it's because she believed in all that that she didn't spot the signs. It was only a headache, she said. Don't make a fuss over nothing. But she was strange in those final weeks. Distant, strange, and secretive. Then came the other symptoms, the pains, the swollen hands and feet. At last, Louis called an ambulance. But it was too late. She died overnight.'

'And – the baby?' I almost said *Edmond*.

He shook his head. 'It didn't survive.'

Poor Margot, I thought. *Poor Louis*. I have grown very close to them both while I have been learning these recipes. I know the flavours that made her smile; the memories she cherished. I know her temper: the broken plate, which was an anniversary gift, chipped when she slammed it down in the sink during an argument with Louis. I know her longing; and now, her loss, that terrible grief that stays alive even after death.

'Probably for the best,' said Tonton, finishing his chocolate. 'I heard there was something wrong with the child. Some kind of genetic something.'

Georges agreed. 'A mercy, yes. Imagine having to care for a—' He bit off the end of the phrase. '*Heh*. Well, I must be on my way. I'm playing *pétanque* this afternoon.' Tonton nodded. 'Yes, me too. Lunch was good. See you tomorrow, *mademoiselle*.'

For a moment I was puzzled at their sudden change in manner. Then I saw that Emile had come in, and was standing by the open door, his cap drawn down over his eyes, his colours as blue as a gas flame. I had no idea what he might have heard, but seeing me, he grinned like a shark.

'What's for lunch? I'm late,' he said. 'I hope you kept some by for me.'

I watched as Tonton and Monsieur Georges hastily picked up their things to leave: Emile settled comfortably at his usual table. He lit a cigarette, and blew foul-smelling smoke into the air. 'Where's Louis?'

'He went to the bank.'

'And left you in charge?'

I nodded.

'*Heh*. Did you get him to go to that chocolate shop?'

'We called by a couple of weeks ago.'

He grinned again. 'I bet he loved that. Meeting your friends, and everything.'

I poured him a glass of chilled white wine. 'Perhaps you could ask him yourself, Emile. Or if you're especially curious, I'm sure Guy could show you around sometime.'

He made a harsh little sound in his throat. 'I'm not a fucking tourist. And I can't afford chichi chocolates.' I smiled. 'You should try. You never know. You might even get a taste for them.'

13

The bar still smelt of grilled sardines. Combined with the smoke of his cigarette, it felt like an assault on my senses as I set Emile's main course in front of him, and went to open the bistrot door to let in a little fresh air, but now the wind had turned cool, and the sudden draught made him look round in annoyance.

'Are you trying to give me pneumonia?'

'I'm sorry. I just needed some air. I'll close it in a minute.'

By then it was almost three o'clock. The dishes were cleared; most people had left. It struck me that Emile's arrival was often the signal for others to leave, although his friendship with Louis means that he is generally tolerated. He ate his lunch in silence, pushing away his main course without comment, waiting for me to bring the dessert even without so much as a smile. Behind him, only a few customers remained, lingering over hot chocolate. I poured a cup for Emile, who pretends to scorn it when Louis is around, and still believes that I have not noticed his appetite for sweet things.

'This chocolate tastes different. I liked it better yesterday.'

'I used coconut milk today. Maybe that's what you can taste.'

He shrugged. 'Perhaps.' He took a navette. 'Make these yourself?'

'Yes.'

'*Heh.*' He has the same mannerisms as Louis, as if through years of proximity. But unlike Louis, he has never changed in his attitude towards me. He is still guarded, suspicious, as if I were something badly made; impermanent; ready to fall. He looked at me from narrowed eyes, his colours low, but blowtorch-hot. He reached into his pocket and brought out a pack of unfiltered *Gitanes*. Most of our other regulars have quietly stopped smoking around me, but Emile is the exception; and the sharp reek of dark tobacco caught in my throat like a fishbone. He must have seen me flinch, because his narrow smile grew broader.

'Something wrong, *mademoiselle*?'

I shook my head. 'Have an ashtray.'

'Good idea.' He grinned again. 'And another cup of that chocolate.'

Herbs to ease a troubled heart. But it will take more than a pinch of spice to ease whatever drives Emile. His anger – glimpsed that first day in July as I came down for breakfast – is a permanent flame in him, unquenchable as a piece of his soul. Anger or – hate. But for whom?

I tried to look through the weaving smoke rising now from his cigarette, but all I could see was the face of a woman seated by the bar, watching me with curious eyes from under a bright silk headscarf.

'Chocolate! May I try a cup?'

She wasn't one of our regulars. In fact, I hadn't noticed her sitting there a moment before. People here tend to wear drab clothes; berets in rusty black and brown; sailcloth trousers; dark overcoats. This woman was wearing a patchwork coat; her brown face was as ripe as a nectarine, with eyes that flashed with mischief.

'Do I know you?'

The woman smiled. I looked at her more closely and saw, with a jolt of surprise, that it was the old woman from Rue du Panier, whom I had last seen in La Bonne Mère on the day of the bouillabaisse. Without her straw hat and basket she looks a lot younger than before – sixty, rather than eighty – with a bright and merry smile all nested in fine wrinkles.

I poured her a cup of chocolate. She drank it slowly, contemplatively. 'I can taste the ocean,' she said. 'Coconut palms on a rocky coast. The sand is gritty and almost black; the air smells of frangipani. Tastes are so good at conjuring place. Place, and maybe other things.' She smiled. 'You're looking well, Vianne. Better than when I first saw you. Pregnancy suits you. Chocolate, too.'

I glanced at Emile. He seemed not to have noticed the woman sitting behind him. The rising smoke from his cigarette bloomed like a corona.

The woman smiled at me again. We might have been alone in the room.

'And yet you gave yourself that name. The name of that village on the Baïse. Names are good at conjuring, too. Names are words of power.'

I said: 'What's *your* name?'

She smiled again. 'Why would I give anyone power over me? But you can call me *Khamaseen*. It's one of the many names I've had over the years, and I'm fond of it.'

'How do you know so much about me?' I said. I was starting to feel light-headed; the smell of Emile's cigarette smoke made my stomach flip like a pancake.

The woman looked sympathetic. 'The smell of chocolate helps,' she said. 'Try it. It kills the nausea.' I held up the pot of chocolate and inhaled the scent. It smelt rich and warm and comforting; calm as an unbroken highway. 'Drink some. It's good for the baby, too.'

I realized I was hungry, and poured myself a cup. She was right; it did help. I felt Anouk flutter like a moth; the reek of smoke diminished. The woman finished her chocolate and set down the cup on the counter. Reaching into her pocket, she brought out a flat parcel, wrapped in tissue paper, and handed it to me.

'She would have liked you to have this,' she said. 'Maybe it will help you.'

I looked down at the parcel. It felt like a book. I started to ask who she meant, who she *was*, but even as I struggled for words, the woman from Rue du Panier had gone, slipping through the open door, light-footed as a leaf in the wind, closing it behind her.

'That's better,' said Emile, stubbing out his cigarette. 'Some people want us all to freeze.'

I looked at him. 'Who was that?' I said.

He poured himself another cup of chocolate from the pot. 'Who?'

'The woman with us at the bar.' I struggled to describe her. 'Grey hair. Headscarf. Patchwork coat. She was sitting here, just now.'

Emile gave me a puzzled look. 'I didn't see any woman there. Sure you didn't imagine her?'

14

20 September 1993

The old woman's gift was indeed a book, bound in faded satin, with the words *My First Album* printed on the cover. Leafing through it, I saw that each page was designed to mark a turning-point in the baby's progress. Headings like – *My Birthday! My Godparents! My Very First Smile!* – were interspersed with printed frames designed to showcase photographs. But there was only one photograph, under the heading *My Parents*: a black-and-white photo of Margot and Louis, standing hand-in-hand on the steps of what looked like a country church. The wind was blowing; a handful of what looked like confetti fretted the air, and Margot's hair had come loose from her veil, and covered half her laughing face. She looked very young; very happy. But Louis I barely recognized: so different was he from the Louis I knew. Here I could see what the years had done to the man in the black-and-white photograph; how grief and loss and loneliness have left their marks in his features. Under the photo, in Margot's hand, I read: *19 July 1959*, and a recipe for *croquembouche*; that wedding cake made up of a pyramid of individual choux pastry puffs, held in place with spun sugar. Such a hopeful picture, I thought. Such a hopeful recipe. What happened to that girl? I thought. What happened to those people?

The rest of the album was mostly entries in Margot's hand-writing. Recipes, for the most part, and spells; and cramped little diary entries.

My little Edmond is three months old; about the size of a plum, they say. Fingernails and earlobes formed. Every night, take valerian tea for restful sleep and healing. And make sure now to speak his name. A named thing is a claimed thing.

My little Edmond is four months old. Louis says I should have a scan to make sure my baby is normal. He's afraid: he doesn't know how we would cope with a damaged child. But Edmond is already perfect. Already he's a miracle. I wish Louis could see it that way. I wish he could let himself love our child without being afraid to lose him.

I can hear her voice so clearly in these diary entries. Clearer than in her recipes, although that's where I heard it first. But Margot's recipes are all the voices of her family: her grandmother's pot-au-feu; her mother's apple turnover, her great-grandmother's cherry *eau-de-vie*, made with the cherries from her own tree. And for Edmond, a special dish: a plum cake, like a *clafoutis*, with Armagnac and cinnamon. *Recipes are like children*, I'd said, on the day of the bouillabaisse. Strange words, from a girl whose experience of cooking came largely from boiling noodles in the kettles of strange hotels, or making soup from packets, or mixing salad dressings. And yet I understand it. Perhaps because I understand *her*. They live on, even when we are gone. And Margot's voice – through her cookery book, and now through this baby album – is strong and warm and comforting, and filled with hope for the future.

Five months now, and my little Edmond is able to hear my voice. I like to read him poetry and sing him lullabies at night so he won't get lost in the dark. This time, I'm sure. I know he'll come. My Edmond is strong. He will find me.

She was so sure her child was a boy. Just as I know my Anouk is a girl; knew it almost from the first, when she was still a seedling. Is that why she named him so early? *A named thing is a claimed thing.* It's the kind of thing my mother would have said, as we moved from country to country, changing our names as we did our clothes, to suit the needs of the journey. But what did naming him mean to Margot? A gesture of defiance? A prayer? Or rather, a cry in the face of God, who had claimed so many children? That list of names in her cookbook. Did she name the others, too? Or was Edmond the only one that she had truly claimed for herself? And why had the woman from Rue du Panier had this book for so many years, when surely it should belong to Louis?

Louis still refuses to use his name. He thinks it's bad luck to name this child before it's born. It might still die. Or worse, he says: be born with some genetic defect. It's common, with women of my age. To name him is to claim him, I say, but Louis doesn't understand. His fear for me makes him angry these days. He barely talks to me any more. But love comes in threes. It completes us. Without a child, there will always be a part of me that stays empty.

Near the end, her writing grows more straggling and untidy. I sense her impatience, her fatigue; I understand her frustration.

Only two months to go now. My little Edmond is almost the size of a cantaloupe melon. And hungry; I can feel him now, dreaming of my kitchen. Light a yellow candle at dusk, and scatter salt by the doorway. Pray to Bonne Mère in her incarnation as Ixcacao: burn cedarwood and dragon's blood to ward off the gaze of the Shadowless Man.

And finally, on the last page, in letters so shaky I can hardly read them, she has written:

My dearest Edmond. I love you more than words can say. Look after your father. He's a good man, but stubborn. He never believed that love alone could accomplish anything. You'll have to change his mind, Edmond. Love him for both of us when I'm gone. Except that I'll never really be gone, not while you're still in the world. My Edmond, I'm leaving this book in the care of a friend who will help you. I hope we can read it together one day. But if we can't, remember this: you were always the best of me.
    Your loving mother,
    Marguerite

It is the last page in the book. But stuck to the inside cover, there is a piece of paper; this time showing a footprint, neatly inked onto the page. Almost too tiny to understand; even smaller than those bootees I bought from the woman on Rue du Panier, perfect in every detail, even to the tiny toes. Underneath, someone has written: *Edmond Loïc Bien-Aimé Martin. 13 October 1973.*

15

23 September 1993

His name is Edmond. Find him, Vianne. But there is nothing more to find. There was no baptism, no funeral. Only that footprint on the card, to show that he existed. That must have been what she wanted of me. That I should see him and understand. Edmond Loïc Bien-Aimé Martin. He would have been my age by now.

I read the cards again last night. I should be gone, they tell me. Nothing good can come from this. Margot's child is out of reach. But I still have her recipes, and I owe it to her to pass them on, to take them with me into the world. I've earned enough money to make a start; to take the first step of my journey. Maybe I'll find a little café in that village on the Baïse. Maybe I'll open a place of my own, serving coffee and *plat du jour*. This will be her legacy; Margot, who has taught me so much about the magic of everyday things. And maybe it will comfort Louis, to know that his Margot's memory will live on in a hundred small, good ways; in the sugary crunch of a crème brûlée; the comforting warmth of a *clafoutis*. Louis' cooking was a monument, frozen in perpetual grief. Mine will be something that grows, that lives, that makes people push their worries aside. Change is life, and life is good, however much pain it may bring us.

And certainly, some things have changed since I began to work here. Guy's chocolate spice is not the only new ingredient in these recipes. My mother's formulae adapt very well to magic of a different kind – a little sign in the air for luck, a whispered word for comfort. Cooking is *meant* to ease the heart; and so many hearts here need easing. Emile's anger: Louis' grief; the loneliness of our regulars, who come to the café for company. Cooking does not *cure* these things; but it does offer some kind of relief. A kind of absolution. Permission to love, and be loved in return. *Some men are afraid to be loved; even more afraid to love.* That's what was missing before I arrived: that's what I'll leave behind when I go. That, and maybe one more thing.

I put my mother's cards back in their box. I do not need them any more. I have a different recipe for working out my future. On Sunday I will light a candle for you at the feet of Bonne Mère. I will leave your Tarot cards there, in the basilica, under the candy-cane arches and the gleaming gold mosaics. And then I will walk away from you, leaving all your fears behind.

16

26 September 1993

It's Sunday today, and Louis has gone to visit the grave of Edmond Rostand. On any usual Sunday I might have gone to see Guy and Mahmed; but this time I went the other way, and walked up the many flights of steps to the summit of the Butte, where the Good Mother looks over the bay with clear and golden compassion. Both Margot's cookery book and the baby book have references to the Bonne Mère, though these are often interspersed with references to Isis, or Venus, or Ceres, or Ixcocolatl. Mothers are holy everywhere. Mothers have the power.

I left my mother's Tarot cards in the place where I found the toy rabbit. The rabbit was gone, and the church was alive with colour, and motes, and sudden shadows, and whisperings. The light here is always magical; dappled with reflections. It looks like a summer carnival, tumbling with confetti. I think to myself that perhaps someone will find her cards and use them. Someone lost – a child maybe – someone who has lost their way.

There is a box of candles at the foot of the Virgin's statue. They are marked at one franc each, with a small wooden box on the wall for the coins. I light one for my mother;

one for Margot; one for myself. As I place them on the stand, I notice a section of the wall given over to gratitudes. Silver charms and written notes pinned to the stone in their hundreds; every one an answered prayer; every one a story. I find myself looking more closely at some of the little offerings. Some of the papers are faded with time; others are still legible. *Thank you for saving my father; my child. Thank you for saving my husband. Thank you for easing my mother's pain: she is with the angels now. Mother, ease my broken heart: for I too have lost a son.*

That last one resonates, somehow. The note is unsigned, like the others, and yet the handwriting could be Margot's. *I too have lost a son.* I try to imagine losing Anouk. Already, the loss is unthinkable. Like Margot, for whom Edmond was fully formed in her mind from the start, my little Anouk has become more real than anything in the real world. I know what she looks like; I know when she smiles. I have seen her at six years old; I see her now at twelve; at nineteen. To lose her now would be to lose every future version of the person my daughter will become. And yet, she is a stranger. To the world, to herself, to me. How strange, that my little stranger should occupy such a large part of me, when she is still so very small. I understand how Margot felt. Why she delayed seeking treatment. How she wanted to give her child the best chance of survival, even at the cost of her life. And I know that in her place, I would have done the exact same thing.

I remember my mother in her last days. She was so frightened of losing me. She talked about it all the time, forgetting that I was an adult now, remembering me as a baby. *A child can be lost so easily. They're so young, so trusting. Easy, to take a child from a pram, or a car, while her mother has turned away. Easy to take her memories, to make her believe she was yours from the start.*

I had to remind her: 'I'm not a child. I won't leave you, ever again.'

Of course, she was strange in those final weeks. She spoke a lot of nonsense. The Man in Black was always close, and even in her delirium, the pain overwhelmed the opiates she was taking. I spent what time with her I could, but I was working to feed us both and to pay for the motel room we shared in the cheapest part of Brooklyn. Every morning she would say: *Promise you'll come back, Vianne*, clinging to my sleeve like a child, her body like an armful of birds. *Promise you won't run away, Vianne*, even though it was thirteen years since I'd run away, even though I barely remembered why I'd run in the first place. Something to do with Molfetta, perhaps. Something to do with that rabbit. The rabbit and the Man in Black; that perpetual mystery. The unsolved equation which has dogged every part of my journey.

I turn to go. My prayer is done. I feel somehow lighter, free in my heart. My mother will always be with me, but she no longer determines my path. I do not need to read her cards to know where I am heading. The wind has grown stronger since I was here. The walk down the Butte feels like flying. I think about that little prayer pinned to the wall on the Virgin's shrine. *Mother, ease my broken heart.* And I know what I will cook tonight; what I will serve tomorrow. *Clafoutis pour mon petit Edmond*: a dish for the broken-hearted.

Cassoulet

I

8 October 1993

September goes by like a schooner, with sails of summer lightning. Now October spreads its wings, and the weather has turned, growing cooler, and bringing with it an altered sky of pigeon-feather purple.

My work in Margot's garden has proved unexpectedly fruitful. And in spite of Emile's prediction, Louis seems not to disapprove. Now we have sage and rosemary, lavender and wild carrot, as well as a riotous tumble of orange and yellow nasturtiums. As well as the yellow *Cyrano* rose, I have discovered three other roses: *Albertine*; *Pleine de Grâce*; and a flame-coloured rose called *Margot* – marked with a metal tag on the stem. The bushes were all hidden and choked with brambles and morning glories, but after some clearing and pruning, I have managed to bring them back: there may even be a few late flowers by the end of the year.

In the kitchen I have almost reached the last of Margot's recipes. Only two main dishes remain – the one she calls *Mon Cassoulet* and *Poulet à la Toulousaine*. So far I have learnt the recipes more or less in the order in which they appear in the book, skipping the ones that call for difficult regional ingredients. This time I chose the chicken first, daunted, perhaps, by the time required to make the other recipe. The Toulousain chicken looked easy compared to some of the things I'd already learnt; a simple roast, with olives and herbs and a stuffing of Toulouse sausage. Louis' double oven would easily take three chickens, I thought, and with some crushed potatoes tossed in oil, I thought it would please our customers.

But for some reason, it did not please Louis. His recent mood has been troubled: perhaps because of the approach of 13 October, the anniversary of Margot's death as well as that of her newborn child. Added to that, it was raining today, and the bistrot was mournful and colourless. Rain is bad for business. Even during the season it discourages tourists, and by now, the summer folk are long gone. Some of our semi-regular visitors have left with them, and as a result, I overestimated the quantities.

'I'll make a *paëlla* tomorrow,' I said. 'I'll use the leftover chicken in that.'

'What, and poison everyone?' Louis made a sound of impatience. '*Bonne Mère*, and here I was thinking I'd taught you something. Today was supposed to be cassoulet. What happened?'

I told him. Louis gave a sniff. 'People like the cassoulet,' he said. 'Next time, stick to the plan.'

I wonder what that plan might be. Louis does not speak of the future. To him, tomorrow is enough. All his planning – and Marguerite's – ended up in Saint-Pierre, in that concrete high-rise locals call *La Cathédrale du Silence*. And yet, here I am, a ticking clock, three months into my pregnancy. I wonder how I fit in his world. In six months' time, where will I be?

Not here, says the October wind. We've already stayed here too long. Margot's book has given up almost all its secrets. Once I have collected them all, I will leave without looking back.

Looking back is dangerous. Looking back, we sometimes see the shadows that we cast on the world. That's why we only move forward; that's why we never stay in one place. But this time is different. This time I can finally step out of my mother's shadow. Vianne, that village with my name, still calls to me from the south-west. That's where my Anouk will be born; where the Man in Black cannot follow. We will find a place to live – maybe a room above a café, or a little *chambre d'hôte*, with an elderly couple in charge – where I will work in the kitchen, or even open a shop of my own, selling hot chocolate and croissants. No one will know us there. No one will connect us with Jeanne Rochas, or any of her aliases. We will live quietly, humbly, without attracting attention. And when the wind changes, we will stay inside and watch the falling leaves, and put on winter sweaters, and eat comforting food, and make hot drinks, and light bonfires against the shadows. I see it so clearly now. I know it will happen. I can smell the fallen leaves, the scent of smoke and petrichor. And when the trees are green again, I'll meet my little stranger.

But first, this cassoulet. The last of Margot's recipes, and one that meant a lot to her. After all she has given me, I mean to do her justice. Louis, too: this is the dish that will open up his heart again, give him the chance to love, and be loved; give him back his future. Margot never wanted him to spend his life in mourning. She wanted him to understand that love is a thing that grows and grows, even as we give it away.

Cassoulet is a dish that needs to be started well in advance. Soak the haricot beans overnight – I found a giant jar of them at the back of a cupboard, still labelled in Margot's handwriting. *Haricots Lauragais*, it says. *ONLY for my cassoulet!*

In spite of their humble origin, I know the beans are important. Guy has taught me the difference between the various cacao beans: the Criollo, the *Forastero* and the rare, white *Porcelana*. According to Margot, these *Lauragais* beans are equally rare: and for this dish, they must keep their shape throughout many hours of cooking. Ordinary beans are too large, she says, and will break up during the process. Only the very best *Lauragais* beans must go into her cassoulet.

Following her instructions, I put the beans in cold water to soak, and checked what else I needed. The difficulty of this dish is the sheer time the cooking takes; three hours for the initial stage, then allow two hours to cool, and warm it again, very slowly, to allow the flavours to combine. That meant I had to start early. I went to the butcher's on the corner of Rue du Panier and explained what I was making.

'Cassoulet tomorrow, *hé*?' The butcher is called André, and he, too, is one of our regulars. 'Madame Martin made good cassoulet. She used her mother's recipe.'

Over the past three months I have learnt that food is deeply personal. Cassoulet, a dish that originated centuries ago in one of our poorest regions, has become an expression of the fiercest community pride. Toulouse has its own special recipe, and so do Castelnaudary and Carcassonne. But there exist a myriad of variants, like wild seeds that have found their home among the ruins of ancient times. Each one represents a life, all but forgotten now except for this – this dish that is more than just nourishment, but a reminder of one who was loved.

'You knew her?' I said.

'She had a shine.'

A shine. Isn't that what Tonton had said? I thought of the woman I'd glimpsed that day in the rising steam of the bouillabaisse. Shining, yes; but troubled, too; racked with grief and longing. The quote on her cassoulet recipe says: *The most beautiful verses are the ones that are never finished.*

Underneath, she has written: *Change reminds us we're alive. Only death never changes.*

André frowned and scrutinized his display of cuts of meat. 'Madame Martin was from Bergerac,' he repeated. 'That means no sausage, no mutton.'

I knew that already: the thick pork sausage is a Toulouse variant of cassoulet; the mutton, often combined with game, is Carcassone's tradition. Marguerite's recipe calls for salt pork, shoulder, rind, goose fat, duck confit. And love, of course; the ingredient that cannot be forgotten.

'Louis always likes to make this dish around the first or second week in October. He says it's the last dish she ever cooked. And the first thing she ever made for him when they were married.'

I sketched a little sign in the air, like pulling at a loosened thread. But André needed no encouragement. He went on: 'Must have been in '73. The year of the Watergate scandal. There was a song called *Angélique* that played all that month on the radio. It was playing when I heard she'd died. She was only forty-one.'

My mother was forty when she died. Or so she said. In truth, I think she was older. We didn't celebrate birthdays. I'm not even sure when mine is – it used to vary between 3 April and sometime in September. But forty-one – I can see Margot now, brown hair touched with tinsel. Margot. She had so much to live for; so much love to send into the world. It lives on in her recipes; recipes I mean to set free.

André wrapped my purchases and handed them to me in a paper bag. 'Good luck, *mademoiselle*,' he said. 'I hope you can make the dish your own.'

I thanked him. 'Yes, I think I can.'

2

9 *October 1993*

I got up at six this morning to be sure of the bakery order. Breakfast is between eight and nine. Fruit, a pile of fluffy croissants, and a pile of hard-boiled eggs, served with *tartines* and coffee. I served our regulars breakfast between frying the garlic and onions, then I blanched the *Lauragais* beans, made stock from the chicken carcass left over from yesterday's lunch, put in some fresh parsley, bay leaves and thyme, then added the beans to the chicken stock to cook while I made hot chocolate.

There were a lot of people today. Not quite as many as during the season, but still more than our usual half-dozen. I noticed Emile (of course), Monsieur Georges, Hélène from the flower shop, her friend Marinette, then Amadou, Rodolphe, Tonton and three young men in Arab dress, whom I did not recognize. I sense that Emile disapproves of this. Emile does not like foreigners. I served the three men, who were shy and polite, speaking just to each other, and returned to my cassoulet, to find that the beans had almost boiled dry. I must not lose concentration, I think. I must not allow distractions to affect the success of this recipe. I managed to salvage the beans just in time, then moved to the bar for a moment to try to relieve the atmosphere. Emile was talking loudly to Louis, and with an unusual relish.

'Time was, when the whole of the Panier was French. Now it's all Chinese takeaways, Turkish bakeries, Arab souks. In ten years' time, you'll be lucky to find a single proper French bistrot anywhere in the Vieux Quartier.'

Louis' eyes flicked to the group of men sitting in the corner. 'I'll still be here,' he said. 'Where do you think I'm going to be?'

'In ten years' time? Who knows?' said Emile. 'By the time you're seventy, you'll be in a retirement home – that is, if you're lucky – and La Bonne Mère will be an Indian restaurant, or a chichi pizzeria—'

Louis' colours flared, and Emile gave a little smirk between gasps from his cigarette.

'You want to start something now?' said Louis. 'You want to start something today?'

'I'm not starting anything,' said Emile. 'I'm not the one who opens his doors to every stray the wind blows in.' He grinned again, and I noticed that both men were drinking shots of cognac, although it was barely nine o'clock. The air between them was clouded with cigarette smoke and hostility. And yet there was some humour there; the kind of aggressive humour that for some men counts as affection.

I hurried back into the kitchen, and emerged carrying the chocolate pot. Scented steam rose from the spout, spiced with vanilla and cardamom. I sketched a sign on the side of the pot – it was *Gebo, a gift*, the rune of comfort and reconciliation.

'Who wants chocolate? On the house?'

'I'll have a cup,' said Emile at once.

'I'll have a cup,' mimicked Louis. '*Heh*. The amount of free food you get from this place, you'd think by now you might have learnt to show a little gratitude.'

Emile laughed, then Louis did too, and some of the tension between them dispersed. The bistrot was starting to clear at last, although between serving breakfast, adding the vegetables to my stock, searing the meat in a cast-iron pan and keeping an eye on my customers, I was already feeling tired. The combination of bar-room smoke, and the scents of garlic and goose fat, onions, coffee and chocolate were almost unendurable, and the heat from the giant skillet in which I had placed the pieces of duck made it feel like midday. Emile was smoking another *Gitane*, and the smoke filtered into the back of the room and all the way into the kitchen. A wave of sudden nausea assailed me like a breaking wave, strong and unexpected. I put down the skillet and clung to the big pine countertop to steady myself.

Tsk-tsk, begone. My mother's spell, to banish bad thoughts, bad feelings. This was no time for morning sickness. Nor could I afford a repetition of the bouillabaisse incident. I drank a glass of water, and felt a little better.

I heard Louis' voice from the bar. 'Vianne! More coffee, please!'

'No chocolate?'

'I said coffee. Do I look like a child to you?'

'Coffee it is.'

'And a cognac.'

I poured it, feeling uneasy. Louis' moods have not so far extended to cognac at breakfast. But twenty years is a long time to grieve. A long time to feel guilty.

Why is he your problem again? Guy's voice, like my mother's, is hard to ignore. But Guy, like my mother, does not understand this need to make people happy. It's the only craving I have had so far during this pregnancy; this need to see light in their faces, to bring joy back into their hearts. And I have the knack, I know: I can ring the changes.

Back in the kitchen, I found the *cassole*, the big clay pot that Margot always used when making this dish. Her recipe makes it very clear that no other cooking pot must be used. It's a very old cassole, probably handed down to her by her mother or grandmother, and the blackened clay still bears the thumbprint of the maker on the rim. *Line the base with the pork rinds, then add the beans, the duck, the pork shoulder in three layers. Add just enough of the chicken bouillon to cover. Bake for three hours. Keep checking the cassole regularly. The surface of the cassoulet will darken and bake to a kind of crust; when this happens, push it down into the mixture, adding stock when necessary. Tradition dictates that you should do this seven times during the cooking.*

You see, there is a ritual in everything. Even this humblest of alchemy; the transformation of base ingredients into something that takes you home. Seven times, to make sure that the tale ends happily ever after. Monsters defeated, lost children found, night terrors banished by daylight. Cooking is predictable; it follows the rules; it keeps to the path. It never has to pack its things and flee under cover of darkness. It has a reason for everything. Everything has its own place. Cooking makes *sense*. It is safe and secure. It never does harm to anyone.

I place my thumb over the print on the rim of the old cassole. *Imagine being that person*, I think. *Imagine leaving a permanent mark. Imagine having a place of your own — a kitchen, with your own pots and pans. And when the Man in Black comes round, imagine serving him chocolate.*

In the bar, the breakfast crowd had mostly dispersed. A few would remain – Emile, perhaps – but most would return in time for lunch. I started washing the breakfast things, while keeping a close eye on the cassole. *Push the top down seven times.* One: a pink rabbit left on a bench on a railway platform in Syracuse. Two: the sound of the wind in the eaves, and my mother talking in her sleep. Three: the face of the Man in Black, who chased us all across the world. Four: the friends we left behind, blown away like dandelion seeds. Five: the scent of unaired sheets, of grubby carpets in cheap hotels. Six: a firework display over the Hudson river. And seven—

Seven needs something more. Something like the thumb-print on the handle of the pot; something to mark this dish as my own. The jar of xocolatl is hidden among the spices; it smells of the court of the Chocolate Kings; the forests of South America. It has a pleasing bitterness; a taste as dark as memory. It calls to me from across the years:

Try me. Taste me. Test me.

I have used it before, of course, in desserts and hot choco-late. But it works best in a savoury dish. I can already taste how it would deepen the range of flavours. Garlic, bay and rosemary, crowned with xocolatl. A pinch or two is all it needs; and already the flavours are shuffling; shuffling like a pack of cards, dealing a different future.

I lift the lid for the seventh time, releasing a veil of steam from the dish. It smells of home, and of history. A fingerprint on a favourite pot. A memory of laughter. The footprint of a newborn child in her baby album. The scent of his head as she holds him there, sweet as blood and chocolate.

I turn off the heat to let the dish rest. Already it looks wonderful. I push down the baked crust a seventh time. By lunchtime, it will be perfect. Here is my gift to you, Margot. Here is my gift to you, Louis. Magic – *real* magic – is not a tool that lends itself to going unseen. Magic makes us visible; that's why we have to keep moving. But I will be moving on very soon: I can afford some fireworks. Unlike Margot, I do not need incense, or incantations. I can already take what

I need through the steam from the old cassole, transforming these base ingredients into something approaching a miracle.

Grief into love. Straw into gold. Mourning into acceptance. Some things can be changed – or called into being. Things – and also people.

Seventh time completes the charm.

I think I'm getting good at this.

3

Certain meals stand tall among the legends of a lifetime. That cassoulet was one of them; served on Margot's good tableware, with garlic bread and a glass of red wine. I could see their faces illuminated from within; their colours like a nimbus in the shadows of the drab little room. Everyone was happy today. The warmth of that good and humble meal was like a benediction.

Of course, it's only food. I know. But Marinette will sleep better tonight; Rodolphe will find his bad hip soothed; Tonton will feel the sun on his face and go for a longer walk with his dog. Even Emile will feel a small unexpected afterglow. And Louis – I have a gift for Louis, which I have been planning since Khamaseen gave me the baby album. Four hundred francs at the funeral shop – more than I expected, but the result is beautiful. I mean to give it to him on the day of the anniversary; a reminder that love is not a place, or a time, or even a memory.

Dessert was a mocha cheesecake topped with crème Chantilly, with black coffee and truffles to finish. The truffles were ones I'd made with Guy, one afternoon at Allée du Pieu, and I saw Louis' look when I passed them around, but he made no comment. I noticed that Emile took three, even though he claimed not to like bitter chocolate; and that Monsieur Georges took an extra one, which he hid away for later.

Traditionally, Louis and I eat our lunch at three o'clock, when our regulars have gone, but today it was nearly half past four when we finally sat down to eat. The weather had brightened, and the sky had veered from grey to washed-out blue, with a net of mackerel clouds that softened the horizon. I thought Louis still looked tense, as if there was something on his mind, and I wondered how many shots of cognac he'd had with his coffee during the day.

'Ready for lunch?' I said at last.

'Not too much. I'm not hungry.'

I ignored his comment, and set the dish of cassoulet in front of him. Slow-cooked regional dishes like this often improve with re-heating. The scent was rich and flavoursome; the meat perfectly silky; the tender beans infused with the flavours of bay, and clove, and rosemary.

Louis tasted a forkful. I waited for his verdict.

'*Heh*. Not bad.'

I smiled. *Not bad* is Louis' highest accolade. Louis Martin is not a man given to lavish compliments. But I could see his colours through the rising steam from the old cassole; the lightning greys of that morning giving way to softer, warmer hues; the pastels of childhood; the palette of hope; the rosy, sunrise tint of love.

'This was my Margot's signature dish,' he said, between mouthfuls of cassoulet. He sighed. 'It tastes like coming home.'

I hid my smile. 'I'm glad,' I said. 'I tried to do it justice.'

He nodded. 'Did you make it last night? It tastes so rich, I thought perhaps—'

It tastes of something he can't place. I can see him trying to isolate it in his mind. I can read it in the steam: a memory of another time, of a time when we were someone else; of laughter and champagne corks, popping like a firework display –

You see, God answers prayers, Louis. In his way, He answers them.

No, Louis was not always the Hermit. On that day, he was different, mirthful as a mad March hare, and she was warm and round as a plum, all filled with the joy of that life inside. My own small inner life responds; Anouk, who has been so quiet of late, now joins the celebration. My little Anouk. I can see her now, in those little pink crocheted bootees. *Summer children are filled with light. God answers prayers. He answers them.*

Louis looked up from his empty plate. His tired eyes were shining. 'That was good. But *different*, somehow. Did you change the recipe?'

I shook my head. 'I followed hers.'

But that's not altogether true. I added that pinch of bitter spice, that dose of something rich and strange. And a hint of my mother's art, that thing that makes us different. The thing that finds what people need. The thing that sees what others miss; that serves it with a smile.

'They finished the cheesecake, I'm afraid. I'll make something else to finish the meal.' I took out my smallest copper pan, added milk and cacao. A generous piece of red chilli, for heat. Grated nutmeg for sweetness. And more than a pinch of the chocolate spice; rich and dark and generous.

'I suppose this means I'll have to start paying you a proper wage. I mean, with the baby, and everything.'

'You've been more than kind,' I said.

'I've been a pain, and you know it.'

I laughed. 'In that case, try my hot chocolate. You'll like it, if you give it a chance.'

'*Heh*. Well, maybe a little.'

4

10 October 1993

I dreamed of my mother during the night. We were standing outside a whitewashed church, the kind you can see in any village in the south-west. A strong wind was blowing, and the sky was filled with pieces of shredded paper. Above us, in the tower, a carillon of furious bells jangled and rang chaotically.

My mother was wearing a kind of robe, like the Empress in the Tarot pack. Her hair was wild and witchlike. A brazier stood before her. And then I saw that her hair was white, and knew that this wasn't my mother at all, but Khamaseen, from Rue du Panier; the Empress's robe like a patchwork quilt swirling and flapping around her.

She shouted over the clang of the bells: *'All change! All change!'* And I realized that the paper that charged the air with particles was ash; the ash from my mother's Tarot cards burning in the brazier; a brazier that was also somehow Marguerite's old earthen cassole, the one with the thumbprint on the rim—

And in my dream I understood that I had done a terrible thing: that all these bells were ringing for *me*, and that somehow by calling for changes for Louis, I had triggered an avalanche, and then I awoke to the sound of bells from Notre-Dame above me, and realized that it had just been a dream, and that it was Sunday.

I pulled on my jeans. They were getting tight. I left the top button unfastened, but I will soon need a larger size. In the wake of the troubling dream, little Anouk was lying low, but below me, the guest room we never use was filled with the sounds of activity, and the morning air through the open window suddenly smelt of autumn. The weather had shifted overnight; the sea was green instead of blue, and a cast of purple cloud was gathering on the horizon. *A seasonal shift, that's all*, I thought – but then I remembered my dream, and my mother's voice, shouting over the voice of the wind:

All change! All change!

I threw on a baggy shirt to hide the fact that my jeans were unbuttoned, and tied up my hair in an old silk scarf scavenged from a charity shop. Going downstairs, I found that Louis had opened the second guest room, and was busily sweeping the floor. Sunlight shone through the windows, and the air was filled with motes. Three unopened cans of paint and a set of new brushes stood by the door, next to a cardboard box containing the rugs and the faded curtains.

He looked round at me and grinned. 'At last, you're up! I was afraid you were going to sleep till noon.'

I was puzzled. 'What are you doing?'

'I thought it was time I did up this room. Air it out, nice lick of paint, clean curtains, maybe a rug—'

I nodded. 'That sounds like a good idea. But – aren't you going to Saint-Pierre today?'

He shook his head. 'I'll go Wednesday.'

'Of course. Whenever you like, Louis.'

That was the anniversary. Wednesday, 13 October. The twentieth anniversary of Margot's death. And yet, although

André had said Louis was depressed at this time of year, he didn't seem depressed to me. Quite the contrary; he seemed to be infused with a kind of chaotic energy. His eyes were bright: he seemed to charge the air like electricity. And he had made breakfast for both of us: just coffee, fruit and croissants, but it was the first time he'd done such a thing since I moved in two months ago.

'I heated up what was left of that chocolate of yours,' he said. 'I think I could get used to it.'

'I'm glad you like it,' I said with a smile, although I was feeling uneasy. The change – whatever change I had worked – was both joyous and disturbing. Louis looked like a man waking up after the best night's sleep he'd had in twenty years of insomnia. And there was a shift in his colours, I saw; something sweet and hopeful and bright, which contrasted with that ominous dream, and filled me with foreboding.

But it was only a little thing!

There are no little things, chérie.

No, there are no little things. I see that now, too late. Too late. That's why she always moved us on before we got too strongly attached. That's why she made me leave my toy on the bench by the railway. Don't put down roots, she always said. Roots drag us under. They take us down. They build their fortresses over us. Roots are what stop us from flying free, and people are the worst of them, always stretching out in the dark, desperate to make a connection. And now, too late, I can feel those roots reaching out so hungrily, and I see what the change in his colours means, and I know why he is repainting the room.

'It won't take long to paint the walls. The gloss work may take longer, but the weather's still good, and we'll air the place out so there's no smell. After that, you can decide what you'd like to put in there. I already have some things you can use. A little crib. Some baby clothes. Toys. They're in the old wardrobe in my room. I never got round to clearing them out, and before long you're going to need them.'

I'd never heard Louis say so much at once. Habitually monosyllabic, this morning, he couldn't stop talking; the words spilled out of him like wine. 'Louis, that's very kind,' I said. 'But—'

'I know, I know. It's six months away.' He grinned. 'To me, that's tomorrow. You're young. But trust me, six months is no time at all when it comes to making arrangements.' He looked at me. 'And you'll need that, Vianne. Because right now, you have nothing. No permanent home, no bank account, no social security number. No health insurance, no family, no wedding ring, no boyfriend.'

'I'll manage,' I said. 'I always have.'

'You don't know what you're saying,' said Louis. 'How old are you? Twenty? Twenty-one? You don't have any family. The moment you have your first check-up, you're going to have to explain to the doctors and Social Services how you're going to care for a child. Otherwise, they'll take him away. Surely you must see that.'

He thinks it's a boy, I told myself, thinking of the pink bootees. *Just as Margot was certain that her child would be a boy.*

I shook my head. 'They can't do that.'

'They can, and they will. But I can help. I can help support both of you. I can deal with the paperwork, the doctors, the insurance. I could serve as a kind of adopted grandfather to the child.'

I stared at him. 'Wait, what?' I said.

'Just to be safe, Vianne,' Louis went on. 'I wouldn't ask anything else of you. For God's sake, you could be my daughter.

But when the baby's born, it means the two of you won't be alone. I've put money aside. Business is good. And you can keep on working here, part-time, and the baby can have this room. It's just under yours, so you'll be able to hear him. And—' For a moment he looked abashed. 'It'd be nice to see him grow. To know I did *something* good, for a change.'

Oh, Louis. I'm so sorry, Louis. It is a kind thought, of course. But it is not his *only* thought. I can feel it all around, distressing the air like the sound of bells. Roots are hungry things, I thought. Like children, all they want is to feed. Through the motes that shine in the air I can see sudden glimpses of the future in his mind: myself, with the child, in a rocking-chair. The bedroom, all painted in yellow and blue. And a pair of blue bootees, hanging from a painted sign on the back of a bedroom door – a sign that simply reads: *Edmond.*

This is what I have called into being. *This* is the change I have summoned. I have brought hope – but at what cost? Love, but what of my freedom? *A named thing is a claimed thing.* And how soon will it be before Louis asks me if I've chosen a name? Before he claims my child as his own? Before the face of my little Anouk is eclipsed by that of a stranger?

'I know it's a lot to take in at first,' said Louis, seeing my expression. 'That's fine. Take all the time you need. Meanwhile, I've asked a friend of mine – a doctor – to come and look you over. He's a good man, and very discreet. He'll make sure you and the baby are healthy.'

'You're very kind,' I said. 'But I—'

'Don't say anything yet,' he said. 'Just think about it for a while. Go have some breakfast. The croissants are fresh. But leave me a cup of that chocolate.'

5

I didn't want any breakfast. Nor did I want to stay at La Bonne Mère, to hear Louis' plans for the future. Of course I'm happy for Louis. I wanted to see him break through his grief, and find a future of his own. But I can't be a part of it. Nor can my child replace Edmond. I realize now how reckless I've been in letting Louis get close to me. I should have seen the signs earlier, known how his protectiveness would soon extend to my baby. But I was too absorbed in my own discoveries – Margot's story, her recipes, my adventures in chocolate – to see the dark clouds gathering. Now I had a new problem; and I could see no solution that wouldn't cause *someone* to be hurt.

And this is why we never stay long, whispers my mother's voice from the Butte, where the Good Mother looks down on Marseille from under a mantle of raincloud. *This is why we don't get attached; why we move with the seasons. Summer is long past, 'Viane. Time to do what we always do.*

I suddenly wanted to talk to Guy. To sit in the chocolaterie and smell the roasting cacao, and hear the sounds of the conching machine, and listen to his stories. Guy has always understood my need for independence. He has never pursued

144

me, and shows only a passing interest in my pregnancy. Not that I needed his help now, but there was something about the chocolate shop that always seemed to calm my mind. And so I made for Allée du Pieu, where I found Mahmed clearing out the mess of litter from a flooded drain. His hair had come loose, his face was splashed with mud, and he looked bad tempered and tired.

'This place. The *work*. It never ends,' he said, shovelling a stack of soaking papers, straw and rags into an open refuse sack. 'Just when you think it's nearly done, you find something else. A broken drain. A leaking roof. A horsehair *wall*, for pity's sake.' He broke off to kick at a piece of sodden chipboard, which flew apart at the contact, and scattered across the alleyway. 'Ouch. *Ouch!*'

'You're busy,' I said. 'Is Guy around?'

He shook his head. 'He's in Toulouse. With his family.'

'Oh,' I said. I was oddly surprised at my disappointment. 'Do you know when he'll be back?'

He shrugged. 'I don't know. It could be a week.'

'I see.' Once more I felt that sting of disappointment. In a week, I will be gone. I won't have the chance to say goodbye. And yet, we never say goodbye. We only turn with the seasons.

Mahmed must have noticed my look. 'Are you feeling okay?' he said. 'Let me make you some coffee.'

He saw my hesitation. 'Come inside. I promise, you'll be doing me a favour.'

I followed him into the chocolate shop. The place is taking shape now, with a counter, a wall full of shelves, and a Plexiglas divider that separates the display area from the workshop, where the conching machine, the moulds, the belt and other necessary tools of the trade will one day be visible to the public. The walls have been painted a delicate ochre colour, with sweeping patterns in red and brown, which are meant to depict cacao pods. There is a coffee machine by the door, which already looks like it's had plenty of use. Mahmed poured himself an espresso and looked at me inquiringly.

'Not for me,' I told him. 'Right now, even the smell of coffee makes me nauseous.'

Mahmed looked abashed. 'Of course,' he said. 'My sister used to be just the same. Hang on a minute—' He went into the back room and emerged a few minutes later carrying a teapot and two little cups. 'It's cardamom chai,' he told me. 'My mother used to make it.'

'What, no chocolate?' I said. I meant it as a joke, and yet it came out sounding mournful.

He grinned, a wide and open grin that made him look like a schoolboy in spite of his greying hair. 'It sometimes feels that way, doesn't it? I have to say, Guy likes the stuff a lot better than I do, but – what can I say? It's his passion.'

He poured two cups of the cardamom chai. It was hot and creamy and good. 'You say his family's in Toulouse?'

He nodded. 'He doesn't see them much. His father's a senior partner in a law firm in the city. I think Guy was expected to take over the family business. That makes it hard for him to go back. I think he's a disappointment.'

I was astonished. 'Guy? *Law?*'

I tried to imagine Guy studying law. But all I could summon was the memory of the day I'd first met him; unkempt in his Hawaiian shirt and battered straw hat, his eyes gleaming with amusement and the lure of distant places. I looked at Mahmed, almost ready to believe he was joking, but his expression was almost sad beneath the rueful little smile.

'You have no idea how lucky you are, not having a family. Not having those expectations. Not being—' He saw my expression. 'Dammit. I'm so sorry, Vianne. I know you lost your mother.'

'It's okay,' I reassured him. 'I know you didn't mean it that way. But what about *your* family? Do you ever see them?'

'*My* parents tell people I'm dead.' He gave that little smile again. 'It's easier than telling them I fled the marriage they wanted for me. Easier than telling them—' He stopped abruptly. 'Easier.'

I took another sip of my tea. A filament of scented steam unfurled like petals into the air.

What's your story?

Look and see. It's not as if you're staying now.

I took a breath of the scented steam. It smelt of roses and bitter cloves. Looking through the vapour, I saw the hand of Tarot cards which has haunted me since I arrived. The Hermit. The Fool. The Chariot. Change. The Six of Swords. The Four of Cups. And the Lovers, still the Lovers, entwined; one dark, one light, a half-familiar face half-turned; embracing on the green, green ground—

How could I have missed it? The easy way they interact. The marriage of their colours. The way he lights up when Guy is around. Behind the shy aloofness, the silent loyalty of love.

'How long have you been together?' I said.

He flinched. 'Is it really that obvious?'

'No, you hid it very well.' I smiled and put down my tea cup. 'I'm glad you found each other,' I said. 'Isn't that all that matters?'

He looked relieved, as if he'd expected something to break between us. He took a sip of his tea, then said: 'I'd rather you didn't tell anyone. It's hard enough to be who I am without having everyone knowing it. Our customers. Guy's family—'

'He's happy with you. Why would they not want that?'

That smile again. 'You don't understand. A son – an only son – is supposed to represent the family. To carry on traditions. To father children. To hold the line. Girls can do whatever they like. But men – they do what's expected of them.'

'Only daughters follow the wind.'

He looked surprised. 'What's that?'

I shrugged. 'Something my mother used to say.' Outside, the weather had turned again, and the sky was a luminous, rain-washed blue. 'I should get back to La Bonne Mère. Louis will be wondering where I am.' I hugged him. 'Give my love to Guy. Good luck with the chocolaterie.'

6

10 October 1993

Over the past few days I have been silently saying goodbye to Marseille. Goodbye to the markets, the Vieux Quartier, the harbour, where the pleasure boats have mostly been put away for the winter. Goodbye to my customers; to Marinette, with her elegant air and love of my hot chocolate; to Tonton and his dog, Galipette; to Emile and his combination of gluttony and resentment. Goodbye to the garden, and the roses that I shall never see bloom; goodbye to Margot's cookery book, and everything she has given me. Only Louis is left, and the gift that I had made for him, a gift I can't bear to part with now, because that would mean saying goodbye.

You should be gone already, 'Viane, says my mother's voice from the top of the Butte. And I know that she is right: I can see the changes unfolding. The guest room – no, the *baby's* room – is completely finished, though Louis tells me the smell of paint will linger for a few days. I chase it away with the good scents of my cooking; apricot tartlets; pan-fried squid with chilli oil; pieds paquets, with saffron rice. Louis has not mentioned our conversation of the weekend, but I feel it always at my side, like the ghost of a promise unfulfilled. I

149

should be gone. I know it, and yet the temptation to stay – just another day, a week – is almost unbearable.

But today is my last day. I have already said my goodbyes, silent as they must be. There is only one place left on my list: the very first place I visited. Over the past months, Bonne Mère has become a part of my life; leaving her now is almost as hard as leaving Louis and the bistrot. And today the weather is threatening; the climb to the summit cheerless; the warm air charged with the rain to come. Halfway to the top of the Butte, I turn to look over the harbour: the wall of purple cloud that stands on the far horizon has acquired a skirt of lightning. There is no audible thunder as yet, but the dark air feels the change.

I hurry towards the summit. A woman by the side of the road is selling Marseille soap from out of a basket. It smells of summer and the sea, and the olive oil used in the process. The woman is middle-aged, nondescript; dressed in the kind of overall so many women here prefer.

I ask, 'How much?'

'Five francs.'

There are so many different scents, so many different colours. Lavender, and vetiver, and patchouli, and seaweed, and rose, all roughly cut and stamped with the words *Savon de Marseille, 72% Extra Pur*. I buy a block of mimosa soap that smells of summer sunshine. She hands it to me in a paper bag. The voice in my head whispers slyly: *One more thing to leave behind.*

It sounds like my mother, but it is not. Perhaps it is the voice of the wind that blows now from the quayside – the *Tramontane*, the *Sirocco*, or in the case of Marseille, the *Mistral* – tugging at my shirttails.

'Vianne, whoever you are. It's time.'

And the mist that blurs the horizon is like the vapour from the bouillabaisse, and the vapour from my dreams, and it shows me that room at La Bonne Mère, in blue and mimosa-yellow, with a bowl of flowers by the bed, and the crib by the open window. And there are toys in that little room: rabbits and teddies and building-blocks, and hand-knitted clothes in the cupboard, and a rocking-horse by the door, hand-carved like the wooden crib.

But the child in the crib is not Anouk. The vapour shows me a little boy, a boy who will not follow the wind, however much it calls him. That boy was wanted. That boy was loved. That boy would have been happy here. That boy would have been at home in Marseille, would have picked the plums from the tree that grew behind La Bonne Mère; would have played by the Old Port and chased stray dogs and dreamed of the ships that went sailing by. But Margot's son did not survive. And the space he has left is *hungry*.

Why, Margot? What do you want? I've learnt your recipes. Read your book. Seen Edmond's footprint on the page. Wherever I go, your memory and his will carry on. But I can't you give you this. Can't change who I am. Can't change who my daughter is going to be.

My mother's voice again: *'Viane. I thought I taught you better than this. A mother is a shark, chérie: if she falls asleep, she dies. You have been asleep for too long. Now you need to wake up, and—*

'Run, before the storm breaks.'

I realize I have closed my eyes. Opening them once again, I see the seller of Marseille soaps fastening the straps on the side of her heavy wicker basket. The purple clouds are now very close; thickly spindled with lightning.

'I'm sorry?'

'I said I'm going to have to run. Before the storm breaks.' The woman hoisted her basket onto her back. 'If rain gets into this lot, there'll be nothing left of me but suds.'

I watched her as she shouldered her wares, and felt a sudden sense of unease. When I was choosing the soap I'd assumed that she was a younger woman, but now I realized she was older than that, and that the braid of hair down her back was not grey, but almost white. It was the woman from Rue du Panier, watching me from eyes the shade of those lightning-spindled clouds.

'Khamaseen. You look different,' I said.

'Sometimes it's useful to blend in.' She smiled. 'So, you decided to leave,' she said. 'You're leaving Marseille, and moving on.'

'How did you know?'

'I see things.' A fat drop of rain fell between us, smacking onto the road like a curse. 'Still, if you're going in search of yourself, be sure not to leave yourself behind. You don't want that for your child, Vianne. Changing direction with the wind, flinching at every turn of the cards. A little boy could be good for you. A good little boy with sea-blue eyes, who loves his mother, and never leaves. A little boy who sleeps at night, and never hears the call of the wind.'

It sounded almost like a threat. And yet, the woman's voice was kind.

I said: 'I have a daughter.'

'Then run,' said the woman. 'Here it comes.'

7

As she spoke, a second raindrop fell on the cobbles in front of me. Then another. Then a third; as large as five-franc pieces. There came a rolling of thunder like the sound of a lorry coming downhill, and a sudden drenching rain, darkening the cobbles. Khamaseen had disappeared.

I ran for the nearest balcony, under which a man was standing. Light-eyed; maybe thirty years old, and wearing a kind of dark cape, revealing a clerical collar. I felt a sudden lurch of alarm – my mother's fear of the Man in Black still lives in me like a splinter – but there was nowhere else to run without risking the downpour.

I saw the man's eyes flick to my face as I ran under the balcony, my shirt already stuck to my skin, my hair in rat's-tails under my scarf. I'd tucked the bag with the mimosa soap under my arm; it felt heavy. I pulled it out; the paper was wet. But there was no bar of soap inside. Instead, I found my mother's cards, neatly bound together with twine, ready to go back into the box in which she'd kept them all my life. For a moment I almost believed that I'd been struck by lightning. I gasped, and felt the cards in my hand shuffle, almost by themselves; caught a scent of mimosa from the sodden paper. How had she found these? How had she known how to return them to me?

The man in the dark cape looked at me. I saw he was younger than I'd thought; not much older than I was. Maybe a *séminariste*, I thought: or a newly ordained deacon.

'Are you all right?' He sounded concerned. 'You're not going to faint, or anything?'

I shook my head. 'I don't think so.'

The young man said nothing. His eyes were a curious shade of pale green, like the harbour water.

'Are you a visitor to Marseille?'

He nodded. I thought he looked ill at ease, like someone who expects to be robbed. Perhaps it was just my interruption of his silent communion with the rain. 'My – ah – colleagues from the seminary all went to see the basilica.'

I notice he did not say *friends*. 'Yes, it's beautiful,' I said.

He shrugged. 'I'd prefer something less – flashy.'

I smiled. 'I thought that was the point.'

'I don't think God needs gilding.' He saw my expression and frowned. 'Did I say something funny?'

'No, not at all. More priests should think the way you do.'

He gave a small and chilly smile. 'I'm not a priest. Not yet. But soon—' His sea-glass eyes seemed to darken. 'My own village priest sadly suffered a stroke. The bishop thinks it unlikely that he will return to his duties. I would have moved back straightaway, but the bishop feels I should take time – to travel the country, to understand all the opportunities available – before going back to my village.'

'That seems sensible,' I said.

He shrugged again. 'I've seen enough. I take no joy in travelling.'

We watched in silence for a time, as the rain hammered down on the cobbles. My bare feet in their sandals were splashed with mud from the dusty street; the awning above us was a drum; the gutters tumbled with water.

'What makes you want to go back there?' I said, as the rain began to abate. 'Why not a different village, at least? Or a city, like Marseille? Or even another country?'

He gave me a look that might have been of pity or of scorn. 'There's no way to explain,' he said. 'You either belong to a place, or you don't. I suppose everyone feels the same about somewhere.' He looked down at my ankles, which were splashed with street mud. 'Even Marseille.'

'Not everyone. Some of us follow the wind.'

'Follow the wind,' he repeated, as if the idea was new to him.

I did not explain. I do not expect the wind to be something he has ever thought about. Some of us are barnacles, made from birth to cling to the rocks of faith, or fear or family. And some of us are thistledown, lighter than the air we breathe – until, perhaps, a thunderstorm drives us into the gutter.

Vianne will be autumnal now, with the plane trees beginning to turn along the banks of the river. I wonder what the priest's village is like. I wonder if he would welcome me there. I wonder what it feels like to belong so completely to a place that all others feel wanting.

'The rain has stopped,' observed the priest.

I looked. So it had. A gleam of grey light pierced the dissipating clouds. 'I should be getting on,' I said. 'This city isn't as welcoming in autumn as in summertime.'

He looked at me. 'I wish you luck.'

'What's the name of your village?' I said. 'Perhaps I'll pass by there someday.'

'You wouldn't know it,' said the priest. 'Its name is Lansquenet-sous-Tannes. No one goes there. I like it that way.'

I noticed he did not tell me that I would be welcome to visit. I stepped out from under the balcony, holding my mother's pack of cards very tightly in my hand. 'Safe journey home to your village, *mon père*.'

I do not know why it felt as if I had made a confession.

8

I never said goodbye to Louis. There never seemed to be a good time: what little time we had was taken up with cooking, or dealing with customers. Nor did I give him his present. I'll leave it here tomorrow, when Louis leaves me in charge while he goes to the cemetery. It's proof of the trust he has in me now, that he will entrust his bistrot to me. I'm not sure I deserve his trust. I have, after all, betrayed it. Pinch by pinch, I have altered the flavours of recipes I swore not to change. The cassoulet. The bouillabaisse. Giving them the quiet call of other places, other loves.

I keep thinking about the priest I met during the rainstorm, the one from that village on the Tannes, too small even to appear on my map. Now I wish I'd asked his name. *You either belong to a place, or you don't. I suppose everyone feels the same about somewhere.* Except that I don't, do I, Maman? You made very certain of that. Perhaps that's why I have taken the name of one of those fortified places. Vianne, that little walled *bastide*, a fortress with a woman's name. What was she like, that other Vianne? Was she also a mother? I open my little map book again, as if to find the answers.

157

Of course, in French, the word for 'map' – *carte* – is also
the word for 'card' as well as the word for 'menu'. *Carte*.
Each word implies a spreading out, an exploration, a connection, a coming home. A welcome. Each one contains magic;
mystery; a glimpse of possible futures. Which one will it be,
I wonder Which card holds my story?

The Tarot cards are back in their box, in my travel bag,
packed and ready to go. It seems somehow inevitable that
they should have returned to me now. Normally, on the eve
of a journey, I would read them, but this time I don't have
the courage to try. Instead I look through the vapour that
rises from my camomile tea, but all I can see is Marguerite,
sitting on the side of the bed, a dish of little sweets at her
side – except that when I look closer, I see that they are not
sweets at all, but *santons*, Nativity figurines; tiny ceramic wise
men and lambs and angels and shepherds and babies. Each one
a whispered secret, a wish, a prayer, an epiphany.

He keeps them now in a wooden box, not unlike the
one in which I keep my mother's Tarot cards, along with a
bundle of letters to him, written in her shapeless hand, and
a lock of her silvery-brown hair, and a dried rose from her
wedding bouquet, dimly scented at its heart with the fragrance
of things past. Tomorrow he will look inside, and take one
breath of that fragrance. Then he will buy a single red rose,
which he cannot place on her grave, and head once more to
Saint-Pierre.

Except that this time will be different. This time, he has
things to say. This time, after he has passed through the
Cathedral of Silence and laid his rose by Rostand's grave, he
will take out a pocket flask, and pour himself a tiny glass of
the *prunelle* he put down the year they were first married,
made with the plums from the little tree that grows behind

La Bonne Mère. The plums are out of season now, but when they are fully ripe they are yellow as honeycomb, and as sweet. He has only one bottle left; and it smells of golden summers, when the world was still gentle, and gilded with possibility.

He will pour the final glass, and drink it there, by the graveside, where her memory is most potent. He will read a passage by Edmond Rostand, something from *Cyrano*, perhaps; and then he will empty the dregs on the ground, to honour the spirit of the place. This is the ritual he performs on the date of this anniversary. But this time, he will say something else. I can almost hear his words.

Margot, he whispers, in a voice that only she and I can hear. *Margot, at last, after all this time, I think perhaps—*

I've met someone.

9

Louis went out before lunch, which was less busy than usual. I'd made red mullet with *ratatouille*, rich with olive oil, onion and herbs, and a pineapple *tatin* to follow. Emile was there, and Monsieur Georges, and Amadou and Marinette, but the rest of the usual patrons were absent, and there were no tourists to take their place.

My things were already packed upstairs. My mother's cards, my papers, the notebook of recipes, the pink bootees, a sweater, a change of clothing, Guy's jar of xocolatl and the money I have managed to save – all packed neatly into the bag I brought with me from New York. The rest of the clothes – those charity-shop blouses and chiffon skirts and summer frocks, all hoarded in the almost-belief that I could wear them next summer – can stay, or be sold, or be given away. I try not to imagine Louis finding them, remembering; keeping them in the wardrobe the way he kept Margot's dresses. I ought to take them with me back to the charity shop, but there are too many to carry now, and time is getting short.

As soon as lunch is over, I thought, I'll shut up the bistrot, and go. *Go.* That urgency, that reluctance, duelling fiercely inside me. Leaving will never be any easier than it is today. Harder, perhaps, but not easier. Louis' present – my gift to him – I will leave in the kitchen. That's where I first met Margot; it's where her presence lingers. The gift is a palm-sized river stone; polished, tactile; river-grey, upon which her baby's footprint appears in miraculous detail, as if he had briefly stepped on the rock with wet feet while crossing the river. Above it, in Margot's handwriting, his name is acid-etched on the stone: *Edmond Loïc Bien-Aimé Martin.*

Margot would have liked it, I think. I hope Louis understands what it means. It means that we all leave our mark, even the ones who leave early. It means that we are connected with each other and with the past; that love does not vanish when we do, but stays; to watch us and to help us grow.

I looked back into the bar and saw Emile, eating lunch alone. He had lingered until the others had gone, and I had cleared the dishes. Then he finished his coffee and brought the cup into the kitchen, where I was starting the washing-up in Louis' big old farmhouse sink, almost as deep as a bathtub.

For a moment he stood watching me, his colours a troubling jumble of greys and greens and resentful purple. I thought he looked unwell today, his face more lined than usual; and yet there was a smile on his face, the smile he usually reserves for when he's about to say something unpleasant. I kept on washing the dishes, but from the corner of my eye I could see him watching me, looking around the kitchen, occasionally touching something – a wooden spoon, a copper pot – with the air of a man testing out a new reality.

'*Vianne Rochas,*' he said at last, speaking as if from a script. '*Vianne Rochas* – if that's your name.'

I turned to him. 'Can I help you?'

He shrugged. He looked both angry and sick, and yet he was still smiling. 'I've been doing some asking around,' he said, 'since you arrived here.'

'Really?' My heart gave a little bump. 'About what?'

The smile became a grin. 'Don't give me that. I know what you are. I knew it the minute you walked through that door. Don't flatter yourself you're the only one who's ever tried to play that game. It's happened before. Did he tell you? That woman from the magic shop, making out she could speak with the dead. He must have given her thousands of francs before he finally realized. And now you. Don't think I don't know. Don't think I don't know what you're doing.'

It was the most he'd ever said to me directly. And I could tell he'd been practising I could feel it in the air, the effort it had taken him, the energy it was costing. He'd dressed for the occasion, too – charcoal suit, leather shoes – Emile, who normally dressed as if he was going fishing. And I could feel the rage in him, and the rage I'd seen on that very first day, a rage that burned like a pilot light, scorching the air with its colours.

'What do you think I'm doing?' I said.

'Don't give me that,' he almost spat. 'You and your hot chocolate. You treat him like a child, and God help him, he *likes* it!'

'I don't,' I said. My voice was calm. 'Louis is my friend. I owe him a lot. And what's wrong with hot chocolate? People drink it all the time. *You* drink it.'

'Louis never did.'

He gave another sick grin, and I remembered what I'd seen in him on that first day at breakfast: something to do with a woman, a child. Louis is not the only one who keeps this anniversary. And in his charcoal suit, Emile looked just like the Man in Black, relentless in his hatred, his pursuit of everything good.

I wanted to say: *I cooked for you. Surely that must mean something.* But all my attention was taken up with the effort of keeping calm. I forked my fingers behind my back. *Tsk-tsk, begone.* But he was still there, watching me, vicious as an autumn wasp. *Wasps are so angry in autumn,* my mother always used to say, *because they know they're going to die. They feel the coming of the cold. They turn on the warm-blooded.*

Emile gave me a sick grin. 'What now? Will you go crying to Louis? Tell him his friend of thirty-five years thinks he's being an idiot?'

I shook my head. 'Why would I do that?'

Emile shrugged. 'It's how you win.'

'It isn't a war, Emile,' I said.

'It is from where I'm standing.'

I shrugged and turned back to the washing-up. I wanted to tell him how wrong he was – but why should I try? I was leaving. Behind me, Emile made a scornful sound. I heard him turn to go. Then a pause.

'What's this?' he said. He'd seen Louis' gift.

'I had it made as a present for Louis.'

He picked it up and studied it for what seemed a very long time. Then I heard him strike a match, and smelt the reek of a *Gitane.*

'You had this made?' he said. 'For Louis?'

I nodded, not quite daring to turn.

Gently, he put down the river stone, and I heard his receding footsteps.

'Goodbye, Emile,' I told him. But I don't think he heard me.

10

13 October 1993

First I finished the dishes. Then washed the pots and pans I had used, drying them and replacing them carefully back in their places. Last of all, I washed Marguerite's copper pan – the pan I had used for the chocolate – and hung it back in its place on the wall. I won't be using it again. Or her favourite slotted spoon, or the cast-iron frying pan, or the chopping-board, or the cassole, or the knives, or the *mouli*. I scanned the kitchen, silently saying goodbye to the sink, the range, the boxes and tins in the pantry, the spice shelf with its hand-labelled jars, the view from the open window. There are new scars on the table now, caused by a clumsy carving knife; a pot I put down with no trivet; a cacao stain sunk deep into the wood.

I did that, I tell myself. *That's the mark of my presence.*

Louis will be back by five. That still gives me plenty of time. Leaving the kitchen spotless, I go back to my little room. I have already stripped the bed and washed and dried the linen, leaving it in the linen chest, along with the baby album. The wind has changed, blowing warm air from the continent. The child in me wails: *Can't we stay?*

The mother answers: *I'm sorry. It's time.*

Together they make a single voice; *my* voice; the voice of the wind that whips me from side to side like a sail, that promises *let's see next time, let's see what happens next time*, as if I were still that child on the bench at the station in Syracuse, sobbing, heartbroken, but already aware that too much baggage weighs you down, and that my mother is watching. Last of all I write a note to Louis, which I leave on the kitchen counter:

Dear Louis,
Thank you for everything. I'm sorry I couldn't stay longer.
Vianne. x

Dal

I

13 October 1993

I can do this. I've done it before. Except that isn't really true. I have never travelled alone. I have never been pregnant before. And yet, there is something inevitable about being on the road again; the familiar weight of the canvas bag, the sounds of the city behind me now; already merging with the past.

The ghost of my mother walks with me through streets that are gilded with danger. Already the sky has assumed the silvery shades of evening; the scent of the sea rises like smoke, and the voices from cafés and restaurants seem incredibly remote, the luminous scenes through their windows like visions glimpsed through cathedral glass. All around the city, children are doing their homework; families are eating dinner; people are curling up together on sofas; having baths; making love; watching television. This is what other people think of as a *normal life.* A partner. A job. Children. A home. Clothes in a wardrobe. A favourite mug. A bowl with your name painted on the rim; a name that never changes.

You had to do this. Remember?

Yes. And yet it hurts to be leaving. But now I hear my name on the wind, the name of that village on the Baïse.

169

And it smells somehow of the carnival, and frying pancakes, and sausages roasted by the riverside on embers made from applewood. And there's Anouk, my little Anouk, her hair like candyfloss in the wind—

I need to get out of this city. Louis will have noted my absence by now. I try not to imagine his reactions; shock, anger, surprise, betrayal. Grief, perhaps. But I had no choice. And he will forget me, I hope, as soon as he finds his routine again. As soon as the taste of my chocolate loses its hold on his memory. But for now, I must put some distance between myself and Rue du Panier. Louis may try to find me; may even report my disappearance to the police. That would be a problem. As Louis says, I have nothing. *No permanent home, no bank account, no family, no wedding ring.* I am an alien in this land where aliens are viewed with mistrust; where a pregnant woman alone is seen as a danger to hearth and home; where I risk losing my child to the State if I cannot show my credentials. Moving around, my mother and I managed to stay invisible. But staying with Louis for so long – making *friends* – was a mistake. Making enemies was worse, although I still do not understand why it is that Emile hates and distrusts me so much. *I've been doing a little asking around since you arrived here.* That sounds ominous, and makes me glad to be leaving. I realize now that my time in Marseille has been like a holiday romance; insubstàntial as candy floss.

Vianne will be different, I promise myself. I will find myself in Vianne. An overnight bus to Toulouse, I think; and then another, local bus, or even a riverboat up the Garonne, where its tributaries, the Tannes and the Baïse, branch off like the tines of a fork. I have enough money for my fare, and maybe a week of cheap hotels. It's enough. I'm used to this. And doesn't it feel somehow *right*, among the sadness and regret, to hear the voice of the wind again, and to go wherever it calls us?

But some places are hard to leave. Marseille, with its many roads, is one. It seems unfriendly at first, with its crowds and the crushing heat of the Butte, and the garbage in the alleyways and the stray dogs on the waterfront, but somehow I have put down roots, so that now it feels as if I am tearing a part of myself away.

Maman, can we stay here?

I'm sorry. It's time.

There is an overnight coach to Toulouse scheduled to leave at midnight. Coaches are much cheaper than trains, and much more anonymous. This is why I find myself here now, at ten o'clock in the evening, in a place crowded with travellers. Even at this late hour, the place is filled with people. Some will spend the night here. I can see their bedrolls, their packs. And the sleep merchants are out in force; they lie in wait for the passengers. Their instinct is unerring; they target the lost, the desperate.

'Room for the night, miss? Very cheap.'

I shake my head. 'No, thank you.'

The man who spoke to me is young; his face is thin and clever. He smells of *Gauloises* and something sharp: his eyes are alert and predatory. I see myself reflected there; so young, he thinks, such easy prey. I flick him the sign behind my back. *Tsk-tsk, begone!* He flinches. I think he feels it like an insect bite; a warning of worse things to come. He leaves me to my reflections, and no one else disturbs me.

The journey to Toulouse takes six and a half hours, with a forty-minute stop in Montpellier. After that, I will be free to choose the rest of my trajectory. Shall I go up the Garonne? Or hitch a ride on the road to Bordeaux? Or catch a train? Or fly like a bird, and spread my wings on the thermals?

One step at a time, Vianne. No need to think too far ahead.
I have some time to kill before the coach is scheduled to
leave. I buy a *croque* at the station café; a bottle of water for
the trip. At this time on an ordinary night, Louis and I would
normally be in the back room of the bistrot, drinking a cup
of hot chocolate or chamomile tea before going to bed. My
bed would be made; the red-and-orange blanket I bought
from a stall on the waterfront spread over the coverlet. The
rising tide would fill the room with its cool and salty scent.
My mother's box of Tarot cards, open by the bedside.

The cards are in my pack, of course, although the blanket
has been left behind. I wish I'd thought to bring it now; the
night is unexpectedly cold. I have no winter clothes. No shoes
but my well-worn plimsolls. I am wearing a denim jacket over
a sweater and cargo pants; enough for the chill of an autumn
night, but too light for the winter. And I can already feel its
call; the storms; the rains; the leaden skies. A summer's day
finds it difficult to re-imagine winter; but here and now,
it's all too easy to sense its approach. I must find a place for
us soon, a place for my Anouk to grow. By Christmas she
will be the size of an avocado. I wonder what Christmas in
Vianne is like. Are there lights along the Baïse? A fir tree in
the town square? Roasted chestnuts on market days, served
in a twist of paper, and the scent of smoke from the brazier
rising in the clear, cold air?

My mother and I never celebrated Christmas. That was
for people who stayed in one place; people with houses and
gardens and cars. People with no fear of accumulating possessions. I remember the Christmas trees; the lights; the garlands
on the doors. Christmas looks different from the outside, the
squares of light from their windows like glimpses into another
world. Other children had log fires, presents, board games.

Family. Other children slept in their beds and dreamed of candied plums and *bûche de Noël*. We had other things, she said. We had the *real* magic. We had the voice of the wind, the shine of glamours reflected in the window-glass of a stranger's house. We had Tarot cards, and runes, and herbal concoctions, and witch's bottles, and hagstones, and spells, and stories from every part of the world, from every belief in history. And when we stood watching their little lives like scenes inside a snow-globe, we knew that we were different; that we were special and set apart.

A memory of myself, very young, outside a church during Midnight Mass, hearing the murmur of voices, seeing the glow of candles and lamps, catching the scent of incense and pine: *Can we go inside, Maman? See the Baby Jesus?*

I don't remember where it was now. Verona, maybe, or Madrid. Or Rome. Or Palermo, or Milan. But I remember the snow-globe light, and the scent of the incense, the pull of the crowd, and the sadness in her voice as she said: *You know we don't do that, chérie.*

But why?

Because we're different.

The incense smells like autumn leaves, like spiced buns from the bakery. And the organ – jewel-box distant, but clear as falling icicles – sounds like music from Lyonesse, or Mahabalipuram, or Atlantis.

Why are we different, Maman? Little 'Viane is tired and cold, too young to be still up at midnight. *I don't want to be different,* she says. *I want to go inside, and see.*

We talked about this, 'Viane. We can't. The Man in Black is watching.

It's a threat I've heard before. The Man in Black; the shadow; the ghoul. But tonight I feel rebellious, and the sounds and the scents of the Midnight Mass are too enticing to resist. And I miss Molfetta, left behind on the station bench. Maman doesn't want me to have toys, or friends, or *anyone*.

"Viane!"

And so I drop her hand and make a run for the open doorway. I am already vaguely aware of the concept of *sanctuary*. To me, it sounds like a distant land, like Faërie or Shambhala. And it smells of autumn sunshine and caramel apples and Christmas Eve, and it looks like a palace of candles and smoke and coloured statues and jewelled glass.

For a moment I look around, expecting the Man in Black to appear. But the only priest I can see is dressed all in angelic white, with thick gold stitching on the sleeves and down the front and on the hem of his garment. The service is already underway. Hundreds of people sit in the pews, some of them holding prayer books. There are children too, children like me, all in their best Christmas outfits. And the music sails in like a galleon laden with beautiful treasures. I look around for somewhere to hide. My mother will be following. I dash down the left-hand aisle and find a little wooden closet; a door just wide enough to slip inside, and a wooden bench, with a curtain drawn against the multitude.

It was a confessional, of course, though I had never seen one. But it was warm and safe inside, and I could hear the music. Through the gap in the curtain I could see the Holy Mother. In her long blue gown, her veil, her hair caught up in a nimbus of stars, she looked nothing like my mother. My mother's face was angular; her hair a mess of tumbling curls. Her face was all extremes; a face incapable of moderation. All her clothes were in carnival prints; clashing flowers and polka-dots and stripes and swirls of bright brocade. My mother was a butterfly in a colony of moths, and yet she knew how to pass unseen, to change her colouring to suit the city's crazy camouflage. It was the first thing I'd learnt from her. *You don't have to blend in to go unseen. You have to look as if you belong.*

But I don't want to look as if I belong. I want a place of my own. A bed that I don't have to share with you. Books. Friends. To go to school. A mother who buys toys, bakes pies, and never has to go on the run.

Once more I looked around me. The tiny cubicle was dark, but there was light coming in through the screen that stood above the wooden bench. Looking through, I could see another bench; a little ledge; the mirror image of my own. It could have been a closet, but there was no rail on which to hang clothes. What then? Storage for prayer books? A place for agoraphobes to sit?

I could stay here. Claim this space. There's room to sleep, and it's private. During the day I'd venture abroad. And at night, when all the people are gone, I could come out and explore, and run along the empty aisles, and climb up into the organ loft, and dance between the pillars.

I was only eight years old. And yet I remember that feeling. At eight, I could already forage for food among a city's markets. I knew where to shower, where to drink, where to find shoes and clothing. So many things are thrown away in a city like this one. All it takes is a sharp eye, and the skill of passing unseen. Yes, I could make this my sanctuary. I could escape my mother.

I know that sounds ungrateful – naïve. Especially now, when I miss her so much. But at eight, the world is a different shape, built around different perspectives. And the loss of Molfetta was still too raw for me to feel any gratitude for our special status. All I wanted was to be like the other children; to have a home, and a toy, and a bed; to put aside magic for comfort. Around me the scent of incense was like a warm woollen blanket. The murmur of voices in Latin was like a well-worn lullaby. And I prayed to Madonna and Isis and Santa Muerte to keep me safe, and protect me so that my *other* mother would finally give up and leave—

Of course, she didn't. She found me. She guessed where I was hiding. Or maybe she used the cards, or the runes, or the vapours in a coffee cup. In any case, I awoke to the sound of voices and movement as the congregation dispersed, and felt her arms around me as she carried me from the confessional – *Oh, chérie! Let's get you home* – her voice a little over-loud, her eyes fixed on the big church door as if someone might try to prevent our escape.

Two hours later we were on a night bus out of the city. I remember it only as one of so many identical journeys; the street lamps arcing incessantly; the roadside coffee and cigarette smoke and the sweat of other people. My mother said nothing about my escapade, but I could see it in her eyes; that fearful expectation. I had tried to leave her once: I would try to leave her again. And later, much later, in New York, when the cancer was working its way through her like a saw through rotten wood, when she was out of herself with morphine, she would still cling to me and say: *Don't leave me, 'Viane. Promise you'll stay. Promise, Viannou. Promise*—

I never realized before what loneliness lies in motherhood. I was a lonely child, of course – siblings, friends and family all sacrificed to the pull of the wind – but it never occurred to me that my mother felt it too. I was enough for her, she said. We were enough for each other. Except that in my darkest heart, I knew that she was *not* enough; that one day I would break away. And now the germ of my daughter sits inside me like a piece of my heart, and I already feel the absence of her, that pull of inevitability. She will leave me, as daughters do, as surely as the dandelion seed will fly from the plant. And my mother's voice says, *See? I said you'd understand one day.* And the streets of Marseille are bracketed with neon lamps, just like that night, and it smells of coffee and cigarette smoke, and we are on the move again, always on the move, and now comes the autoroute – *superstrada, freeway, snelweg, Autobahn* – all those names for the same long road, a road that switches back and forth across decades and continents, and somewhere along it I fall asleep and dream of the confessional, and awake at first light in Toulouse, alone in another new city.

2

14 October 1993

They call it *La Ville Rose*, on account of the terracotta bricks that make up so many of the buildings. That day it didn't look rosy at all; under the persistent rain it was as grey and cheerless as any other strange city filled with tourists and students and people at work, and strangers and casual labourers and refugees and lost souls.

I was already feeling grubby. Travelling attracts a certain special kind of grime; the kind that gets into everything. And I was gritty with sleeplessness and already homesick for Marseille, where the markets would be waking up all around the Vieux Port, and stray cats slinking from the Butte, and the bells ringing out from Notre-Dame under the Virgin's mantle sky. I recovered my travel bag from between the seats and got off the bus into a rain that was thin and cold and somehow inescapable.

Why does it always feel so strange, arriving in a new town? I should be used to it by now. The sadness of being in transit; the unfamiliar smells; the altered sound of the traffic; the indifferent crowds. I have seen so many towns; so many railway stations and bus depots. And people are not so different. Everywhere in the world there is kindness or indifference, anger, suspicion, comfort. This town will be like that. Here – at least for as long as I stay, for a night or a week – will be home. And yet it doesn't feel that way. Home still feels like La Bonne Mère. Perhaps I'm still grieving my mother. I tell myself I need to grow up. No one is coming to save me. But I feel cold and lost today, and not at all ready for what's to come.

Oh, Maman. I wish you were here. I miss her more than words can say. If only she had known that on the day I tried to escape from her. If only I could have told her that she would be with me forever. But for now, I need a place to stay. For now at least, I have options. Nearly two thousand francs in cash, earnings from La Bonne Mère, as well as tips from my regulars. Bar work pays well when you're a witch. *Charm the coins from their pockets, 'Viane. Let your smile reflect the sun.* Except that I don't feel like smiling right now. Right now I feel alone and afraid. Inside me, Anouk is a nautilus, curled up in silence. In less than six months I will see her. I will be able to speak to her. I will teach her everything I know about being in the world. We will build a home in a tree, or in an abandoned cottage. We will eat berries and woodland fruits, and sleep on a bed of sweet summer hay. We will be the best of friends. I will be such a good mother.

But that's the child in me dreaming. For now, the practicalities. A bed for the night. A meal. A job. Everything costs more than you think. My two thousand francs will not go far. *One step at a time, Vianne.* It has been hours since I last ate. There's a café near the bus station: its name is *Café Pamplemousse*, and a *café-croissant* costs eight francs. I wash myself in the bathroom, and brush my travel-tousled hair. The croissant is stale and overpriced; the coffee makes me feel nauseous, but I fill my pockets with sugar cubes. The middle-aged woman behind the bar gives me a suspicious look. I know how I look to her; laden, unkempt, dishevelled, as if I have slept in my clothes. My smile reflects nothing but sadness. I'd like to ask her if she knows of a boarding-house or a cheap hotel, but I already sense her hostility. She is tired-looking; grey-blonde; maybe fifty-five years old. She does not return my cautious smile.

Suddenly, her face comes alight. Another customer has entered. It must be a regular, because the woman behind the bar greets her with what looks like genuine pleasure.

'Sophie! The usual?'

'*Salut*, Cécile!'

The woman is polished, professional. Smooth dark hair to her shoulders. Grey pinstriped skirt-suit, well-cut enough to reveal a neat figure. Patent black shoes, too high to walk in comfort. She must work nearby, I think. She doesn't like to walk in those heels. No wedding ring. There's someone, though. Those shoes have a kind of eloquence. Her usual is *café-croissant*, with strawberry jam from a little jar. The croissant looks fresher than mine was: Cécile looks after her regulars.

Suddenly I don't want to go back out into the cheerless rain. I want to sit here for a while. I put down my bag, which suddenly feels unusually heavy. Cécile looks at me with suspicion. 'You can't stay here without ordering.' Her voice is very different to when she was speaking to Sophie. 'I'm not a waiting room, you know.'

It shouldn't have made me angry. I've heard that tone so many times, in so many different places. But today I am feeling raw, as if I am missing a layer of skin. Perhaps it's the hormones of pregnancy, or the changing seasons, or homesickness, or just this terrible fatigue that feels like so much more than mere sleeplessness. I clench my teeth and fork the sign against malchance behind my back.

'I'll have another coffee.'

'Five francs.' She gives me a look that would sour beer.

I reach for my purse, which has fallen to the bottom of my bag. It springs open as I pull it out, spilling small change over the floor. The woman in the high-heeled shoes looks at me from her table. I pick up the coins, my face burning. The last coin has rolled beneath the table at which she is sitting. If it were a ten-centime piece, maybe I would have left it there. But it's a silver five-franc piece. Too much to abandon.

I say: 'Excuse me,' and reach for the coin, on my knees on the pitch-pine floor, which has not been cleaned in a long time. A wine stain like an open eye stares at me accusingly. Another joins it, alarmingly bright. And another.

That isn't wine. I lift my hand to my face to find that my nose is bleeding. The woman at the bar gives a cry of mingled surprise and disgust. I struggle to my feet, the coin under the table forgotten. Blood falls in fat red drops from my nose down the front of my shirt.

'I'm sorry.'

I shouldn't apologize. And yet I feel compelled, somehow. I have always been sensitive to the discomfort of others. I try to pinch my nose, but the blood refuses to be silenced. It trumpets its presence, exuberant; splashes onto the pinewood floor.

The woman at the bar says: 'That's enough. Get out of here. Take your bloody nose elsewhere.'

There's no point in getting angry. And yet it's so unfair. The voice of my younger self in my mind is raw with unspoken anger. *We didn't do anything wrong, Maman.* Why are people like this? Is it our skin, our hair, our clothes, our scent of other places? Is it simply that they are afraid, and that we are different?

I turn to face her, unspeaking. My nose is still bleeding heavily. My head feels like a helium balloon, tugged and tumbled by the wind. Cécile's colours are threaded with disgust and indecision. That, and a kind of entitlement, that says: *I belong here. You don't.* I look a little closer into the woman's colours. Not at what she *wants* me to see, but at what she is trying to hide. I wouldn't normally do this – Marseille should have taught me that – but today I am not in a normal place. That sense of missing a layer of skin, the blood from my nose that wouldn't stop, the sense that to her, somehow, I might as well be invisible—

What do you see, Vianne? What do you see?

I see a girl in a hospital room. I see a woman living alone. I see some self-importance; some loneliness; some aggression. I see guilt, and fear, and regret. Most of all, though, I see loss – a very *familiar* kind of loss – and that kills my anger.

I say: 'It wasn't your fault, Cécile.'

She bristles. 'What are you talking about?'

I said: 'You were fifteen. Only a child. They all decided what was best for you and her, between them. They thought you'd get over it, that you'd forget. They never knew about the times you lay awake, feeling her inside. The dreams you had of the two of you. The secret name you gave her.'

'What's this?' Her voice rises suddenly. 'Who have you been talking to?'

I should have looked away by then, but somehow I couldn't stop myself. Perhaps it was fatigue, or distress, of that blood that wouldn't stop. I held out screaming, scarlet palms like those of a bloodstained oracle.

'You called her *Ondine*, in your dreams. In life, you never saw her. Nothing but the sheet they held over you, to hide her. You never held her in your arms. You have no proof she was even there, except for those silvery marks on your skin, which faded with time to a dappled brown, and the memory of her fading cry, right at the end of the corridor. But you never forgot her. And you never forgave yourself for letting them take her away from you.'

Cécile sags like a ruptured balloon. I see her jellyfish colours blooming and fading fretfully. Sophie in the patent shoes is frozen in place, hesitant. I sense she is struggling to cope. So many things need attention. The dropped coins; the blood on the floor; the breakfast coffee growing cold; and now, Cécile at the counter, and the girl with the nosebleed saying those things, those bewildering things—

Suddenly I feel very dizzy. Maybe it's the nosebleed, or the fact that a stale croissant is the only thing I've eaten today. But I feel somehow *divided*, like a river forking towards the sea. On one side, a bowl with my name on the rim. On the other, the Man in Black. But which is Vianne? And is Vianne me?

The lights in the café seem very bright; the sound of the rain is deafening. And I can still feel her memory, which has somehow become my own, with all the midwives clustering around the wailing parcel, ready to repackage it and send it out to someone else, to someone who *deserves* her, and I feel a sudden conviction that I am about to lose my child, that this is the price you have to pay for misusing our kind of gift—

'Help me,' I said, and sat suddenly on the floor, pulling the tablecloth after me. The words seemed to float around my head like a cloud of butterflies. 'Please help me. I'm pregnant. My baby—' And then, for the second time that year, I passed out on the floor of a backstreet café, with the taste of blood in my mouth, and the sound of the autumn rain like thunder in my temples.

3

I woke up in the ambulance. A nurse was holding a mask to my face; a blood-pressure cuff was around my arm. I tried to sit up. The nurse – a young man with long hair and a beard – gently pushed me back into place.

'Don't try to move. You're going to be fine.'

'My things—'

'I left them with your friend.'

I wanted to say: *I don't have any friends.* But I was still too confused to speak. My heart was racing, my head was sore and my shirt was dark with half-dried blood. I felt a sudden panic as I realized my trousers were also wet, but it was not blood, only coffee, spilt as I pulled at the tablecloth.

'A lot of people get nosebleeds in the first trimester. We'll just get you checked over, and then you can be on your way.'

I nodded and said nothing. Inside, I was thinking furiously. I had no papers with me; nothing to prove my identity. Of course, I had no insurance; but no one asked me for details. Instead, they asked for my name and address: I told them Sylviane Rochas, and gave an old address in Nîmes, an empty house behind the old fish market. Arriving at the hospital, I was given a series of tests, including an ultrasound that showed them my baby was healthy, and some blood tests that revealed nothing but a moderate iron deficiency.

'Plenty of leafy vegetables,' said the doctor who saw to me. 'Also, red meat. And chocolate. Did you know that chocolate contains as much iron as spinach?'

I did, because Guy had once told me, and for a moment I felt a powerful sense of longing for him, and for Allée du Pieu. Now I would never see the chocolaterie up and running. I would not see the Christmas lights along the Vieux Port, and the candle-lit processions up the Butte to Notre-Dame. I would never see Mahmed and Guy on the night of their grand opening. That's always been our fate, of course: to see so many stories begun, and to leave so many unfinished.

'I'd like to keep you overnight, just to make sure,' the doctor said. 'Your blood pressure is a little low, and in your condition, we need to take care.' He smiled. He was kindly; balding; plump. 'Would you like to call *Papa*?'

For a moment I thought he meant *my* father; a man whose name I'd never known, and of whom my mother had never spoken. Then I realized who he meant. The *baby*'s father in New York. The man with no name.

I shook my head.

I thought the man looked crestfallen. I'd seen the way he looked at my hand, noting the absent wedding ring. Then, he smiled again, and said: But most importantly – boy or girl? Would you like to know?'

I started to tell him I already knew, but I could see he was trying to lift my mood, and it seemed unkind to refuse him. I nodded.

'Well, you're having a *boy*!'

I stared at him. I know he's wrong. And yet, once more I feel that troubling sense of *forking*, as if my life were divided in two. On one side, my little Anouk, so very like myself at her age; moving from town to town in my wake, just as I did with my mother. On the other, a little boy. A different life entirely.

'You're disappointed?'

'No, I – no.' I managed a smile. 'I'm just – a little tired.' In fact, what he'd said made no sense. My Anouk is already so real in my mind that to tell me she doesn't exist seems absurd: like denying the rising sun. I said: 'I don't suppose these tests are ever entirely accurate?'

'Completely accurate.' He beamed. 'You can start knitting those blue bootees.'

I thought of the pink bootees in my bag, and of what Khamaseen had said: *A little boy could be good for you. A little boy who sleeps at night, and never hears the call of the wind.*

But I'd escaped that, hadn't I? I had averted that destiny. I had followed the wind. I had done everything I was meant to do—

So perhaps Anouk doesn't want you, whispered an evil voice in my mind. *Perhaps she knows what you're really like, and wants nothing to do with you. Perhaps because she knows you don't know how be a mother.*

I took a shaking breath. *You're wrong. I'm going to be a good mother.*

Like your mother was to you? Dragging you halfway across the world? Changing your names in every town? Running from every shadow?

That's unfair. She did her best. She taught me everything she knew.

And what do you know, exactly? Where were you born? When's your birthday? Who was your mother? What's your name? Are you really telling me that your child would be different? That you'd give them security? That you'll never change their name, or tell them: the next town will be better?

I lay awake for a long time, listening to the hospital sounds like music from a seashell, and when at last I fell asleep, I dreamed of a railway station bench, with the sounds of the distant trains in the dark, and a lemon-slice moon hanging overhead like something from a fairytale, and Khamaseen's voice in the distance saying: *If you're going in search of yourself, be sure not to leave yourself behind.*

4

15 October 1993

In the morning, I awoke to find that my clothes had been washed, and breakfast brought to me on a tray, along with a prescription for iron and zinc supplements and a sheaf of forms to fill in.

'All we need now is some paperwork,' said the nurse who brought them, putting a clipboard down by my bed. 'Your *Sécu* number. Things like that.'

Of course I don't have one, or any real proof of identity. But I'm used to situations like this, and I have my mother's instincts. I smiled. 'Of course. After breakfast.'

'Take your time. I'll be back in ten minutes.'

Breakfast was a coffee and a roll, some bottled water and some fruit. I drank the coffee, ate the fruit and the roll, got dressed and picked up the clipboard. I put the bottle of water in my jacket pocket and, carrying the clipboard, walked purposefully out of the room and down the busy corridor, where doctors and nurses came and went, and no one gave me a second glance.

Invisibility isn't a cloak, but an attitude, my mother said. And she's right. It's not about blending in. It's not even about going unseen. It's about making people believe that you have no place in their life. In a hospital, all that means is looking confident and not in need of assistance. I saw the nurse heading back to my room; changed direction to avoid her. Then I made for Reception, left through the front entrance and continued to walk at the same brisk pace until I rounded a corner, after which I disposed of the clipboard in a bin in an alley and altered my gait to match that of the tourists around me.

The thin rain of the previous day had set in, becoming a steady downpour. Even now, my memories of Toulouse are always of that rain, which dulled the famous rose-pink stone to a sullen madder. I had no money for a Metro fare, no travel bag, no possessions. And so I made for the station once more, hoping the woman at Pamplemousse would know what had happened to my bag. But when I reached the café at last, around midday, I found it shut, and a neat little sign on the door that read: *Closed.*

I went to the back of the café, where a row of bins were lined up under a plastic awning. I found my bag in the last one, on top of a bundle of old magazines. It had been opened, but a further search revealed my things were still in there – my mother's cards, our papers – the little leavings of a life in which even a book or a stuffed toy can be too much to carry. I found Guy's spice jar, open, but whole, releasing its fragrant contents, and I was back in the chocolate shop, with the gentle hum of the conching machine and the scent of cacao everywhere. But the cash and the pink bootees were nowhere to be found, and I knew that this was the price of my small demonstration of power.

Never cast a shadow, 'Viane, my mother used to tell me. *People who cast no shadow are free.* But once again, I have broken the code. I have made myself visible. I have no one to blame but myself if this has made me vulnerable. I went through my bundle of papers to make sure nothing else was missing. Passport, forged documents: my mother's newspaper clippings. The death certificate in the name of Jeanne Rochas. Her photograph. It's the only one I have of her; a Polaroid taken when I was fourteen, at a fairground somewhere in Italy. Startled by the flash, both of us are laughing.

I sheltered in the alleyway and considered my situation. Of course there was no question of reporting the theft to the police. I needed to stay invisible. And besides, there was no proof that Cécile had taken the money. Except that she had; I knew she had. The loss of the pink bootees proved it. I tried to recall what I'd seen in her colours that day; the interplay of grief and loss, resentment, fear and denial. I could see her in my mind's eye, half-indignant, half-afraid; scrubbing my blood from the wooden floor, angry at my intrusion into her life, her memories.

If I were back at La Bonne Mère, I would make a cup of tea, and look through the vapours for Cécile; but all I have here is Guy's half-empty jar, which still smells poignantly of his shop, and the plaster dust and wood chips of his labour. In this place it smells nostalgic; sweet as a childhood I only knew from books collected on the road. My favourite was a book about a group of English children for whom a long bike ride or walk in the woods counted as an adventure, whose fathers smoked pipes and whose mothers baked cakes; who had extravagant picnics with lemonade and chocolate. To a child who had never known the security of a permanent home, whose mother had never baked a cake, this was a fantasy akin to Narnia or Middle-Earth; and by the time my mother made me leave it behind in a hostel in Pavia, I already knew the words by heart, and would speak them silently to myself, like a prayer, as I went to sleep. I don't remember much of it now, but I do remember the scent of stale sheets, the aching sound of the traffic outside, the neon lights of the hotel sign blinking on and off through the night, and the thought of those other children — the ones with beds and sheets of their own — sleeping somewhere alongside me, and maybe dreaming of *my* life, just as I always dreamed of theirs.

A voice jolted me out of my reverie. 'What you got there?'

It was a man; maybe sixty-five, in a disreputable woollen coat and a felt hat that had seen better days. His face was lined; his eyes the faded blue of stonewashed denim. He was carrying a rucksack, as well as a wicker basket, from which came the sound of a persistent and angry mewing.

I've met a lot of homeless people on my travels. Most are harmless, although some are pushed to violence by necessity. But this man's colours showed only caution, humour; some concern. I realized what I looked like to him; hair wet with the rain, my sweatshirt still bearing the shadow of yesterday's bloodstains, searching through the bins at the back of an alleyway by the station.

'Don't mind me,' said the man, with a grin that revealed a number of missing and discoloured teeth. 'I'm Stéphane. This here is Pomponette.'

I looked into the basket and saw a large and fluffy black-and-white cat, glaring out at me through the mesh. 'If you're hungry, I know a place,' went on the man, coming closer. 'The Indian van. It comes every week. It's okay. If you like lentils.'

I was at the same time startled and touched. 'Thank you,' I said. 'But someone stole my bag yesterday. They dumped it in this alleyway.'

The man's eyes went to the jar. 'What's that?'

'A spice. I used to add it to food, when I cooked. When I *cook*.' Not the past tense. I will cook again, in this town, or another. I closed the spice jar tightly and slipped it into my pocket. Just for the memory, I thought. A tiny pinch of sunshine.

Stéphane shrugged. 'Well, the lentil van comes at twelve o'clock every day. Round the back of the station. It's foreign food, of course, but it's hot. Better than the *Miséricorde*.'

Well, yes. Catholic charity often comes with a side order of condescension. Maman and I encountered it often, on our travels. I carefully repacked my travel bag, making sure all my mother's cards were there. The man with the cat watched me as I counted out the major and minor arcana, scattered in a careless arc across my rifled possessions.

'Do you play cards?'

'It's not a game. I use them to—'

'Tell the future. I know.' He took a step closer. 'Go on, tell mine.' Now I could smell him; the scent of wet wool, old tobacco, old sweat, and over it all the bitter caress of the spilled xocolatl, nostalgic as fallen leaves. 'They'll tell you I'm heading straight to hell.'

'I don't believe in hell,' I said.

'You will if you stay here long enough.' He gave a gappy, cheerful grin. 'I'm guessing you're new to Toulouse?'

I nodded. 'I'm Vianne.'

'Go on, Vianne. Tell my fortune.'

It's one of the things my mother and I used to do for money, when we were on the road. Everyone wants to know their fate; even those who don't believe. And so I took his hand, and smiled, and set out the cards in their old pattern, the one my mother called the Tree of Life.

Ten cards in three columns; present, past and future. It's easy to make the connections; easy to awaken the imagination.

We do not read the cards, says Maman; *we only read their reactions to them. We see the light in their eyes, the small reflections in their faces. We use these painted images, but in truth we could use anything: a dish of ink; a bowl of steam; the rising smoke from a candle. People show more than they realize. They share a world of history. The Hermit. The Lovers. The Six of Swords. The Chariot. The Four of Cups—*

'Wait.'

These are not his cards. They're mine. I have allowed my mind to stray. I have read the cards to myself for so many months that now they flock at my command, like birds expecting to be fed. I cut the pack again. Change. The Six of Swords. The Tower. Death.

Stéphane gives me a look. 'That's nice. Just what I was hoping for.'

I smile, and put the cards away. 'I'm sorry, Stéphane. I can't do this. My mind isn't in the right place just now.'

He shrugged and opened the basket, allowing Pomponette to come out. 'Lentils it is, then. Come with me.'

5

The lentil van was easy to find, and was painted with big orange flowers. Inside, a young man of about eighteen served out scoops of yellow *dal* in colourful plastic dishes, while a woman – his mother – made chapatis on a hot plate. A line of thirty people or so waited more or less patiently along the kerb, some carrying their possessions in heavy-duty shopping bags, some huddled in thick overcoats. Most were men, but I saw two women, both of them older than me, one in a wheelchair, one pushing her, along with a mountain of baggage.

Stéphane and I took our place in the queue, while Pomponette, who had followed us, went to explore the back of the van. 'A man was drowning some kittens,' said Stéphane, who had followed my gaze, 'She was the only one who survived. She once bit my hand so hard that I nearly lost a finger. But now we're good friends, because she feels safe.'

'Won't she get lost?'

He shook his head. 'She always comes back. She likes lentils.'

We waited our turn in the queue, and I watched the people as they took their food. Some were homeless – I know the look. Some were merely in transit. Some knew Stéphane, and greeted him with nods and muttered exchanges. Some of them watched me suspiciously. Most did not make eye contact.

'Bring the dishes back, please,' said the young man in the van, handing me my portion, along with a chapati wrapped in a piece of paper. I saw him looking at my hands, and realized they were deeply stained with the spilt contents of Guy's xocolatl jar. The scent of the spices still lingered; nostalgic in the cool, damp air.

I smiled at the young man. 'Thank you. I'm Vianne. What's your name?'

He looked surprised. Maybe he wasn't used to being seen as anything but a provider of food. 'I'm Bal,' he said at last. 'And this is my mother, Abani.'

The dal was comforting; warm and good. I scooped it up with the chapati. I saw that Stéphane ate his own with a spoon he pulled out of his pocket, leaving a share for Pomponette, who finished the portion, purring. The others took their food elsewhere; an alleyway; a bus shelter; the little park I'd already seen at the back of the railway station.

'They never bring the dishes back,' said Bal, as I brought him my bowl. 'They're always leaving them around. Sometimes, they complain there's no meat. As if we didn't do enough.'

Abani gave him a sharp look and said something in Hindi. Bal looked mutinous, but said nothing and returned to his pot of dal, which by now was almost empty. I thought how tired both of them looked; the young man in T-shirt and faded jeans, the woman with the dark-red scarf slipping from her greying hair. They do this every day, I thought. Every day, in a different place.

'I'll have a look,' I told them. 'See how many I can find.'

I went to look for discarded bowls, and with Stéphane's help, returned them all. Pomponette followed us eagerly, in hope of finding uneaten food. Abani fed her a piece of rolled-up chapati, which she took under the van to eat.

Bal gave me his cautious smile. 'Thanks,' he said. 'You've saved me a job.'

'How long have you been doing this?'

Bal watched as the last of the crowd dispersed into the rainy streets. 'My father started it, years ago. This was his van. He painted it. He used to tell us that prayer is about putting good into the world. Not sitting in your best clothes, listening to someone talk about the afterlife.'

'Your father was a good man.' I found myself suddenly on the brink of tears. That's nonsense, of course. I never cry. But little Anouk has ideas of her own, and sometimes clamours to be heard. And the scent, the scent from the spice jar, lingers like a memory, and it is warm and sweet and good as kindness from a stranger.

Putting good into the world. Not thoughts and prayers, not preaching. I thought of my mother, who taught me, almost aggressively, to *look after Number One — because no one else will,* she used to say, with a laugh that sounded brittle and harsh, like a flock of seagulls. But *putting good into the world —* that sounds so right, so simple. Making the world a better place, with nothing but lentils, and flour, and love.

'Do you have somewhere to go?' he said.

It was a pertinent question. With money — even a small amount — there are still options for someone like me. But with no money at all, we find our options greatly reduced. Without money, everything costs. Water, the chance to wash your hands, permission to sit in a public place without attracting attention. All of these things are permitted to those who belong, which means money. Without it, the things that we think of as free — free restrooms, free seating, free bread rolls with soup, free water, free movement to all kinds of places where only the moneyed are welcome – all of these things that ordinary people take for granted suddenly need to be paid for.

'There's a women's shelter I know. If you need it, here's the address.' He passed me a little yellow card. 'Tell them I sent you.'

I thanked him. My face was suddenly hot. I know how hard it is to find a shelter in a city this size. And today I was feeling especially raw. The doctor, saying my child was a boy; the looting of my travel bag; the theft of my cash and the pink bootees – all this had left me with the unsettling feeling that somehow my future was slipping away, stolen, by the sly north wind. I turned again, with the scent of those spilled spices fretting the chilly air, and set out into the city streets, as red as powdered chocolate.

6

Any vagrant will tell you this. You have about twenty-four hours in any given place before being marked as undesirable. That's twenty-four hours of relative peace and comfort in a waiting room, or on a railway platform, or on the crowded concourse of a busy coach terminal. Use it wisely; because once you have been identified as one who is not merely passing through, officials will make it their business to force you out, harass you, drive you from the safety of the shelter into open streets, where police will move you from place to place, take your blankets, your bedding, your tent; and finally drive you to settle in worse and more dangerous places, until at last you are driven to seek another town entirely, where the whole process will happen again – and again – for as long as your strength endures.

The trick is to keep moving, and not to come to rest for too long. Furthermore, to convince other people that you belong, you have to first convince yourself. The narrative of self-loathing is one that I have encountered many times. Treat a person like garbage, and soon they will end up believing they are as lazy and worthless as society believes them to be. *Why do they not get a job? Why do they simply sit around doing nothing?*

But what I have learnt is that homelessness is a full-time occupation. When you have nothing, everything costs; everything must be accounted for. Days are spent looking for food; keeping warm; searching out facilities. Some people are aggressively independent; others seek the company and security of others. Some people seek the comfort of alcohol or substance abuse, and are judged for this by those who believe such things should be reserved for those with homes and productive employment. But a job, a home, a family – anyone can lose these things. Loss is not linked to virtue, whatever the Church may tell us. Everyone has a story.

Stéphane tells me all of this as we sit outside the coach terminal, with Pomponette on his shoulder, sheltered from the rain by his coat. He has been homeless for nearly four years; ever since his marriage broke down. Alcoholism, depression, bad luck and trusting the wrong kind of people have all played their part in his circumstance; and yet he is curiously upbeat, in a way that I almost recognize. 'No one lives rough for more than five years. That means my luck must be turning.'

Stéphane was originally from Marseille. He spent his first eighteen months with friends, sleeping on sofas and in spare rooms, but in the end their friendship ran out, and he ended up with the sleep merchants, and then in a home-built shelter in one of the city's *bidonvilles*.

'That was a bad time,' he tells me. 'A township built from garbage, filled with humanity's rejects. Live there long enough, and it feels like there's nothing else in the whole world. And so I hitchhiked to Toulouse – it took me three weeks to get here – and now here I am, unable to leave, surrounded by tourists and churchgoers.'

He and his friends sleep by the Garonne, one of the city's rivers. There are green spaces here, places to camp. Some people have built shelters. It isn't quite a *bidonville*: but it is a kind of community. And of course, he has the cat. The cat, he says, is everything.

'I'll help you, if you want to stay. Fix you up with materials. You can find all kinds of things. Plywood, plastic sheeting. Just as long as you know where to look.'

'Thanks,' I said. 'But I'm waiting here.'

'What, here in the terminal?'

It isn't safe, he tells me. All kinds of undesirables overnight in the terminal. The irony is not lost on him – he grins as he says it, but is not deterred. 'Sleep here, you're apt to get robbed.' I tell him I need to talk to Cécile.

'Okay, then I'll stay with you. I promise you'll be safe with me.'

7

We lasted there until midnight before an official moved us on. Alone, I might have passed unseen, but Stéphane was a familiar face in and around the terminal. Long-term homelessness can have a look: and there was no missing Stéphane's leathery skin, the missing teeth, the greasy-elbowed, threadbare coat. Even so, I'd hoped to pass unseen for a little longer: outside it was still raining, and the night was unexpectedly cold. Once more I found myself thinking of the blanket I'd left at La Bonne Mère, and of the people I'd left behind; and of my mother, and how we swore we'd always be together.

A memory, bright as Christmas lights, of the two of us in some hotel room: she and I holding plastic cups filled with some kind of sparkling wine. I am eighteen, and she is already starting to show the signs of the cancer that will kill her. *To us!* she says, with that smile of hers. *To us, Viannou, and nobody else!* And the laughter is bright as broken glass in that grubby little room, and her eyes are filled with disaster and fear and hope and love and defiance. *To Florida! The Everglades! Disney World! And us!* And I laugh, because that's what we do, and because the idea of my mother's death is outside of my comprehension. *Here's to leaving things behind*, she says, and laughs, and drinks her wine, and the scent is like juniper and the sea, and the lingering smoke of her cigarettes, and the cards are spread out on the bed with its grubby candlewick bedspread: The Tower. The Hermit. The Chariot. Death.

Stéphane protested at being moved on. 'We're not hurting anyone here,' he said. 'Why are we your business?' But the official – a man in his forties, with a little official's moustache – was not open to argument. A uniform will do that, you know. The less real power it confers, the more dogged a person is likely to be in wielding their authority. The Man in Black is more likely to be a traffic policeman, a ticket collector, a parking attendant, a social worker, even a priest – which is why we have always tried to avoid such people on our travels. These are the people who confiscate tents and rolls of bedding; who lock public restrooms at night; who take children from their mothers; who guard the bins outside supermarkets for fear that the hungry might raid them. These are the people who think of themselves as honest, decent citizens; who cannot imagine themselves in need; who go to church on Sundays and think of themselves as generous. These are the people who reconcile this with their cruelty to others because they do not really think of those others as people.

'Why are you my business? Because I have a job to do. A job, to protect these premises. So move on before I call the police.'

Without Stéphane, I might have tried to charm the man from his bitterness. But the lines were already drawn. Stéphane was getting angry, shaking aside the restraining arm of the man with the little moustache. Pomponette had retreated back into her basket, from which she watched with eyes like moons.

The official stayed hatefully calm; his colours like petrol

on water. I could see the contempt in his eyes, the nervous hostility in his posture. 'I have a job to do,' he said. 'You wouldn't know about that, I suppose.'

'Come on.' I took Stéphane by the arm. 'Come *on*. There's no point arguing.'

I manoeuvred him out of the terminal, and found myself under a rain-scribbled sky, at the mouth of the alleyway at the back of Café Pamplemousse. The dim orange glow of firelight reflected onto the wet stones. I went around the corner and found two women – one in a wheelchair, the other with a rucksack – sheltering there under blankets. The fire was in a metal bin, throwing sparks at the sullen sky. I recognized the women from the food van, and smiled at them, with no response.

'Don't take it personally,' said Stéphane. 'They never talk to anyone. Let me show you where to go. I know a place by the river. There's water. Stuff to build shelters with. There's even electricity – some guy from one of the river boats managed to hook up a lamp-post.'

I shook my head.

'But *why*?'

'I'm fine. I mean it, Stéphane. You don't have to stay.'

He shrugged. 'One shithole's as good as the next. At least let's find somewhere out of the rain. Pomponette doesn't like it.'

There was shelter next to the bins, and a stack of cardboard boxes. Stéphane let Pomponette out of her basket and started to collect dry cardboard and newspapers for bedding. The two women from the lentil van gave me a look of suspicion.

'Do you mind if we join you?' I said.

'Can't see how I could stop you.'

The fire was only paper, which burns hot, but only briefly. I added some pieces of plywood scavenged from the nearby bins. Searching once more through the debris I caught the fleeting scent of chocolate spice from the spilled spice jar. In the damp of the alleyway it seemed to bloom, like night scented stock. I've noticed that about this blend; it lingers like perfume, like memory. It teases out confessions.

'What are you doing here, anyway? You don't look like one of us.'

The woman's voice is illuminated with the sunny accent of the south-west. It is the one in the wheelchair; a short-haired, narrow-faced woman who might perhaps be forty-five. Her friend is a little older; grey hair chopped to jaw-length under a black knitted cap. Both have the look of people who have lived outside for too long to pass. It is a look that goes beyond grubby clothes or neglected teeth: it is the look in their eyes that says: *I have been treated like dirt for so long that I have begun to believe it.*

Maman once told me the story of an English socialite, who lived homeless for two years, surviving on the canapés from the parties she attended each night. A woman in a party frock on the streets of London seldom attracts attention; and the young woman knew her world, and was able to take advantage. As a child, I thought the story sounded like a fairytale. Now, I suspect that the socialite mostly slept on sofas, and in the bedrooms of people she met at those fancy parties. She had a change of clothes. She had make-up and jewellery. She had the privilege of her class, and her race, and her connections. There is a world of difference between homelessness and sleeping rough. City streets are not glamorous. They stink of sadness and despair. In twenty years, my mother and I slept rough only a handful of times, in parks and railway stations, and never for more than a night or two; never long enough for that look to etch itself onto our faces.

I shrugged. 'I'm in between places right now.' From my backpack I pulled out the bottle of water I'd been given at the hospital. 'Want to share?'

The woman in the knitted cap gave me a suspicious look. 'Is it open? Can I see?'

I handed her the water bottle with its unbroken seal. She checked it and nodded, satisfied. 'Some people leave out bottles of contaminated water,' she said. 'The way they leave poison bait for the rats.' She dug in her rucksack and brought out a tin. 'Okay. That's good. I've got coffee.'

'Coffee sounds fine.'

8

15 October 1993

The coffee was weak and bitter, brewed in a tin pot that had seen better days, and served in scavenged paper cups. I added the packets of sugar I'd taken from Café Pamplemousse, and the last pinch of Guy's xocolatl spice.

'What's that?' It was the suspicious woman, the grey-haired one in the knitted cap. Her name is Roxane, she tells me, and her friend in the wheelchair is Poupoule. Not their real names, I suspect; but names are things of power, not to be given away lightly.

'It's a spice blend. I use it for—'

'Not drinking that.' Roxane pushes her cup away as if I'd admitted to poisoning it.

Stéphane shrugs and sips from his. 'It's fine. It's actually nice. Tastes a bit like—'

Fireworks. The Fourth of July. The scent of smoke; the taste of tears; her ashes in the slipstream. The warmth of a stranger's hand in mine: the taste of him, like peaches.

She reaches out and takes the cup. 'Whatever. I'll have it. As long as it's hot.'

She drinks, then passes a cup to Poupoule. 'Hmm. I guess. It's—'

What is it? Sweet? Evocative? What does the scent of it mean to her? Her colours are like the firelight, reflecting fitfully onto the stones. A memory, caught like a moth in a flame, of childhood, and sadness, and the sound of her mother sleeping next door. Roxane had an unhappy childhood. A carer to her mother, perhaps. Now she cares for Poupoule instead. What is their relationship? Too close to be family, they speak in a series of shutter-quick shorthand glances and single words. Poupoule is the gentle one; small-featured, oddly birdlike, she has a kind of patience that complements Roxane's brittleness. Both of them drink with the wary look of people not used to pleasure.

'*Mocha*,' says Roxane at last. 'Tastes like some kind of mocha.'

I wish I could have made them the drink I used to make at La Bonne Mère; hot milk, sweet vanilla, allspice, nutmeg and cardamom. But this is the best I can do right now. I send Roxane the tiniest flash of something bright and comforting. Her smile is almost peaceful. I wish I could do more for them, but this may be enough for now. It occurs to me that maybe I am *putting good into the world*. Perhaps that's why I feel warmer now, although I feel a sting of unease. *He smells it, Viannou. The Man in Black. He knows when you begin to care.* And yes, I care, I realize. I care about my new friends. I care about the old ones, too; Guy, Mahmed, Louis, even Emile. It's a strange and dangerous feeling, but I do not want to leave it behind. I pour Stéphane the last of the brew. It smells of leaves and woodsmoke. Good things put into the world. Afterwards, Roxane and Poupoule unpack a little clamshell tent and a couple of bedrolls to sleep on. Stéphane has already made a place for us under the shelter by the bins. He offers me a blanket. The fire is dying, but warm enough to give the illusion of comfort. Pomponette sleeps between us, street-cat regal and unconcerned.

I never sleep well on the streets. No one really does, I suppose, even with blankets and bedrolls. The air is damp; the ground is hard and pitted with irregularities. But tonight it feels safe. The scent of burning paper and the lingering scent of chocolate overpowers the smell of the alleyway. Here I will wait. Tomorrow will tell where the path will lead me next. Beside me, the cat twitches in her sleep. For a while I hear Roxane and Poupoule talking in lowered voices.

The rain has stopped. The fire burns low, and the night shuffles by like a pack of cards, interleaved with sounds, and scents, discomfort, and troubling memories, although I must have slept a while, because I dreamed of Molfetta, except that in my dream I never left her behind, but stayed there on the station bench, and waited for the Man in Black, and when I awoke he was standing there, right at the end of the alleyway.

9

16 October 1993

My first thought was: *He found us! He's here!* – and yet I sensed no immediate threat, no danger from his presence. Roxane and Poupoule were both alert, peering from under the flap of their tent like birds attempting camouflage. The fire was out, though the rain had stopped, and the sky overhead was marble-pale. I guessed it to be about six o' clock. There was a smell of cigarettes, and soot, and ash, and mildewed stone, and bread, and coffee, and garbage. Pomponette was drinking from the end of a dripping drainpipe, and Stéphane was smoking a cigarette. I thought he looked tired, and wondered if he had slept, or whether he had spent the night watching over the rest of us.

The Man in Black lifted a hand, as if in greeting. I sat up feeling cold and stiff. During my time at La Bonne Mère I have got used to my comfortable bed; my blankets; my nightdress; my pillows. A single night sleeping rough had left me feeling sick and exhausted. I wondered how many nights my friends had spent out in the open; not camping, not in transit, but in all weathers, and every day. I reached into my pocket for the card that Bal had given me. I smiled at Roxane, who was now busily packing up the tent and bedroll into her rucksack.

'Thank you for last night,' I said. 'I thought you and Poupoule might want this.'

She looked at the yellow card in my hand. 'He gave you a card for the *shelter*?' she said. 'Do you know how rare that is? Why the hell didn't you go there?'

'I told you. I'm just passing through. Take it,' I said when she seemed to hesitate. 'I promise you, I'll be fine.'

I hoped that was true. The Man in Black was still watching us from the mouth of the alleyway. Behind him stood the woman Cécile; I recognized her colours. I pulled my jacket closer, squared my shoulders, smoothed my hair. Then I stood up and walked towards the figure of the Man in Black. His face was still in shadow, but I thought he looked familiar. The dark suit and black shoes were new. His hair, habitually unkempt, had been cut short and slicked back. But his eyes were the same; very bright, very blue, and filled with lights and reflections.

'Guy!'

He laughed. 'You look surprised. Good God, did you spend the night back here?'

'I didn't have the choice,' I said. 'Someone took my money.'

Behind him, Cécile seemed to flinch.

'Never mind that now,' said Guy. 'We've found you. That's what matters.' He laughed again at my expression. 'What? Did you really think we'd let you go without even saying goodbye? Mahmed phoned two nights ago. Said Louis from La Bonne Mère had been over, demanding to see you. Said you'd packed your things and left. It wasn't hard to find out where. People seem to remember you.'

I looked at Cécile. 'What people?'

He grinned. 'I'll admit it. I had help. Cécile found your papers.' He gave me an energetic hug. 'You dope. Why did you run away? I've been looking for you all over the place.'

'Why?'

He gave a comical sigh. 'Don't you know? Vianne, you have friends. People who care about you.'

I thought: *That's what I'm afraid of.* And Guy looks different in a suit. Almost as if he's in disguise. I said, addressing Cécile: 'I found my bag in one of your bins.'

A flash of alarm in her colours. Her face reflects uncertainty. 'Someone must have dumped it there. I—'

Guy gave her a quelling look. 'For now, let's get Vianne some breakfast.' He turned to Stéphane and the others. 'You, too. Let's get croissants and coffee.'

We followed him into the little café. Roxane and Poupoule came warily; Stéphane with the same cheeriness that characterized all his actions. Cécile moved as if she were under arrest: bringing the coffee and croissants without making eye contact. I wondered what she was thinking. She knows him, I thought. She isn't surprised at the way he looks. I thought of the Hermit; his furtive smile; his not-entirely-trustworthy gaze.

'You look so different,' I said.

'Basic camouflage,' said Guy. 'Forget it. Drink your café-crème.'

I wondered why he'd said *camouflage*. Who was he trying to deceive? I'd always thought him so open, so straightforward in his dealings. But none of this was my concern. The road to Vianne led away from him. And there was something *wrong* here; I could feel it in the air.

'I'm sorry for all this trouble,' I said. 'I should have said I was moving on.'

'Moving on?' he said. 'But why? Did something happen in Marseille?'

I thought of Emile, on that last day. *I've been asking some questions.* How can I explain to him? Moving on is what we do. We never cast a shadow. Except that I've already broken that rule. And somehow it feels different. As if I'm leaving something behind. Something I should have remembered.

Vianne. 'I'm going to Vianne,' I said.

'But why? What's there?'

I shook my head.

'Is this because of Louis?'

I shrugged.

'Mahmed told me you came round a few days ago. He said you looked worried. He asked around.' He lowered his voice. 'Seriously, Vianne. If it wasn't working out at the bistrot, you could have found somewhere else in Marseille. I mean, you had a life there. Friends. You had *us*, if you needed someone.'

I shook my head. 'You don't understand.'

Of course he doesn't. Guy makes friends wherever he goes. He is effortlessly sociable. He never seems to consider the effect of himself on other people. My mother used to say that we should pass through the world like a stone through water; frictionless, leaving no trace. Guy passes through his world unaware of the burrs that attach themselves to him, the undergrowth he tramples. I envy him that. His carelessness. But that's why he'll never understand. People like us are different. People like us have to take care. And yet, isn't that what I wanted? To leave my mark, and be marked in my turn? Why am I then so fearful of the ripples I leave behind?

'Come back with me to Allée du Pieu. Stay in the guest bedroom. You could help us out in the shop. You already know the basics.'

I said: 'Are you offering me a job?'

He laughed. 'Why not? You're capable. Intelligent. Good with people. Given time, you could learn how to run a business. What?' He saw my expression. 'You don't think you could? I've seen what you did at La Bonne Mère. You brought the old place back to life. You could do the same with a chocolate shop. With my shop. With *any* shop. Come back with me to Marseille. Learn how to be a *chocolatier*. The van's just outside, we could be home by tonight.'

Home. I thought of La Bonne Mère, and of Emile's words to me; and Marguerite, and Louis, and Edmond, and Khamaseen, who had told me: *If you're going in search of yourself, be sure not to leave yourself behind.* How much of myself have I left? And how much more do I have to lose?

My little Anouk has been silent since I went to the hospital. I have not felt her, dreaming; warm; or fluttering with impatience. A little boy, the doctor says. My child will be a little boy. But Anouk is real. I claimed her. I dreamed of her, by the river, in Vianne. I thought that, by moving on, I would secure that future. Instead, I fear I am losing her, just as I lost the pink bootees.

'Come on, Vianne,' Guy told me. 'You were doing so well in Marseille. I was going to teach you how to temper chocolate. How to make rose creams, and pralines, and almond cracknell, and Turkish Delight—'

I felt a sudden, tiny, little movement under my ribs. A flutter, like that of a moth's wing. My little Anouk is listening. How strong-willed she is already, I thought: how quick to express her preferences.

'Come on, Vianne. Till the baby's born. There's space for you above the shop. I'll pay you a decent salary. I'll teach you everything I know about chocolate, and running a business. Then, if you like, you can move on – or not, whichever choice you make. Does that sound good?'

That flutter again. She hears him, I thought. She hears him like the call of the wind. Maybe my little stranger knows better than I do what we need. And maybe being a mother means more than simply being afraid.

I nodded. 'It sounds good.'

'Then it's decided,' Guy said with a grin. 'I'll get the van. We're going home.'

IO

I got up to follow the others, but found Cécile at my elbow. 'Wait,' she said in a low voice. 'I have something that belongs to you.'

I followed her into a back room that smelt of mould and sadness. Shelves of provisions. Tinned goods; giant tubs of coffee. A neon tube stuttered overhead, casting a cheerless brightness. Cécile looked both sullen and jaded, as if bad things happened every day, and I was only one of them. I thought she looked very tired, as if she, not I, had slept outside.

'Are you okay?' I said.

She flinched. People like Cécile often think that they deserve no better. Then she turned away from me and began to fuss with a shelf of tins. I waited there: some people need time.

Finally she turned and said: in a low, fierce voice: 'Are you *her*?'

I thought of the papers in my bag, papers that she might have seen. Then I saw her expression, and the colours threaded with longing, and understood her question.

Oh. The loss of a child is more than grief: it is the loss of a piece of yourself; a thing that can never be replaced. Her child – *Ondine*, in her secret heart – has made of her an empty room, with all doors open to the wind.

'I'm sorry. I'm not your daughter.'

She sagged. 'But you knew. You knew her *name*. And then when Guy said he knew you—'

'You know Guy?'

'I know his family. Everyone knows his family. And Sophie, of course.' I remembered the woman in the high-heeled shoes, whom Cécile had greeted so warmly. 'I thought you might have heard something. Or maybe you even knew her.'

I shook my head. 'I'm sorry,' I said.

Cécile was crying quietly. 'I knew it wasn't really you. But I dreamed of her last night. She looked like you. She'd be about your age by now. And now she'll never, ever know how much I tried to keep her.'

I put my arms around her. She smelt of coffee and cigarettes. Very like my mother, in fact; as if the grief of losing her had somehow taken human form. I lost my mother. You lost your child. But love – love finds a way to stay. To shine, and to remember.

'She knows,' I said.

'You think?' Her eyes were blurred with mascara. 'I mean, I don't even know her name. Whoever adopted her will have changed it. Why would she care about me?'

I said: 'I think that love stays in the world. It colours what it touches. Putting love into the world is more important than anything. You put it in, it comes back to you. It makes the world a better place.'

She laughed. 'What good have I ever been? The one good thing I had, I lost. Worse than that. I gave it away.'

I shook my head. 'You didn't, Cécile. You've kept her in your heart all this time. Love has a way of finding us. And you deserve love, as does everyone.'

She looked at me. 'You really believe that hippie crap?'

I smiled. 'My mother taught me that. I hope I'll teach my child the same.'

Cécile looked thoughtful. Her eyes were red, but her colours seemed to be clearing. 'I wish I'd had your mother,' she said. 'Mine was a judgemental bitch. I sometimes think I'm like her.'

'You don't have to be,' I said. 'We can make our own recipe.'

She held my gaze for a moment. I caught the sudden fleeting scent of cacao powder, cardamom, black pepper, star anise – the scent of Guy's xocolatl spice, clinging stubbornly to my palms. A potent blend, calling me back to my room at La Bonne Mère, and the blue sky on the Butte, and that feeling of *possibility*—

I had a sudden memory of Margot, in the kitchen. *Find him. Bring him home*, she'd said. But instead of that, I had fled: and ever since, I had felt disconnected – to my life, to my child, to my future, to myself. What had I missed, in my need to escape? What promise had I left unfulfilled? Cécile reached into her pocket. 'Here. I know I shouldn't have kept these. I'm sorry.' And she brought out an envelope – my envelope with the two thousand francs – and a pair of knitted bootees. But these were not pink. Instead, they were blue; blue as a fold of the Virgin's robe. Then I looked again, and they were the bootees I'd bought on Rue du Panier, still quaintly scented with lavender, delicate as spider silk, pink as eglantine blossom.

It was just the light, that's all. Just the light in the storeroom.

And yet I knew I'd seen something real; as real as Margot's voice from her book; as real as that footprint on the page. And at last I understood *why* I had to go back to Marseille: why the doctor had seen a boy, and not a girl, in my future; why every step in pursuit of Vianne was also a step away from myself.

His name is Edmond. Find him, Vianne.

Margot's son was still alive.

Mendiants

I

16 October 1993

I found Guy waiting in the van, with Stéphane in the back with Pomponette. During the time I'd been with Cécile, Guy had changed from his business suit into a pair of baggy shorts and an orange Hawaiian shirt with a frangipani design. Apart from the newly cropped hair, he looked just as he had when we first met, and I felt a pinch of unease. *Camouflage*, he'd told me. But why?

'Stéphane needed a lift,' said Guy. 'I said I'd drive him to Marseille.'

I thought about the *bidonvilles*, and the sleep merchants, and the vendors at the Vieux Port. 'I needed a change of air,' said Stéphane, revealing his disconnected teeth. 'And besides, you never know, there might be work at the harbour.'

Roxane and Poupoule had already left. I hoped the shelter would take them in. I thought about the lentil van; Bal and his mother; the band of homeless people around that cheerless station. Suddenly I wanted to be gone from this city of desert-rose and its scent of desperation. I wanted the ocean wind, the sound of morning traffic from the Canebière, the markets and fishmongers of the Vieux Port, the kitchen at

La Bonne Mère. I wanted my room, with its woollen throw. My pans. My knives. My piece of sky. And Edmond, the lost boy, the boy I promised his mother to find.

'A change of air sounds good,' I said.

We set off into the traffic.

The van smelt of cacao and rust, and the damp wool of Stéphane's overcoat. The little blue-eyed glass charm dangled from the mirror. We drove through the rosy streets of Toulouse in silence until we reached green space, and the long grey stretch of the *autoroute*. Stéphane seemed to go to sleep; Guy kept his eyes on the road, and the van made small, unsettling sounds as it rattled over the carriageway.

Finally, I asked him. 'Guy, how did you find me so quickly?'

'I told you. I know people. Besides, Cécile's a family friend. You chose a good place to pass out, Vianne.'

'A friend?'

'Well, more of a client, I guess. My father's firm helped her out once or twice. Abusive husband, messy divorce.' He shrugged. 'The usual story.'

'Your family's firm,' I repeated.

Guy pulled a face. 'Lacarrière, Maurel. It's been going for sixty years. My grandfather founded it with his friend. It's quite an institution.'

I nodded. 'It must be strange, coming back here.'

'It's like being a flamingo, trying to blend in with a murder of crows.'

I laughed. 'That explains the haircut, the suit. I almost didn't know you at first.'

'I barely know myself.' He smiled. 'But that's what it's like, when I come back here. Some places never let you change. It's like coming back to your childhood. Everyone knows you. Or thinks they do. Everyone makes assumptions.'

He drove on in silence for a while, and the fields and the trees went by. Finally, I asked him: 'Guy, does your family know what you do? Do they know about Mahmed?'

A pause. 'Well, not *exactly*,' he said. 'It's sometimes easier to blend in than to be who you really are.' He smiled. 'But we can talk about that later. For now, try to sleep. You're exhausted. I'll tell you about it another day.'

2

16 October 1993

It was already dark as we reached Marseille, and I felt a pinch of *déjà vu*. My life so far has always been a series of rear windows; of places never revisited, of friends made in transit, left behind. It seems so wrong to be coming back to a place I have already left; and yet it feels like coming home. As if the events of the past two days had been nothing but smoke and shadows.

Remember why you left, says Maman; and yet, I feel no anxiety. Only a sense of gratitude and warmth for this community. The people in the windows, faces pressed against the glass. The people on the streets, the regulars in the cafés. *Remember why you came back*, I thought. *This is how you learn to be Vianne.*

We found Mahmed still hard at work in one of the back rooms of the shop. There are several of these, once-store-rooms, now adapted to contain the stages of transformation: the winnowing, grinding and conching that turns cacao beans into chocolate. The scent that seemed part of the woodwork lay heavily on everything; a canopy of vanilla spice over a base of petrichor. It takes so many of those beans to make even a dozen bars, but Guy maintains that this is the way artisanal chocolate should work: not mass-market produce at supermarket prices, but specialist, high-value goods, made to be enjoyed by those who understand its complexity.

Mahmed is rather more practical. 'We made just fifty bars last month, working every single day. We'd have to charge a hundred francs a bar just to break even.'

'But we're not selling bars,' said Guy. 'We're selling dreams. Indulgences. *Magic*, Mahmed. Fairytales.'

'Next time I go to the bakery, I'll see how much bread *that* buys.'

Guy laughed. 'You need to believe, Mahmed.'

'I do. I just don't believe in – what the hell is *that*?'

That was Pomponette, who, on being released from her basket, had followed us into the room, and jumped up onto the conching machine to sniff tentatively at the drum. Mahmed flapped his hands at the cat, who stared at him contemptuously before jumping back onto the floor.

'Vianne brought a couple of friends with her,' said Guy. 'I said they could stay for a while.'

'Waifs and strays,' muttered Mahmed.

Guy grinned. 'You were a stray yourself.'

Mahmed said something in Arabic. Guy laughed, and Mahmed laughed with him. And it felt so good to be back with friends that I almost forgot my initial unease at his casual transformation and allowed myself to be seduced by friendship, warmth, and chocolate.

3

My room above the chocolate shop is small compared to La Bonne Mère. There is nothing here but a cracked sink and a mattress on top of three packing-crates. There is no view but the alleyway; not even a glimpse of the ocean. But give me a week and I can make it into something better. A little paint; some posters; maybe a second-hand rug on the floor. The building is old and sprawling, with more little storerooms than Guy can use. A central living area; a kitchen; a double bedroom he shares with Mahmed.

Stéphane and his cat have claimed a converted storeroom in the back. It smells of fermenting cacao beans, and there is no bed, just a sofa; but nevertheless he is overjoyed. It is the first time he has had four walls around him since his divorce, and although this is not a permanent home, he has already begun to refurbish the place, with paint he found in the basement and some items salvaged from a skip.

'It's amazing, what you can find if you know where to look,' he says, showing me the bookcase and chair that he has recovered and brought home. 'They're battle-scarred, but so am I. That's no reason to throw them away.' He promises to look out for more: maybe a table; another chair; maybe even a cradle. I think of the crib Louis promised me. The toys, the baby clothes, the things put away in his wardrobe. That was another life, I think. That was another future.

Mahmed does not approve of Stéphane. Stéphane sees this, and tries to please. But Mahmed is not easy to placate. *My* moving in to work is one thing, it seems, but Stéphane – a homeless man, with no connection to the shop, or the art of chocolate-making – is something else altogether.

'Waifs and strays,' he mutters, when he thinks Guy is not listening. 'Dogs and cats belong on the street.'

His mood was further darkened today by the noise from the takeaway next door. 'It stinks of cooking oil back there. It's going to affect business.'

'It's only a takeaway,' says Guy.

'It's an eyesore.' Mahmed glared at Stéphane. 'I don't want you bringing that food in here. The smell gets into the chocolate.'

Stéphane looked abashed. 'I'm sorry,' he said. 'I won't do it again.' He bought some fried noodles home last night, which he shared in his room with Pomponette. Since then, he has been looking for ways to make himself useful in the shop. While Mahmed works in the back rooms, he has been decorating the front. And with Guy's approval, he has found the perfect piece of wood from which to make a sign for the door.

'I used to be pretty handy at this,' he tells me. 'I had a workshop. Made things in my spare time.'

He has not shown us the sign yet. He wants it to be a surprise. But over the past couple of nights I have heard him at work in his room; the sound of the fret saw; the restless, whispering sound of sandpaper during the night. Sometimes, if the sound is especially persistent, Pomponette will come into my room and crawl into bed beside me. It feels good not to be alone.

I know I need to talk to Louis. I know it won't be easy. I need to make him understand why I had to leave, and why I am staying at Allée du Pieu, the place he so despises. But I keep putting off the task. It's childish, I know. But I'm afraid of what he might say. I am not used to facing up to my responsibilities. Besides, no one knows I am here. Allée du Pieu is an island, far from the dangerous currents of gossip that stir all around Le Panier. As long as I stay here, I am safe from sight and speculation. I keep thinking of Emile, and his words to me on the day I left. And there's so much work to do here that I can almost forget why I came, and those blue bootees in the overhead light all seem part of a dream of Toulouse, a dream I can barely remember.

Besides, there's so much here to learn, so much to discover. Chocolate is endlessly variable. Tender or brittle; bitter or sweet, fondant or creamy or crunchy or plain, there's something here for everyone. I have a talent for this, Guy says as I sort the roasted beans. He can always tell these things. I have an affinity.

Today, I learnt the first of three ways of tempering couverture chocolate. This one requires a marble slab and a lot of energy, but nevertheless it is simple enough, and the result was acceptable. Using a series of button moulds, I made those simplest of chocolate shapes, and when they were cool, I showed them to Guy, who checked them for taste and consistency.

'Not bad, for a first try,' he said. 'Now let's try a recipe.'

It is the simplest of recipes, after pralines and chocolate ganache. He calls them *mendiants*, those chocolate discs studded with raisins, and almonds and candied lemon peel. He tells me they're named after the mendicant orders of monks, who used to sell them door-to-door during the Middle Ages. It's a word I have heard before, though never in this context; instead, I remember it flung like stones in our wake as we passed through some long-ago village. It's a surprise to find this word – this *slur* – thus sweetened by circumstance, harmlessly translated into the language of chocolate.

First, melt the chocolate in a bain-marie. Strange, how the Virgin seems to bless even this most secular of baptisms. Then, on greaseproof paper, place tablespoons of the chocolate to make round discs, the size of the Host. On this still-cooling chocolate, add the traditional dried fruits and nuts that symbolize the Orders. Fat raisins; yellow sultanas; cherries; toasted almonds; pistachios and hazelnuts, like jewels on a medallion. Now leave them to cool, at least for as long as it takes for Stéphane to steal one.

'Stop that! I just made them!'

He grins at me. 'Delicious. Let's call it payment in kind.'

'For what?'

'It's a surprise,' he says. 'I left it in your bedroom.'

It is a crib, hand-carved from wood, and a child's small rocking-horse. Both are seemingly unused; the workmanship careful, but amateur. 'Where did you get these?' I said at last.

'Found them round the back of a bistrot somewhere up on the Butte. Left out with the rubbish.'

'Which bistrot?'

He shrugged. 'Does it matter?'

4

This morning, I went to La Bonne Mère, bearing an offering of mendiants. I found Louis with Emile, in the bar, drinking pastis and smoking. Louis' colours were muddled; combining anger and relief. But Emile was a gas flame; I could feel it across the room.

'Oh, look, it's the prodigal. I thought you'd taken off for good.'

I forked the sign against malchance. 'I need a word with Louis, Emile.' He glared at me. 'Alone, please.'

Emile downed his pastis and slammed down the glass. 'Don't let me get in your way,' he said, pushing past me towards the door. 'But if you think Louis is going to fall for you a second time, you're mistaken.' And then he left like a sullen child, kicking the door on his way out.

I waited until he was gone. The bar was otherwise empty. It smelt of pastis and cigarette smoke, and from the kitchen – no longer mine – came the smell of Margot's bouillabaisse. Louis put down his glass and pretended to wipe the counter top. But I could see the averted gaze, the stiffness of the shoulders. I said: 'I'm sorry, Louis. You've been so kind. I shouldn't have left the way I did.'

'You think?' His voice was cold.

'I ran away. It was stupid.'

He shrugged, still wiping the counter top. 'Don't expect to collect your things. I gave them all to the Croix-Rouge.'

I nodded. 'It's okay. I'll get more.'

He made a hard little sound in his throat. 'I should have known you'd be trouble,' he said. 'In fact, I knew. I knew from the start. I had a life before you came. I had a routine. It all made sense.' He scrubbed at the spotless counter top with a kind of desperate rage. 'Emile tried to warn me. He said nothing good could come of it. And he was right. I was a fool. Now even *food* doesn't taste the same.'

'Please.' I put my hand on his arm. 'It isn't what you think, Louis. You've been so kind, so generous. But—' How could I explain it to him? How could I tell him that Maman and I had always fled their charity? And charity is the hydra-headed mother of duty, and gratitude, that clips our wings in kindness as it tucks us into our feather bed.

'You don't need to explain. I get it,' he said. 'You probably did me a favour. Go back to Lacarrière. I'm sure he'll be understanding.'

I sighed. His words were so at variance with his colours and his tone that I knew I was not forgiven. *This is why we never go back*, said my mother's voice in my mind. *This is why we never stay long enough to get attached.*

'It isn't like that, Louis,' I said. I put down my box of mendiants. 'I made these for you yesterday. Call it a peace offering?'

He shrugged. 'No need for any of that. You worked for me. I paid you. Now you don't owe me anything. Except—' He seemed to remember something. Reached for a moment under the bar. Came back with the river stone, etched with the tiny footprint and the name in Margot's handwriting.

'Here.' He put it down on the bar. 'Take it. I don't want it.'

'But – it was a present,' I said. I've never given a present before. I've never had anything of value to give.

For the first time, his gaze was direct. 'I don't care what it is,' he said. 'What were you thinking, anyway? It was the darkest day of my life. Why would I want a souvenir?'

I tried to explain, but suddenly I found myself too close to tears. My throat was tight; my head ached; I wished I'd stayed at Allée du Pieu. I tried to say that love is the place where you go to find yourself; that everyone makes a mark on the world; that forgiveness has to start with the self, but all I could think of was Cécile, saying: *You really believe that hippie crap*, and I suddenly wasn't sure if I even believed it myself.

Louis went on, in a voice that was both cold and unbearably gentle: 'My Margot died, and with her, our son. I think about that every day. I don't need a fucking paperweight to remind me. Now go back to your chocolates, and don't come round here ever again.'

I picked up the river stone; it felt very smooth in the palm of my hand. I thought of her words in the baby book: *A named thing is a claimed thing.* I turned towards the door, and saw Louis, his face immobile. But his colours were eloquent; speaking to me in the language of things unspoken, things unfound.

My Margot died and with her, my son. And I knew, for whatever reason, Louis Martin was lying.

5

21 October 1993

I read the cards again last night, in my room above the shop.
Change. The Hermit. The Lovers. The Fool. And now, at last,
after all these weeks, a newcomer; the Nine of Cups, card of
peace and fulfilment. The picture in my mother's pack shows
the cups as flower-heads; petals shed, bellies swollen with the
growth of the new seed. Little Anouk inside me agrees; I made
the right decision.

But at night, all my doubts return. Since my conversation
with Louis, I have not been able to sleep. Perhaps it's the light
at my window from the fat October moon; or the sounds in
the alleyway, or the distant rumbling of the conching machine,
day and night, spinning cacao into gold. Whatever it was, I
awoke last night to the moon shining in through the skylight. A
moon like half a pumpkin, casting golden shadows. October is
my favourite month: soon it will be Hallowe'en. It's a night we
always celebrated, my mother and I. It belonged to us. Other
children had birthday cards and coloured candles on a cake: I
had Tarot cards; black candles; incense on the day of the dead.

I was never afraid of death. If you keep moving, my mother
said, death can never catch up with you. *Stay for only as long*

233

as it takes for dust to fall on the mantelpiece. A single layer is all we leave before the Man in Black comes round. I read somewhere that dust is mostly flakes of human skin. How many layers of myself have I already left in this room? How close am I to summoning the very thing we fled for so long? These thoughts were what kept me awake; that and the memory of Louis, saying *Margot died, and our son with her,* while his colours said something different. At Hallowe'en, she used to say, the skin of the world is paper-thin. The voices of the dead can be heard whispering through its pages. But it is not her voice, but Margot's, that speaks to me now from between the worlds, telling me that to find myself, all I have to do is stop running.

I get up, pull on my dressing-gown and go down into the kitchen. A cup of hot chocolate, I think, might help me off to sleep again. There's a comfort to be found in this most elementary of rituals: the heating of the whole milk in a copper saucepan; the adding of the nutmeg, cloves, cinnamon, chilli powder. Guy has taught me that chilli was what the Mayans used in chocolate; that cold and bitter forerunner of the drink we enjoy today. Chilli has special properties: it's a powerful antioxidant with antibiotic properties, and like *Theobroma cacao*, it boosts the immune system, lifts the mood and makes the senses more alert. Chilli and chocolate are soulmates, just as some people are soulmates, bound together through centuries. *Heat the milk to a shiver, then add the grated chocolate*: Guy only uses the darkest kind, but I prefer something sweeter. Brown sugar to combat the heat, and cardamom, for freshness.

The vapour rising from the pan is ghostly in the darkness. In the days before Hallowe'en, the dead gather around in readiness. If I concentrate, I can see our faces in the vapour;

the people we were, and will be again, reflecting each other down the years. Narrowing my eyes, I see a stretch of river; some boats; a row of wooden shacks on stilts, straggling along the water's edge. My little Anouk with her candyfloss curls. And behind her, a man in black—

I banish the vapour. No more of that now. There are no ghosts as troubling as the ghosts of our possible selves.

'Can't sleep either?' It was Guy. He moves surprisingly quietly; not even the vapour remembers him. 'I'm sorry. Did I startle you?'

I shook my head. 'I'm just tired.'

'Sleep is overrated,' Guy said, moving closer to inspect the contents of the copper pan. 'And Mahmed snores.' He grinned. 'This smells good.'

I said; 'I adapted your recipe.'

He poured the last of the chocolate into a small espresso cup. 'Yes, I like this,' he said. 'It's light. Not as strong as I make it. How are you feeling?'

'Much better,' I said, 'since I started the supplements.'

He nodded. 'I thought so. You look better, too. More relaxed.' I was surprised. I hadn't thought my anxiety would be so clearly perceptible. 'You don't need to worry, you know, Vianne. I want you to think of this place as home.'

I smiled. 'That's a word I don't really use. I've always been – a traveller.'

He thought about that. 'You know what's weird? I've never really travelled. I'd like to see Chichén Itzá, and the Temple of Kukulkan. I'd like to see Sao Tomé, and the chocolate farms of Principe. I'd like to see chocolate grow in the wild, and taste the fresh cacao pulp taken from the growing beans. Instead, I travel *this* way—' he made a gesture that encompassed the whole chocolaterie. 'Through recipes and stories.'

'I do that, too,' I told him, thinking of the maps that marked my childhood. 'I never really had a home. Just a series of passing places.'

He smiled. 'My home was the opposite. A place so fixed and set in its ways that even the air was rationed. My only taste of freedom came when I went to visit my grandfather in Moncrabeau. I used to go there every year and stay with him over the summer. He used to pick me up in his car and take me with him, and every year, for a week or two, I used to pretend things were normal.' He smiled. 'It was Pépé who introduced me to the art of chocolate. He had a friend in a village nearby who ran a chocolaterie. I used to go there and watch them making all the different kinds of praline. I promised myself that's what I would do, as soon as I could get away.' He paused for a moment. 'But *getting away* isn't as easy as it sounds. My family all studied law. My sister was a natural.' He paused to look into the dregs of his cup, as if in search of answers. 'I wish we could choose our families, instead of just being born to them.'

I thought of my mother. 'I think we do.'

He looked at me. 'Did you never have anyone but your mother? No father? Not even a boyfriend?'

'No one,' I said. 'We were enough.'

I saw him turning the thought in his mind like a truffle on the palm. 'That sounds good,' he said at last. 'Mahmed and I, we can be enough. We don't need their approval.'

His colours told me otherwise; I read volumes of sadness there. *What's your story, Guy?* I thought. *Why are you someone else in Toulouse?*

I reached for the vapours in my cup; *Try me. Taste me. Tell me.*

6

'In Moncrabeau,' Guy told me, 'there is a Liars' Festival. An old tradition, dating back to the eighteenth century. It's famous all over the region, and every year on the first of August, people come to Moncrabeau to watch the liars' contest. I always went with Pépé: there was a market, and music, and dancing, and a parade of the Liars' Academy in their ceremonial robes, with banners and pennants and pageboys in their red and white livery; and all the mayors and clerics of the different towns and villages along the Garonne would arrive in state, wearing their full regalia. And in the evening, the liars would tell their most extravagant stories; and the winner would sit on the Liars' Throne and be crowned as King of Lies.

'The throne itself was a stone seat, built into the wall of one of the narrow streets of the *bastide*, and I used to dream of sitting there, and being awarded the traditional scroll and bag of salt awarded to the winner, and the official certificate, stamped by the Mayor, that gave the winner the freedom to lie − to anyone − for the rest of his life.

"What would you do with your prize?" said Pépé. "Who do you want to lie to?"

Guy paused in his story. 'I think this story needs a little more than chocolate, don't you think?' He opened a cupboard and brought out a bottle of Armagnac. Setting out two shot glasses, he poured out a measure for each of us, then, seeing my expression, grinned.

'Sorry. Force of habit.' He drank his shot, then picked up mine. 'I just don't like drinking alone. Now, where was I?'

'Lying.'

He nodded. 'Right. But that was a game. Just part of the Liars' Festival. And in September I always went back home to Toulouse, and my father.' He took a mouthful of Armagnac. 'My father. He was so certain. So very sure of who I was. Never a doubt in his mind that some day, I would take his place in the firm. And so for years I believed him. Pretended to take an interest in law. Hid my collection of recipe books. I even dated girls, for a while. I'd always known my sister would be a brilliant lawyer. And then Anna died, in a car crash, three weeks after her twenty-second birthday, and suddenly there was only me to carry on the tradition.' For a moment he paused, and I saw his eyes all filled with reflections. I saw his sister; his father; his fear of letting down the family. 'The thing about lying,' Guy went on, 'is how often it comes in disguise. We lie to protect other people. To make them happy. To earn their love. Well, Vianne, I've been lying ever since I can remember. It's my greatest talent, I think; even more than making chocolate.'

Guy had gone to study law at the Faculty of Aix-Marseille. 'My father would have preferred the Sorbonne. But I loved Marseille. The city, the sea – everything but the course itself, which was dry, and depressing, and filled with the kind of young person my father would have loved me to be.' He grinned. 'So I dropped out without telling him, and took a cookery course instead. But I didn't want to be a chef. I wanted to be a chocolatier.'

'And you met Mahmed.'

He nodded. 'He was working as a delivery driver at the docks. We met in a bar. We clicked. That's all.'

'But you didn't tell your father.'

'No.' He gave me his wry and wistful smile. 'My father would never have understood. Would never have forgiven me. I was all he had left – my mother had died when Anna was five, and I barely remembered her. The business was all he cared about, that, and carrying on the name. He'd even selected a girl for me – Sophie, his partner's daughter. And so at first I just let them believe that I was studying law in Marseille. It was so easy. I played the part. My living allowance was generous – although he'd have stopped that straightaway if he'd ever suspected the truth. But every time I went back to Toulouse I promised myself I'd tell him the truth. And every time, I told myself that this time wasn't the right time. Do you understand?'

I think I do. My mother and your father are not so very far apart. I could imagine Guy's father now; a physically imposing man, like his son, but without Guy's humour. A monolith of his childhood; remote as a god on a mountaintop. Receiving offerings of lies, disguised as filial duty.

'But what about graduation?' I said. 'How did you manage after that?'

'I did what every student does. I rented some robes. Had some pictures taken. My father still has one of them, framed, on the wall of his study. I was still trying to find the right time. The right words. But they never came.' He paused, and I saw him struggling. 'And then, he fell ill. It was cancer. How could I tell him the truth then?'

Unlike my mother, Guy's father had been as aggressive in his fight with cancer as he was in pursuing his cases. There were therapies, hospitals, treatments. 'I'd always known the old man was tough,' Guy said. 'I'd thought him immortal. But when he fell ill, I started to think that the right time would never come. Not for him, and not for me.'

Guy had told his father that he was planning to stay in Marseille in order to gain some experience before returning to Toulouse. He told him that he was working *pro bono* along-side a barrister who specialized in immigration law. Marseille has many immigrants, both legal and illegal, and although his father complained about Guy's tendency to pick up waifs and strays, Guy could tell that he was proud.

'Thinks he's a working-class hero,' he said. 'I used to be just like that, once. Let him get it out of his system. There's time.'

'That was eighteen months ago,' went on Guy. 'Since then, he's back in remission. He's passed his cases on to Sophie. And still—' He sighed. 'I meant to tell him this time. I really did. I was going to. But I want him to see my business thrive. I want him to know it's a success. Give me six months, and I'll show him what we've achieved together. Prove to him that I'm serious. That I lied to him for a reason.'

'Sophie.' I knew the name rang a bell. 'That woman in Café Pamplemousse?'

He nodded.

I thought about her patent shoes; my feeling that she was making an effort for someone. 'She likes you,' I said.

'What can I say? I'm likeable.'

There was a pause, during which I thought about what Mahmed had said to me about Guy being a disappointment. 'What does Mahmed know?' I said.

'Mahmed doesn't know about this. He thinks my father knows about us, and the chocolaterie.' Guy pulled a face. 'Listen, Vianne. I know it's a mess. I never meant it to go on for so long. I'll tell my father as soon as the chocolaterie breaks even. And it hurts to lie to Mahmed. He's the most honest person I know. But I still need that allowance, and he's always been so sensitive about my family's money.'

He paused, and seemed to listen for a sound in the passageway. 'Did you hear something?'

I shook my head. 'Probably just the wind in the eaves.'

He seemed to relax. 'Just nervous, I guess. I don't know why I'm telling you this, but somehow, you inspire confidence. It isn't always easy, being optimistic all the time.'

I thought about that. I suppose I'd always taken his certainty for granted. Now I saw his self-doubt, and felt a sudden kick of sympathy. 'You'll do it,' I said. 'I know you will. I'll help if I can.'

He smiled. 'Thank you. I'm glad of your help. You were so good for Louis Martin. I thought maybe you'd do the same here. You're so good with people, Vianne. You know how to bring them in.'

I wonder about that, though. He seems to have such faith in me. But ever since I returned from Toulouse, people have been different. This is a close-knit neighbourhood; it's hard to avoid seeing people. Those who were once almost my friends now suddenly seem not to notice me, and the shopkeepers, the market-traders, the fishermen at the harbourside – all reflect a secret contempt, a kind of veiled hostility. The sound of whispering as I pass. The sudden silence as I approach. What can I do to win their trust? To charm them from their suspicion?

I smiled. 'Of course. I'll do my best.'

Outside, the wind's soft laughter.

7

The last half of October brings sullen skies and storms from the south. Lightning stalks the harbour at night, and the rain brings a flotilla of plastic bottles and beer cans down Allée du Pieu straight to our door. My skylight is leaking; a steady drip comes through the frame and falls into a flowered chamber-pot supplied by Stéphane from wherever he goes in search of abandoned objects.

Next door, the Chinese takeaway has been shut down by inspectors. Apparently someone has complained that they were pouring cooking oil into the drain at the end of the street. This is a lie, says Madame Li angrily, in her broken French. They have always put the oil into drums, to be taken away by the refuse collectors. But the inspectors came to check, and although they confirmed that this was true, they also discovered some other problems that must be addressed immediately. As a result, Happy Noodles is shut, with a warning sign on the door; and the familiar smell of spiced roast pork and frying garlic and cooking oil is absent.

'Good,' says Mahmed. 'Let's hope it stays that way.'

This is a habitual refrain: relations between Mahmed and the Chinese family are not cordial. But the Chinese family are dismayed. Madame Li tells me that they must refurbish the premises completely before they are allowed to reopen. 'That could take three months,' she says. 'Very, very difficult.'

I can see from her manner that she blames Mahmed. I have seen her watching him coming and going behind the shop. I sense that to her, he looks frightening; his height; his long and greying hair; his scowl of fierce concentration. I have seen her calling her girls inside when he is working: beside him, they look tiny; almost painfully fragile.

'If there's anything we can do to help, please ask,' I say.

She smiles and nods politely. I know she will not ask. I wish I could tell her that Mahmed is not responsible for their troubles; that he would never do such a thing; that beneath his look of ferocity, there beats a kind and gentle heart. But the Chinese family remain aloof; nothing I can say breaks through their veil of polite suspicion.

Meanwhile, our own refurbishments are coming on apace. Stéphane has found me a chest of drawers, which he has painted primrose-yellow; and he has repainted the walls of my room in the same sunny colour. The result is bright and cheerful: and he has promised to fix the leaking skylight as soon as he can. A little picture in a frame – an icon of the Virgin and child – hangs above my makeshift bed, and I now have a pair of blankets, slightly moth-eaten, one sky-blue, one lemon-yellow, as well as a couple of cushions. I also have some second-hand clothes to suit the colder weather; a couple of sweaters; a corduroy skirt; a pair of comfortable boots.

This urge to collect is dangerous. But I have always done it. Menus, stolen from restaurants where we could never afford to eat. Seeds, planted in our wake, in the hope that one day I might see them grow. Mahmed has made me a window-box in which I will plant daffodil bulbs: by Christmas I will see

243

their shoots. Until then, I have planted a little windmill in the soil, a child's toy left by the roadside, which flashes bright colours as it turns. Today the windmill is turning so fast that I can barely see the colours – a sign, my mother would have said. The wind is always changing.

Let it change. I am safe here. And I am learning so much about chocolate and its origins; its history, its legends; its many different grades of beans. Guy makes me spiced hot chocolate every day instead of my usual coffee. It's better for the baby, he says. Perhaps it is; coffee does not seem to agree with me as it once did, and the chocolate is sweetened and made with milk to make it more palatable. Guy and Mahmed both take theirs black; but Stéphane likes the frothy *chocolat au lait*, which reminds him of his mother, and his childhood home. Breakfast together has become another of our rituals; with croissants or *tartines* with apricot jam. We take it in the back of the shop, where there is a little kitchen. And we talk, and go over our plans for the week, and the opening in December. I like it; having a routine. Having a kind of family. Were it not for one thing, I would be completely content. And still the quiet days roll by like waves upon a sandy shore, and we build our castles in the sand, and dream of Christmas chocolates.

8

A week has passed since my return, and still I feel no closer to achieving what I came back here for. And yet the thought of finding Edmond is never far from my mind. The paperweight – my gift to Louis – is on the floor beside my bed, along with the crib and the rocking-horse Stéphane found in an alley on the Butte.

I have no doubt that the bistrot behind which he found them was La Bonne Mère. Louis made these things, I am sure of it. And after keeping them all these years, Louis chose to throw them away. I wish I could believe that this means he is finally moving on. But from his words to me, it seems more like a rejection. He does not want to remember the child. Margot's album told me as much. *Louis still refuses to use his name. He thinks it's bad luck. He wishes I had given up.*

I've tried asking questions around the Panier: everyone knows Louis Martin, but no one wants to talk to me. André at the butcher's; Marinette at the florist's; all those people who were almost friends now look at me with suspicion. There is no sign of Khamaseen in any of her usual haunts. Once more I am a foreigner; my accent jarring; my manners, subtly different. I wonder what Emile has said about me in my absence. I wonder how I can find my way back into this community.

Guy seems optimistic. He likes me; thus I am likeable. The chocolaterie is progressing well. And of course he assumes that his chocolates will be impossible to resist. I am less certain; the people here like what is familiar. Not everyone wants to travel, I say. Not everyone loves stories.

Today, he is wearing an oversized shirt with a design of pink palm trees. A checked bandana around his hair – he has been making dinner. The rich scents of olive oil, red wine, bay, basil and sage fill the air. Guy does most of the cooking here. He laughs when I appear surprised.

'What, did you think I brought you back to have you cook for us? When we first met, you didn't even know how to choose fish for bouillabaisse.'

I laughed at that. 'I'm learning, though. I even used your chocolate spice.'

'You did? In what?'

'In everything. In cassoulet, and *tapenade*, and scattered over café-crème. You were right; it isn't sweet. But it gives an extra something.'

He smiled. 'I knew you'd enjoy it. Later, I'll teach you the recipe.'

I wondered if I should tell him that I already know it. *Spice to calm a restless heart: Cardamom, cinnamon; vanilla, star anise, chilli.* But for now, Guy is planning a leaflet campaign for All Saints on 1 November. 'We need to target the holiday crowd. The tourists. Tourists love chocolates. Maybe you could hand out some samples to people coming out of church.'

Mahmed has his doubts about this. All this means money, he tells me, and we are already far beyond budget. 'Guy never

thinks about money,' he says. 'It's all very well to experiment, to advertise, but in the end, we need to sell product.
Guy doesn't think of this as product. He thinks of it as *story*.
As *art*. As *magic*.' He made an impatient sound. 'As if magic
could pay the bills.'

'We just need to get to the end of the year,' says Guy,
waving aside his objections. 'Just till we get up and running.
First, we build up a customer base. Then, we start earning
properly. I promise you, in six months' time, we'll be the
Chocolate Kings of Marseille.'

I made up some boxes of mendiants to hand out as samples
next Monday. I gave one to André, one to Stéphane, and
one to the Chinese family. Madame Li and her mother are
laying tiles in the kitchen: the girls are collecting rubbish into
a couple of heavy bags. They accept the gift with smiles and
nods, although they look bewildered. Madame Li is wearing
overalls over her faded jeans; her hands are chapped and
reddened. It's hard to tell how old she is; her face is drawn
and unhappy. Her daughters are beautiful, in that casual,
unfinished way that only teenage girls can achieve, but I can
see her shadow in them, like a foreknowledge of sorrow.

'I'm learning to make chocolates,' I said. 'I hoped you'd
help me test them.'

'Test?' said Madame Li uncertainly.

I smiled and nodded. 'You know. Try some. On the house.
Tell me if I've got it right.'

Madame Li nodded and thanked me again. Her colours were
muddled and anxious. She spoke in Chinese to the eldest girl,
who was watching from the door. Black hair in a ponytail
tied back under a spotted scarf; dark eyes guarded and wary.

'*That's* what you're making? Chocolates?' The girls both
speak perfect French, and with a strong Marseille accent.

I nodded. 'I'm Vianne. I live next door.'

The girl glanced at her sister. 'That's the man who made the complaint. Who reported us to the health police.'

'Mahmed wouldn't do that,' I said.

The girl simply shrugged and made no reply. Her mother said something in Cantonese which sounded like a reprimand. 'As you say,' said the girl to me, and went back to picking up rubbish.

9

24 October 1993

I caught sight of Louis again today. Just for a moment, as I came out of the bakery with a bag of croissants. He pretended not to see me: I saw it in his colours. It makes me unhappy to see him like this. I liked him – *still* like him, in spite of all his efforts to the contrary. But he did not acknowledge me, and from the looks I've been getting from people in the neighbourhood, he – or more likely, Emile – has been spreading rumours. Rumour is our currency here; and I can sense the hostility in faces that until now were friendly. What whisperings have they heard? That I tried to seduce him? That I made a fool of him, and then disappeared without a word? That, having failed to persuade him to give me what I wanted, I simply found someone else?

Some men are afraid to be loved; even more afraid to love. And yet such people are surely the ones who are most in need of it. It's there in Margot's cookbook. *Spice to calm a restless heart.* I can't help thinking that this is the heart of the chocolate spice Guy calls xocolatl: just add it to ground cacao, and let the flavours rise like smoke. In any case, it had an effect on my regulars at the bistrot: perhaps I can introduce it somehow to prospective customers. I took my croissants back to the chocolaterie, thinking hard to myself all the way. Then, after breakfast, I headed for Rue du Panier and La Bonne Mère, taking with me a box of mendiants, tied with a scarlet ribbon.

Mendiants. It seems appropriate. I come here as a supplicant, with offerings of sweetness. But arriving at La Bonne Mère, I found the bistrot deserted, except for Emile, who was eating a *tartine* dipped in coffee, with his usual cognac on the side. He gave me a look of sour triumph, reflected in his colours like the brightening of a gas flame.

'If you're looking for Louis, you're wasting your time. He left me in charge while he went out to buy something for lunch.'

I looked around at the empty bar. No crumbs on the tables, used crockery, or any other sign of life. I said: 'How's business?'

'Like you care.' The cape of rage that surrounded him seemed to tighten a little more. 'You made him dependent on you. Made him think you were going to stay. And then like that—' He made a dismissive gesture, and I wondered briefly how many of those shots of cognac he had drunk, under cover of his café-crème. 'Like that – *pff!* – you were with someone else, without even a word of thanks for everything he'd done for you.'

'I didn't mean to hurt him,' I said. 'I told him that already.'

He gave a dry little hacking laugh. 'That makes it all better, then, doesn't it? Well, never mind. He's found someone else. A new man to help around the place. Someone who won't let him down.' I supposed he meant himself. Emile is a painter-decorator by trade, but seems to be mostly retired, preferring to sit in La Bonne Mère rather than seek work elsewhere.

He glanced at the box of mendiants. 'What's that?'

'Chocolate,' I said.

'For Louis?'

'For you.'

At last, I thought he looked surprised. 'For *me*?' His colours flared suspiciously, as if he expected trickery.

'I'm learning to make chocolates,' I said. 'I need someone to test my work. You were the first to try my pralines. You always enjoyed my hot chocolate. I thought perhaps you could sample these. Market research. On the house.' And with my hand, behind my back, I made a little coaxing sign; like sunlight on the counter. *A pretty.*

Emile looked suspicious. 'I've never heard of such a thing.'

'You'd be doing me a favour,' I said. 'Chocolate is Guy's passion, but he doesn't know what the public wants. And so I thought – a volunteer. Just to provide some feedback.'

Emile made the sound again. 'I don't know shit about chocolate.'

'But that's what makes you so perfect,' I said. 'There's no point making chocolates for a handful of experts. We need a layman's opinion. An *educated* layman, of course.'

Emile opened the little box. The scent was strong and earthy. I saw a slight surprise on his face. *Try me. Taste me. Test me.*

'Dark chocolate,' he said. 'I prefer the other kind.'

'Try it anyway,' I said. 'Leave it to melt on your tongue.'

Emile ignored me, but slipped the whole chocolate into his mouth. I heard it crunch between his teeth and thought about the sound a dog makes when it crunches a bone.

'We use the finest beans,' I said. 'We buy them from all over the world. We make the chocolate from scratch, to control the whole of the process. That way we—'

Emile pulled a face.

'Well?'

He shrugged. 'Too bitter. I have a sweet tooth, to go with my sweet nature.' He gave a mirthless grin, which showed the nicotine stubs of his teeth.

251

'I see. Well, thank you for your time.' I reached out to take back the box, but Emile pulled it back. 'I'll keep hold of these. Who knows? The taste might grow on me.'

I smiled at him. 'Of course,' I said. 'Next time, I'll bring something else.'

10

26 October 1993

'You're wasting your time with him,' said Mahmed, when I told him about my experiment. 'I know that guy. He's a rattle-snake gourd. Noisy as hell, but empty inside. You won't win him over, or change his mind if he's decided you don't belong. Stick to making chocolates for people who might actually want to spend money here. Those old codgers from Rue du Panier wouldn't know artisan chocolate from soap.'

I have to admit that my first attempts to make friends in the community have not been very successful. Samples of my mendiants have gone to all the shopkeepers and stall-holders in the Old Quarter, without any noticeable effect. I'd hoped for some reaction, at least, from Madame Li and her daughters, but the whole family remains aloof, watching us with suspicion. I found my gift of chocolates unopened, in the rubbish bin at the back of Happy Noodles. So much for building bridges. I suppose the family still think Guy and Mahmed are responsible for their misfortune. Mahmed, especially, does nothing to alter their opinion of him. Could he really have made the complaint? Over the past couple of weeks, he has been increasingly anxious about the opening

253

JOANNE HARRIS

in December, and especially about what he considers Guy's cavalier approach to money.

'It's not a game, you know,' he repeats. 'A railway set in a back room. A hobby to be abandoned. It's a business, and should be run professionally. You can't just keep on giving out freebies and taking in every stray that comes around.' A pause. 'Not you, Vianne, of course,' he says, his dark eyes softening. 'But Guy has a habit of taking in people who take advantage. People who see his kindness and mistake it for stupidity. He trusts people. He assumes they're good.'

'If this is about Stéphane,' I said, 'he's really making an effort. Look at all the things he's done. The paintwork at the front of the shop. The things in my room. The sign he's making for the shop.'

'Yes, the sign. Who asked him to do that, anyway?'

I said: 'It's his way of thanking you. It's not an attempt to take over.'

He shrugged, and his mouth twisted bitterly.

'Guy *loves* you. That's not going to change.'

He made a dry sound in his throat that somehow made me think of Louis. *Some men are afraid to be loved; even more afraid to love.*

I said: 'My mother taught me to take what I could from the world, and move on. Don't get invested. Don't make friends. Never stay in one place too long. When I arrived here, I never thought I'd still be around in October. Guy did that. For the first time, he made me feel as if I belonged.'

Mahmed's eyes softened. 'He has a way of doing that.'

'You, too, Mahmed. You're a good man.'

The glimpse of softness disappeared. 'Well. I have work to get on with. You, too. See you later.' And pulling back his hair into its usual messy bun, he vanished into the back rooms like a hermit crab into its shell.

I stayed a while in the kitchen, and made myself a cup of tea. Cardamom tea, or chamomile, or peppermint, or green tea with lemon and ginger always seem to do me good. It occurred to me that perhaps I could use my window-box, or the strip of ground at the back of the shop – too small to be called a garden – to grow something that I could use. There wasn't as much space here as there had been at La Bonne Mère, but the urge to make things grow was just as strong as it had been there. I finished my tea, and went to check what space there was available.

I found a narrow strip of earth, measuring maybe six by three feet. Most of it was hidden under boxes and assorted junk. But moving this aside, I found that here too there had once been flowers; shaggy-headed asters; buddleia; nasturtiums; lavender, gasping for the sun. And a single stunted rose, almost leafless, bearing a barely legible tag that read, in tiny letters: *Vianne.*

Cacao

I

26 October 1993

A rose with my name. What can it mean? I rubbed the rusty
metal tag between my fingers. Maman and I had a lifetime of
reading runes and Tarot cards and mystic contrails in the sky.
But something like this – a rose with my name – I've never
seen anything like that before.

'Of course, she's named after Vianne d'Albret,' said a voice
above me. 'Founder of that bastide we know. And yet, it *could*
be a sign, of course. Margot loved her roses.'

Khamaseen has changed again since I saw her last; now she
was wearing a fisherman's smock over a patchwork skirt, and
a knitted cap over her hair. She also looked younger than
before – no older than fifty – and the hands that had seemed
old and frail were square and brown and capable.

She smiled at me. 'I'm glad you're here. I miss my little
garden. It's always surprising to see what survives in the worst
of conditions. And plants are always such hopeful things. All
they need is a little space.'

I looked at her. '*Your* garden?'

Of course. I should have known who she was as soon as
she gave me Margot's album. The herbalist, the friend of

Margot's, whom Louis seemed to resent so much.

'This must have been your shop,' I said, indicating the chocolaterie. It looks a lot better since Stéphane replaced the original door and window frame, although the shop front is still unmarked, and covered over with newspaper.

'It was,' said Khamaseen. 'For ten years. I moved here back in '64. My shop sold herbs and spices, Tarot cards, incense and teas. Sometimes I told fortunes. It was popular back then. And Allée du Pieu was a colourful place, filled with little businesses.' She indicated the row of shops, long boarded over, signs faded grey. 'That was a barber's shop,' she said. 'That was a tattooist. A hardware store. An Iranian restaurant.' She pointed at Happy Noodles. 'What happened to that place? It looks closed.'

I explained about the forced closure of the takeaway. 'It's never been easy, settling here,' said Khamaseen. 'People are wary of foreigners. There were always so many rumours about me in the old neighbourhood. First of all, that I was a witch.' She gave a small, mischievous smile. 'Then, that I poisoned Marguerite with my spells and potions. That I lit the fire myself to cash in on the insurance. That I was the reason no one could make a business work in Allée du Pieu – I'd somehow put a curse on the place. In fact, there was no insurance. I lost everything in the fire. And Margot died to save her child, the child she'd always wanted.'

'I heard the baby didn't survive.'

She smiled. 'Is that what Louis told you? You and I know better, of course. Men are so predictable. Margot was told by the doctors that another miscarriage might kill her. But she persisted. Did everything to make the child stay with her. And then, when she started to bleed again, she simply didn't tell anyone. The child was born six weeks early, and Margot bled out in the taxicab. And Louis – poor, grieving, *stubborn* Louis – refused to even look at it. A child that had caused its mother's death, a child he thought was imperfect.'

'Imperfect, how?'

She shook her head. 'What does *perfect* mean, Vianne? The child was a child, who deserved to be loved. Children give love where they find it. But to love his son, Louis would have had to give up his anger.'

I thought of Louis, suspended in grief like an insect in amber; knowing that his son was alive. Knowing that the key to his heart had always been there, just out of reach. *Some men are afraid to be loved; even more afraid to love.* Margot had seen that in him, I thought; had written it as a warning.

'So what happened to Edmond?'

'They gave him into the care of the State. It was the only thing to do, without a father to claim him.'

'So he was adopted? Who by?'

She shrugged. 'How would I know? They changed his name. Gave him a different future. He'd be about twenty now. A good age; everything's possible. We can hope that Margot's son had loving parents; a happy home. We can hope he feels safe and loved. But Louis will never know him. Not unless the boy seeks him out. And really, why would he want to?'

2

29 October 1993

The second way of tempering chocolate is the seeding method, which involves melting some of the chocolate in a double boiler, then seeding the rest into the already heated mixture, moving it constantly to achieve the correct temperature and crystalline structure. It is a less time-consuming method than the first, on the marble slab, although the results were less pleasing, and I overheated the process so that the chocolate was scorched. Guy watched me and shook his head, and told me I had to start again.

'Chocolate is moody,' he tells me. 'It loses its temper. It seizes. You need to get the heat just right. That's why we use the thermometer: even a degree makes the difference between chocolate with a good shine, a clean snap, and murky chocolate that blooms like the plague.'

The different grades of chocolate all work at different temperatures, too: fifty degrees for dark chocolate, forty-five degrees for the milk. The vapour that rises is volatile; subject to sudden changes in mood. It's funny, to think of angry chocolate; and yet, it speaks to me: to my uncertainty; to the life growing fiercely inside me. I have started feeling nauseous in the mornings. I take a spoonful of cacao nibs to combat this morning sickness, and it works. It gives me energy and focus for the day's work.

I have even begun to get used to the bitterness, to appreciate the complexities of the different cacao beans. The *Forastero* is lighter in taste; the *Trinitario* warmer, but more likely to be bitter; the Criollo deeper and more complex. The rarer varietals – the *Porcelana* and the *Nacional* – are even more subtle, with floral, woody, citrus notes suspended in the bitter water.

'You have a good nose,' Guy tells me. 'That's good in a chocolatier.'

I wonder, though. My handmade chocolates have not had all the success I hoped for. I wonder if I am lacking something. If there's some part of the recipe that somehow doesn't reach them. Perhaps it's the tempering method; or maybe the beans I am using. Or maybe it's the recipe itself; the combination of flavour and form that speaks directly to the heart.

Everyone has a favourite. Just like Margot's recipes. Emile likes pissaladière. Tonton loves grilled mackerel. Marinette loves anything sweet. If only I could apply what I see in people to making chocolates. But only Emile comments, though never in a positive way. So far I have tried: mendiants (too bitter); milk chocolate truffles (too powdery); mint cracknel (an old woman's chocolate, apparently). Today I have been making rose creams; unlikely to be his favourite, although he has taken to hanging around Allée du Pieu when he knows I am making a batch.

'No need for Louis to know,' he says, cramming a chocolate into his mouth. 'You've already upset him enough. What is this?' He stops mid-mouthful.

Rose fondants, made with Turkish rosewater; coated in 70 per cent couverture chocolate from hand-sorted *Porcelana* beans. I remove the embryo myself in order to limit the bitterness. Eighty-five hours conching; then tempered on marble, my favourite way, then dip the fondant, leave to set and add a crystallized rose petal on top. The result smells like roses; chocolate-red; full-throated; the petals like the bloom on a grape. I see the surprise in Emile's face, surprise now tempered with softness.

'Not bad,' he said. 'It reminds me of—'

Show me. What do you see?

A night at the theatre in '59. Ice cream in the interval, champagne in the bar afterwards. She was wearing a rose-coloured dress. I couldn't keep my eyes off her.

I heard his answer as clearly as if he had spoken the words aloud. I saw it in his colours, like a display of Northern lights. I saw *her.*

Margot?

You were in love with Margot?

Of course I couldn't ask him: all I could do was watch him. The narrow face; suspicious eyes; the dark, insatiable hunger. And beneath it, a bitterness so intense that I could almost taste it. *Some men are afraid to be loved; even more afraid to love.* Did you ever tell her, Emile? Or was it enough to be near her?

He finished his chocolate, savouring the last of it like a lingering glimpse of home. I thought his voice was slightly altered as he said:

'Yes. This is good. Keep the recipe.' Then, he turned and strode away, pausing only to doff his cap as he rounded the corner.

3

30 October 1993

The third method of tempering chocolate is *sous-vide*, in a waterproof silicone bag. The trick here is to get the temperature of the chocolate just right; and it works, it's easy; but I still prefer the marble slab, the feeling of connection with the medium. It engages all the senses; the cold of the slab; the warmth of melted chocolate; the rhythm back and forth; the scent; the sound of scraper and marble. Guy says I should go with my instincts – they're good. And he likes to see me experiment with different fillings and fondants; and has even shown me how to make my own chocolate moulds from silicone plastique. These things are surprisingly easy, once the magic has been demystified. I have already made moulds from several small objects around the house, as well as from something I borrowed from La Bonne Mère when I left: something for which I have high hopes when All Saints' Day comes along.

Mahmed thinks I spend too much time messing around with details. He thinks we should stick to familiar things: chocolate bars, and Easter eggs, and maybe a small selection of truffles, which are easy to make, and require little skill, and which will not confuse our customers.

'This isn't art,' he tells me, seeing me working on a chocolate cameo; a woman's face, picked out in white chocolate
against a dark medallion. People are going to be afraid to eat
them if they look too fancy.'

I disagree. Food *is* an art. I learnt that at La Bonne Mère.
Food engages sight and sound and texture, not just scent and
taste. And food is the most elementary expression of human
connection; love without complications. Travelling with my
mother has taught me the value of perspective. A simple dish
can become ridiculously elevated by an elegant turn of phrase.
Bread with a square of chocolate inside becomes a pâtissier's
chocolatine; two dozen snails from a woodpile become *escargots
en persillade*.

Maman used to laugh at my little collection of menus.
Vermicelle à l'eau, she would say, when she made instant
noodles. *Served with a sprinkle of sel de mer, and maybe some
poivre noir and a packet of ketchup à l'américaine you stole from a hot
dog stand in New York. Or maybe sandwich à la manière Rochas,
with moutarde à l'anglaise and beurre du café du coin? Or pizza à
la Genovese, scavenged from a table outside a swanky roadside café?*

I still hear her voice best from her cards. And at this
time of year, when Hallowe'en comes around, I find myself
reaching for the pack, even though I know what she'd say
if she knew what I was planning. I was reading the cards in
my bedroom when Stéphane came looking for Pomponette.
'What's this?' he said, seeing the cards spread out over the
coverlet. 'Checking out our future?'

'Not the future, exactly,' I said. 'More of – a meditation.'

We already know the future, Viannou, so my mother used to
say. *The cards tell us what we already know.* And yet I don't
know anything. Will Xocolatl be a success? Will I see the
Vianne rose bloom? Will Edmond Loïc Bien-Aimé ever know

who his parents were? Although my talk with Khamaseen confirmed what I already believed, I still have no idea how to find the child Louis gave up for adoption. And all the cards are meaningless blanks, reflecting nothing. I looked up to see Stéphane watching me with interest. 'My wife was into that,' he said. 'All yoga and meditation. On Tuesdays she used to go the gym. It took me a while to realize that *Jim* was the name of her lover.' He picked up Pomponette, who had been sleeping at the foot of the bed, and pressed his face into her fur. 'Even my cat sleeps with someone else. Come on. I have something to show you.'

This dry, almost existential humour is very much Stéphane's default position. Over four years of homelessness have failed to dent his optimism. Like my mother, he seems to live from day to day, taking from it what he can, scavenging rubbish from roadsides and skips to give it a new purpose. Along with the crib and the rocking-horse he found for me behind the bistrot, he has also brought me some faded brocade cushions, a woven multicoloured rug, a bookcase and some paperback books he found in a box by the side of the road. Thanks to him, I have never had quite so many possessions. He has also mended the skylight, and finished repainting the woodwork. His own room is already filled with things that he has rescued and mended; and tonight he finally showed me the sign he has been making for the front of the shop: a piece of mahogany, polished and oiled, incised with a fretwork geometric design that looks vaguely South American. The name of the shop has been chiselled expertly into the wood and highlighted with gold paint: *Xocolatl*. It is a beautiful piece of work, and I know how many hours of polishing, planing and finishing it has taken him.

'What do you think?'

I touched the wood. 'I think you're an artist, Stéphane.'

267

He shook his head. 'There's no money in art. But maybe this will show Guy and Mahmed that I'm not just a pretty face.'

'What did you do before all this?'

'This and that. Mostly that, to be fair.' He saw my expression and went on: 'I used to work in marketing. My company made office supplies. I spent the last eighteen years of my life trying to make paper clips sound exciting.' He gave a rueful smile, which revealed another glimpse of those shocking teeth. 'That feels like a very long time ago. At the same time, it feels like yesterday.'

I know that feeling. I know what it's like. The man has reinvented himself. Is Stéphane his real name? What drove him to alcoholism, and later still, onto the streets? I know better than to look, although I could if I chose to. But he is entitled to privacy. He deserves this chance to become someone else; to build anew. And he is good at building things – the shop has never looked better. Even Mahmed, in his way, has come to acknowledge his usefulness.

I took out the last little box of rose creams and handed it to Stéphane. 'Here. I made these. What you think?'

He sniffed the box. 'Smells like perfume.'

How very odd, I tell myself. Their magic only works for Emile. Stéphane will try all my chocolates, but these are not his favourites. Stéphane prefers the mendiants, the beggar's sweets, in dark chocolate. Simple enough for a child to make; little circles of happiness. It occurs to me that my chocolates are not so different to Tarot cards: each one brings out a different mood, a different kind of story. In my mother's hands, the cards were a dangerous magic. Maybe this is a safer one: a means of reaching out to those in need of a little comfort.

Small comforts. Yes, I like that. It reminds me of the lentil van, of Bal and his mother Abani, putting good into the world.

If I ever have a shop of my own, maybe that's what I'll call it, I think. The thought startles me from my reverie. That I should even consider such a thing – a chocolaterie of my own – is outrageous. Impossible. My savings add up to no more than a few months in a cheap hostel. I have no materials, no stock, no building to rent. I have no allowance from an indulgent father. And yet Guy promised to teach me a trade. Said I had skills. Encouraged me.

I've seen what you did at La Bonne Mère. *You could do the same with a chocolate shop. With my shop. With any shop.*

And maybe I could. I'm putting down roots. I even have my own garden. I have a headful of recipes; a room of my own; a future. I have a flair for chocolate, he says; a knack for thinking up new ideas. And of course, I have other skills. Skills my mother taught me. Skills she meant for life on the road, but which can be adapted. I have no reason to hide any more. I have spent too long being afraid; watching with envy, when I could just reach out and take whatever I want. Whatever I need.

It isn't wrong. I know that now. I want to put joy into the world. I want to help my friends, to build a future for my daughter. This is the time to put aside those things that try to hold us down. Time to say goodbye to the dead, and to celebrate the living. Everything is ready now: candles from the market, lined up in wine-bottle holders; incense from my own supply, ready to sweeten the troubled air. Salt and sand, for the circle. My mother's cards in their sandalwood box. And a dozen little red sachets, made from scavenged scarlet silk, one for every month in the year, and filled with a combination of herbs: lavender for peace of mind; marigold, for friendship; strawberry leaf for good fortune; hawthorn for protection; mandrake for power; cedar for strength; and in each, a scrap of paper with a secret invocation to the dead: a prayer for future prosperity; a light against the darkness.

I always loved this time of year best. It was our birthdays; our Christmas. It was our leap into the dark. And now, Maman, I must do it alone; for my friends and my daughter. Willow, for a broken heart. Mustard seed, for endurance. *Broken bread at the threshold of the home and the bedroom. Scatter salt around the house to ward off evil spirits. Sing a gentle lullaby—*

V'là l'bon vent, v'là l'joli vent—

Now I know what I have to do.

4

All Hallows' Eve, and the wind has changed. Winter is waiting in the wings. The soft wind from the sea has become a harrying, urgent tug from the east, all charged with the cold from the mountains. At Xocolatl, all of us feel that sudden sense of urgency: even Stéphane seems less mellow, somehow; his round face pocked with shadow, like the last moon of the season.

In the back of the shop Guy is hard at work, making bars of couverture and singing tunelessly to himself. Mahmed tends to the machines, and frets. I sense the tension between the two, as well as the affection. Guy believes implicitly in his product, and in his own genius. Mahmed believes in good accounts, and investing in the future.

I pack the chocolates into boxes and sachets as well as making my own new creations: mendiants, painted with gold leaf and jewelled with Malaga raisins and Seville orange peel; strawberry violet fondant, caramel, with pink peppercorns; green tea truffles, with sea salt. Mahmed isn't sure about any of them. The combinations are too strange; even the names are unusual. '*Nipples of Venus*. What kind of a name is that? Are you trying to get us shut down before we even open?'

'Names are important,' I tell him. 'Half the taste is in the name. And nipples of Venus were a famous treat in seventeenth-century Italy. I read about them in one of Guy's books. Try one.'

Mahmed shrugs. 'These fancy names. Why can't we just sell chocolates?'

'Because it's never just chocolate,' says Guy. 'It's dreams. It's magic. It's a story that started a thousand years before Christ, and which is still unfolding. We're not just selling chocolate. We're selling *Theobroma cacao*, the elixir of the gods.'

Mahmed gave a reluctant grin. 'Whatever it is, Guy, you're full of it.'

Guy laughed again. 'I hope so.'

We celebrated Hallowe'en with a version of Margot's chocolate cake, and cheap red wine in plastic cups, and one of Guy's chickpea curries. It feels good to do this with someone else; to feel this sense of family. I belong here, I tell myself. Anouk and I could belong here. But for that to happen, Guy must make his chocolaterie a success. He needs his independence from his wealthy, controlling family; we need him to bring us together, to keep us all from drifting away. And I already owe the man so much; I want to help him if I can. Such are the good intentions that lead us into the path of the wind. Such are the songs of the Man in Black, and of those who summon him.

Back in my room, I pushed back the bed and cast a circle in salt and sand. First the circle, then the star; drawn in thick, unwavering lines. A candle at each point of the star; one for each of the elements, and red silk sachets at intervals all around the circle. It's a ritual I've watched my mother perform for us so many times, in cheap hotel rooms and in deserted lay-bys, in the scent of incense and diesel fumes, with the scuttling clouds across the moon. And always when we had no choice, because, as she said, *there's always a price. The world must stay in balance. It gives, but only to take away.*

I never really believed in that. But she did: believed that whatever she did to ease our path would tear away at something else: her health, her child, her safety. *That's why we can only help ourselves,* she would tell me afterwards. *Helping other people is a risk we cannot afford.*

Except that you were wrong, Maman. We *can* bring good into the world. Bal and Abani taught me that, with their orange-flowered van. We are like trees, which, branching out, nourish each other in time of need. Crown-shy, we keep our counsel. Rooted, we keep each other safe.

I sit inside the circle, cross-legged on the tiles, my mother's box beside me. I have some dried eucalyptus leaves, picked from a garden on Rue du Panier. Their scent is still fresh and powerful; a potent, natural incense. I light one of the leaves; it smells fragrant and faintly medicinal, like cold winter nights under blankets and warm summer evenings in the park. The smoke is light and moonlight-pale, painting frost-flowers in the air. Orange flowers; a fleeting smile behind the battered counter. The lentil van, with its message of hope. I open the box and take out the cards.

Come to me.

The wind gives a sigh.

Come to me. Bring me the future.

I draw the Two of Wands. A good card; a card of plans and projects. A good sign for the chocolate shop; for all the plans we are making. The smoke grows slightly more opaque. Now it smells of Sicily, and the hedges of eucalyptus that grow on the sides of the mountain. The brush fires that ravage the island have the same gentle fragrance; their smoke is almost invisible, like a heat-haze from the hills.

Another card. The Lovers, reversed. I think once more of Guy and Mahmed. More hangs on the success of this shop than financial independence. Another card. The Hermit. Louis. I see him in winter sunlight; his face is almost gentle in repose. And he is holding a dish of cacao beans – no, not beans, but the *santons* that Margot kept beside her bed. As I watch, he puts one in his mouth. I banish the card with a gesture. His card – the Hermit – keeps coming up like an unpaid debt. I draw another card. The Fool. A young man on a hill, smiling into the summer sky.

Outside, the wind rises and falls in tune with the sound of the ocean.

The next card is the Tower. It stands on the corner of Allée du Pieu, all flashing red neon and gleaming glass. Hard to tell, through the thickening smoke, if the neon sign reads *Xocolatl* or *Happy Noodles*; the design seems to hold a little of both; a cacao pod that might also be a noodle bowl; a filament of rising steam which could also be a column of smoke. The Three of Cups: a generous card, which reminds me once more of the lentil van, with the big orange flowers on the side, and the colourful plastic bowls of *dal*. And finally, the last card, Death. Death, which is an ending, but also the chance to start anew.

Outside, the wind is rising. Its voice sounds like a lullaby. And as the last of the scented smoke drifts across the circle, I see reflections of a town; a bridge across a stretch of river; some boats, one with a filament of smoke rising from the chimney; another with a line of washing drying from the bows. And there are trees by the waterside, and the spire of a church in the distance, and the scent of woodsmoke on the air, and the sweetness of fried dough and candyfloss. And I hear music from the smoke; the jangle of a carousel warring with the church bells, and I think: *This must be Vianne.*

The eucalyptus smoke has dispersed, leaving a pallid, sick-room smell. My movements in the chalk circle have blurred and broken the outline. Two of the candles have blown out; a draught comes from the open door.

I looked up, feeling suddenly cold. Stéphane was in the doorway. His face was Hallowe'en-pumpkin yellow in the candlelight. 'I'm sorry to disturb you,' he said. 'I was looking for Pomponette.'

I put the cards back in their box and climbed to my feet. It's getting harder to do that now; my pregnancy is starting to show. I was suddenly conscious that I was barefoot, dressed only in my nightgown. I pulled one of the blankets from the bed and drew it around my shoulders. Pomponette was not on the rug, nor in her usual place under the bed. 'She must have slipped out,' I told him. 'I'm sure she'll be back in the morning.'

Stéphane looked uncertain. 'You mind if I stay here for a while? I don't sleep too well nowadays.'

'Of course.' I handed him my other blanket. 'You want me to make you some chocolate? It often helps when I can't sleep.'

He gave a painful, toothless smile. 'You know, chocolate doesn't solve *everything*.'

'No, but it's warm on a cold night.'

'Okay. You twisted my arm.'

I put on my slippers and went into the kitchen to make the chocolate. Seventy per cent couverture, with whole milk, sugar, grated nutmeg, vanilla seeds, and a whole bird's-eye chilli, scored to release its warmth into the milk. Let it steep for a minute or two. Drink it in a flowered cup, with the steam rising in the candlelight. Watch Stéphane's face lose its anxious look, the fine lines around his mouth start to fade. Hear the wind at the window, like the voice of my mother.

'Viane. Think what you're doing, 'Viane.

But the new voice inside me is stronger. It feels like the voice of a Vianne that has been waiting forever in the wings, a Vianne who chooses her own path, who takes control of her destiny. And the voice of this Vianne calls: *Come to me. Come to me. Bring me power.*

5

All Saints; and the bells from Bonne Mère ring out in celebration. A chill wind blows from the north-east, bringing the
promise of snow from the steppes, and people who seldom go
to Mass come out in their winter finery. There are a lot of tourists here. Nylon backpacks and cameras among the fur collars
and cashmere scarves. The autumn sun is cold today; the Virgin
and her infant shine above the city in scintillating gold.

On the steps of the Butte, Stéphane gives out fliers for the
shop, and I give out samples of chocolate: dark, and milk and
white (which is not strictly *chocolate* at all, but cacao butter,
and sugar), and we tell them about our Grand Opening. My
latest creation stands on display on the table of gift sachets: a
figurine of the Bonne Mère herself in 70 per cent couverture,
holding her infant son in her arms, the fine details of face and
crown picked out in a lighter shade. I'm still quite new to
making moulds, but I'm proud of this recent effort, and Guy
has praised my lightness of touch, and the ease with which I
have adapted his technique to make it my own.

'This one isn't for sale,' I repeat, handing out my samples.
'But when we open, you'll have the chance to buy figures

277

like these, and lots more Christmas things besides. Look out for us on the fourth of December. We'll be having our grand opening then, with free gifts and surprises!'

We gave out two hundred fliers today, and all my little samples. 'If even a tenth of those people drop by, then we'll be in business,' said Guy, as we sat down to dinner – a generous *biryani* prepared by Mahmed, silky with saffron and turmeric, with crunchy chickpeas, fresh lemon juice and lentils with cumin and cardamom. Mahmed's food is always as vivid and as flavoursome as he is cautious and distant. Today he was especially so in the face of Guy's optimism.

'You'll be lucky if any of them come. Most of those people were tourists. They'll be long gone by the time we open. Handing out free samples is one thing, but getting folk to put their hands in their pockets will take a lot more than that.'

'He's right, though, Mahmed,' said Stéphane. 'Tourists come and go, and the shops that serve them come and go as well. What you need is a proper foothold in the community. Something to bring folk together. A library, or a favourite bistrot, or a local bakery—'

Once more I thought of the lentil van, with its pink and orange flowers. Last night I saw it in the smoke; and ever since I left Toulouse, it has never left my mind. Bringing good into the world is not as easy as it sounds. Sometimes the world does not listen. Sometimes, you have to shout louder.

'Maybe – we could have a van,' I said slowly.

'We do have a van,' said Mahmed.

'I mean, like the lentil van in Toulouse.' I looked at Guy, who was smiling. 'We could take it out one day a week. We could serve hot chocolate.'

Mahmed looked suspicious. 'Why?'

I told him about the lentil van, and Abani and Bal.

'So – this chocolate would be free?'

I nodded.

Mahmed's lips tightened a little. 'Look. I get that you want to create goodwill. But there's a difference between giving out samples to people who *might* buy from us later and doling out hot chocolate to homeless people who never will.'

'Maybe that's the point,' said Guy.

Mahmed's impatience seemed to grow. His colours flared from sullen green to an angry burnt-orange. 'I don't think you're listening,' he said. 'All these things you're giving away cost money that we can't afford. Cacao beans from ethical farms at ten times the price of the regular kind. Advertising brochures. Mixing machines. Not to mention this place – I know it's a shithole, but still, it's not cheap – plus power and utilities. And none of that even starts to cover time, and labour, and living costs.'

'Not everything is about money,' said Guy.

'Tell that to the people we owe it to.'

'Have a little faith,' said Guy. 'Magic doesn't follow rules.'

Mahmed gave a sigh. 'No. *You're* the one who doesn't do that. You've never been short of money. You always think you can pick and choose. But some of us don't have the luxury. Some of us have to be *practical*, and balance the books, and buy groceries. Some of us don't have the luxury of grand schemes, or magic, or bringing home every stray that happens to catch your attention—'

'What does that mean?' said Stéphane.

'It means that we're spending far more than we earn. We already were, when you first arrived. Now we have two extra mouths to feed, a cat, and a baby on the way. *Stop it*—' This last remark was to Guy, who seemed about to protest. 'Just stop dreaming, and face the truth. You can't keep giving stuff away. We're not a charity.'

I said: 'You're right. We're a business.' I smiled at Mahmed's look of surprise. 'And that's why, as a business, we need to make an impact in the community. Earn ourselves some goodwill. Agreed?'

Guy was smiling. 'I think I do. We can manage without the van for one day a week. Let's see how it goes.' Then, to Mahmed, whose face had turned stony and expressionless, he said; 'Come on, man. What harm can it do? It's only a bit of hot chocolate.'

Mahmed shrugged and turned away. Guy put a hand on his arm, but Mahmed pulled away angrily. 'You have no idea how much I do – for you, for this shop, for the business. You're used to it. Like so many things. You wouldn't survive a week without me.'

'I know,' said Guy, still smiling. 'Who else would keep me honest?'

Mahmed did not smile in return, but pushed his chair back and stood up, his long hair hanging over his eyes.

'Where are you going?'

'Out for some air. Everything stinks of chocolate here.'

6

Last night, no one slept very much. I heard Guy pacing in his room until well after midnight. Stéphane was anxious for Pomponette, who has been missing for a couple of days, and I heard him walking about downstairs, opening doors and closing them, until Mahmed came in, very late, and I heard him, saying: *What the hell?*

I listened to the rise and fall of voices in the kitchen, and then at last Stéphane went to bed, and Mahmed stayed alone downstairs, and there was an unquiet silence. But all night I felt the call of the wind, as if the power I invoked has taken an unexpected turn, bringing discord and resentment into my new family. I've never been happy with conflict. My mother shrugged off unpleasantness like a rain-wet garment. *That's why we move on, Viannou. We move between the raindrops.* But I am always caught in the rain. And I lie awake during the night, while the people I am learning to love tear each other apart, piece by piece.

But that can all be fixed. The cards have promised me a solution. Already, my little red sachets have been placed all around the chocolate shop, with a circle of sand and salt cast around the building. The Lovers will be reunited. The Three of Cups will bring us success. And the Hermit – I have my plans for him, too. I know where to look for him. Today is All Souls, and the bistrot is shut, and Louis will go to visit Margot. That's where I mean to find him – alone – to heal the rift between us. Louis knows the neighbourhood, and if I am to win back my place, then his approval matters.

There was no one downstairs at breakfast today. Guy and Mahmed must have been asleep. Stéphane was not in his room – I supposed he must have already gone out. I slipped into the bakery to buy fresh bread and croissants, and then, after a hasty, solitary breakfast, pausing only to pick up a box of my most recent chocolate creations, I went out into the windy streets in pursuit of Cyrano.

I knew exactly where to go. I took the same route, the same bus, the same walk across the cemetery, past the *Cathédrale du Silence*. I was a little surprised to see how naturally it stands above the necropolis; the patterns of the arches, like futuristic space capsules. I was also surprised at the size of the place; a city for the dead, with its own streets and alleyways and slums, and this, its high-rise housing for nearly two hundred thousand people. All the alcoves are the same: the five blocks nearly identical to those designed for the living, but without the human details; curtains in the windows; pot plants on the balconies; litter in the doorway; the ramshackle trappings of life.

This place is almost indecently clean, from the cloisters to the central court, and seemingly empty of visitors. There are no flowers, no furnishings, no offerings from loved ones. The dead here are democratic: all of them nothing but names and dates inscribed on identical plaques. I find it strangely moving, and yet I can understand why Louis refuses to come here. Grief is not democratic. Grief demands a gesture. Grief demands the illusion of singularity, of permanence.

I think of my mother's ashes, drifting on the slipstream of the soft wind over the harbour. The wreath of fireworks overhead; the sound from the cheering holiday crowds. I remember wondering how many other people had done the same with the remains of their loved ones; how many secrets the Hudson held quietly in its dark embrace. We're all the same, really, aren't we, Louis? We want to believe we are different. We want to believe our loved ones are special, unique; that they will be more than ashes. But we are all of us carbon: stars, and ash, and coal, and diamonds. And in the end we all return to the same collective stardust.

Edmond Rostand's tomb is a family plot which has fallen into such disrepair that the inscription on the plain stone cross is barely even legible. Rostand was always derided for his Marseillais background: the literary world never forgave him for being the son of this city. His tomb stands in an alley of gracious monuments some distance away from the main drag. It is humble in comparison to the mausoleum that shields me from sight. Without Louis, I would not have noticed it; next to the other tombs it looks drab and relatively unadorned. A marble cross; a scroll underneath: a raised stone section at the foot on which now rests a single rose. And Louis there, in his Sunday clothes, which have nothing to do with going to church, sitting at the foot of the grave, reading softly from a book.

> *'Mon cœur ne vous quitta jamais une seconde,*
> *Et je suis et serai jusque dans l'autre monde*
> *Celui qui vous aima sans mesure—'*

I can't hear the words, but I know them. Cyrano's final love letter; filled with unspoken longing and loss, the words like the sound of a river at night, with fireworks in the distance. Poor Cyrano, I think. Poor Louis. *Some men are afraid to be loved.* And some women need reassurance that their love is acceptable; that it nourishes the ground instead of simply draining away. But some men only realize what they had when they no longer have it, and their love has nowhere to go any more, except into the wilderness. Cyrano would have understood that, too. Cyrano, of the golden voice, hiding his face in the shadows.

Poor Marguerite. I see her so well. I see her all-consuming need to love, and be loved, unconditionally. A woman loved by two men, neither of whom understood her. And now Louis keeps this ritual – Louis, who despises magic – and Emile watches from the wings, to ensure that Louis can never move on, or earn a second's happiness. *This* is the bitterness he hides. I saw it in the vapour, and in his colours when he tried my chocolate rose fondants. What it serves me to know this is a mystery for the moment. Maman never encouraged my skill of looking into people.

'Vianne? What are you doing here?'

I must have made a movement. I stepped from the shadow of the tomb and came to stand by Rostand's grave. 'I knew you'd be here,' I told him. 'It's All Souls' Day.'

He faced me, angry; bewildered. 'You followed me?'

'I knew where you'd be. I wanted to give you something.' From my pocket I took out a box.

'What is it, another paperweight?'

'I made the moulds myself,' I said. 'I thought maybe I could do something to celebrate Margot's memory. Her recipes have taught me so much. I wanted to mark that, somehow.'

I saw him stiffen. That suspicion of his is always so close to the surface, and yet there is so much in him that wants to let it go. Some men find it hard to trust because their trust has been betrayed. Some men find it hard to trust because of their own betrayals.

'She's dead,' he said in a low voice. 'Nothing we do can bring her back.'

'And yet, you come here. That means something. You keep her recipes alive. You read her favourite poetry and buy her favourite flowers.'

He made a dry, dismissive sound. '*Heh*. Much good it does her.'

I smiled at him. 'These things are not to please the dead. These monuments, these memorials – they're all to comfort the living. To keep a part of them with us. To remind ourselves that death is only one part of our journey.'

He looked at me contemptuously. 'And you think chocolate will do this?'

'Just try one,' I said. 'I thought perhaps I could call them – *Santons de Margot.*'

He opened the box. I'm proud of this work. I used Margot's *santons* as a template; those little ceramic babies transformed into 75 per cent cacao; dark and sweet and tempered just right in order to achieve the snap that makes for the very best chocolate. Brown, and plump as plums on the branch, they lie side by side in the little box, smiling, irresistible.

Louis looked at the chocolate *santons*. His narrow face was expressionless. In the autumn sun they shone: *Try me. Taste me.*

'Try one,' I said.

'I'm not hungry.' He picked out a *santon* from the box. 'She collected these,' he said. 'Not the other figurines – the shepherd, the washerwoman, the kings. Only the babies.'

'Yes. I know.'

The scent from the open box was starting to come alive now. It is a scent I have come to know well; the dusty scent of cacao beans hoarded in cedarwood caskets; the spicy scent of cacao liqueur whisked to a froth in an abalone cup; the hot scent of chillies, and cumin, and mace; the sweet and rich vanilla scent of innocence and childhood. Chocolate is like wine, I think. Like wine, it unleashes the tongue. Like wine, it has its rituals. Like wine, it opens the mind to different possibilities.

'She wanted a child so much,' he said. 'My Margot would have done anything. Hormone treatments, vitamins, prayers. An army of doctors and herbalists. Cold-water baths. Hot-water springs. And then, that Arab woman.'

'The one from the shop on Allée du Pieu.'

He made the dismissive sound again. 'I suppose you heard that from Emile. That idiot never could hold his tongue. I suppose he told you she duped me? Told me she could contact Margot? Took God knows how much money from me?'

'Didn't she?'

He shook his head. 'She wouldn't take it. All those other people she helped, all those spells and potions, all those séances behind closed doors, and she wouldn't even talk to me.' His voice was small and pebble-hard. 'She knew I didn't approve of her, or believe in her methods. This was her revenge.'

For what? But I already knew the answer. Revenge for giving up Edmond. For having rejected Margot's gift; the child she'd always wanted.

He put the chocolate in his mouth. Held it for a moment there. Felt the sweetness of the bean without its bitter embryo. 'I would have paid whatever she asked. I would have given her anything. I didn't believe in her nonsense, but I would have tried anything. For a single word from her. Even a letter. Even a lie.'

'What happened to her?'

'She moved away.'

Of course, there's more to it than that. A burning rag, through a letterbox, which had spread to some dried herbs, then to a plastic curtain, and then like an evil spell, torching the air, leaping and dancing from place to place—

I remembered him saying to me: *Should have burnt it to the ground.* And now I could see how he blamed himself, though someone else had started the fire; blamed himself for what he'd said to turn the others against her. The fire could have been anyone – local youths, one of his regulars – but his resentment had lit the fuse. I could see all this in the motes that danced in the air like fireflies; this, and his sullen conviction that he would do it all again—

'She moved on. So can you,' I said.

Chocolate is confessional. Like the sacrament, it is occult. Like the Host, it is holy. Most of all, it is transformative; passing from euphoria to regret, from grief to consolation in the space of a heartbeat.

Louis finished his chocolate and looked up. '*Santons de Margot,*' he said. 'I think she would have liked that.'

I let the thought hang in the air between us, like a bauble. Then I said: 'I hope you'll come to our opening on the fourth of December.'

He gave a brief, one-shouldered shrug. '*Heh.* I might be busy.'

I smiled. 'I'll see you there,' I said.

7

It was late afternoon when I got home. A small cold rain had started to fall, and my hair was all barbed with raindrops. Guy was sitting in the kitchen, drinking coffee. Stéphane was round the back of the shop, doing some kind of work on the van. Mahmed was nowhere to be seen.

'He hasn't been in all day,' said Guy. 'Went out sometime late last night, and hasn't been back.'

'I'm sorry,' I said. 'He'll be back soon.'

'Of course he will.' He gave a wan smile. 'And your idea for the van was a good one. I've got Stéphane working on it right now.'

I touched the coffee pot. It was cold. 'Here, I'll make another.'

'Thanks, but I should get back to work. Someone broke a window last night. I've had to order a new one.'

'Did someone try to break in?'

He shrugged. 'I don't think so. Just vandalism.'

He led me to the front of the shop, where the front window had been smashed. A messy pile of glass fragments had been swept against the wall, along with the half-brick that had been used to do the damage.

'Why would anyone do this?' I said.

Guy shrugged. 'Any number of reasons. This isn't the first time we've had hate for who we are, what we're doing. That's why it's important for us to fit into this community. People look out for each other here.'

I thought of the Tower, all neon, and the scent of euca- lyptus smoke, and wondered how Khamaseen had fitted into the community. *She moved away.* I wonder why. People didn't look out for her. She was a foreigner, a weed in this garden of roses. The scent of eucalyptus smoke is more than just a memory. It's like a seam of something dark running through the walls and floors; a hint of something dangerous trembling on the edge of the air.

'I wonder if she felt that too,' I said. 'The previous owner. The herbalist.'

He shrugged. 'I never met her. The property's on a long- term lease. I took it over when she left.' He looked at me. 'Why this curiosity?'

I explained about Marguerite, and Louis' long-harboured resentment of Khamaseen, and all she stood for.

'So that's why Louis hates us,' he said. 'You don't think *he* could have done this?' He indicated the broken glass.

I shook my head. 'He wouldn't do that. In fact, I think I've made progress.'

I told him about the cemetery, and the *santons de Margot*. Guy listened, and the drawn look softened into a little smile. 'I knew you were good at this,' he said. 'You have a knack.' He paused, then went on in an altered tone: 'Did you know that the Aztecs associated the cacao pod with the human heart? Not in a romantic way, but in sacrifice and blood. Funny, how over centuries it has been tamed and sweetened. But underneath, the truth remains. The heart is anything but sweet.'

It was an odd thing for Guy to say, and I wondered what had prompted it. I still sometimes find it hard to believe the lie he told his family. But lies, my mother used to say, will seed like dandelions in spring: overrunning the roadsides; sinking their roots into everything. A lie has a hundred different names; it crosses over continents. It grows from an infant into a child, then into a mother with lies of its own, each with the face of an angel.

The wind brought you to me, she said. *The wind could so easily take you back.* That's why we take up as little a space as the world will allow us. Because if the world knew, then everything would be taken away from us. Who we are. Who we chose to be. Of course at the time I didn't know the fear my mother was nursing. To me, it was just a story. But now her voice is just as strong as it was when she was alive, and it tells me: *Children are on loan. The world will always try to take them back. That's why we keep moving, 'Viane. That's why we change with the seasons.*

I suppose on some level, I've always known. Even as a child, I knew. The memory of that Christmas night, that night in the confessional, keeps coming back: the stricken tremor in her voice, the scent of books and incense. My own voice rising, furious, from inside the wooden box: *You're not my mother! Get away! I know you're not my mother!* And later, in our room, her tears; her soft cajoling, her promises. *I promise I'll find Molfetta,* she said. *I should never have left her behind. I know that now. Give me a chance to make it right with you again.*

We never found her, though we looked for her on every bench; on every train; aboard every bus; in every lost-luggage department. But I kept her close in my heart; whispering to her in the dark; sometimes glimpsed from the tail of my eye as we moved through the faceless crowds. Sometimes, Maman saw her too, especially in those later years. *Your invisible friend*, she called her. *Remember your invisible friend?* But we both knew what Molfetta was. She was the secret my mother had carried with us all my life, the thing that follows, and bides its time; the thing from the confessional.

I swept up the broken glass into a dustpan while Guy went back into the conching room. The constant burr of the machine was like the sound of the sea in a shell. And the scent of chocolate, so much a part of the fabric of the building, now seemed to have tempered to something almost acrid, almost burnt. A memory of sadness, perhaps; chocolate responds to emotions. But then I heard Guy's voice from the back room, rising and falling in the rhythms of profanity, and went in to see what was happening.

The acrid scent was stronger here: a kind of scorched and angry scent. Guy, in his chocolate-stained overalls, was peering into the conching machine.

'What is it?' I said.

'The chocolate has seized. Water must have got in, somehow.'

I looked over his shoulder. The chocolate in the machine looked like cinders; rough and bitter and calcified, with none of the gleaming smoothness of correctly tempered chocolate. Water in the machine will do that; and yet there was no sign that the mixer had been tampered with in any way.

'The whole fucking batch is ruined,' said Guy. 'There's no way I can salvage this.'

Sometimes, chocolate that has seized can be brought back to life again, but not to the standard it was before. 'We can still use it for ganache,' I suggested, but Guy shook his head impatiently. 'I know you want to help,' he said. 'But just leave me with this for now. Maybe go for a walk or something. I'm no fit company today.'

I nodded. A spoilt batch of chocolate is not the end of the world; but for Guy, it represents more than that. The cacao beans deserve better than this, after everything they've been through. The fact that he can start again does not dispel the sense of loss. And there is the financial aspect of this to consider. Our profit margins are already low. This only adds to the pressure.

'I'll see if Stéphane wants a coffee,' I said.

'And if Mahmed comes back, send him in here.'

8

I found no sign of Stéphane outside. He must have gone to fetch supplies. Glancing into the decrepit hangar round the back of the shop, I could see that he must have been doing some bodywork on the van. The air still smelt of hot metal and solder and primer paint, the van doors were open, but Stéphane was nowhere to be seen.

Old Madame Li, the grandmother of the family next door, was putting out rubbish at her back door. More building debris, by the look of it, tied up in a black plastic bag. She gave me a nod as I went past, but I thought she looked suspicious. I remembered my gift of chocolates, thrown away unopened, and her granddaughter saying that Mahmed had reported them to the health inspector. I was still not ready to believe that Mahmed had been responsible, but I could see why they might not be inclined to be friendly.

I smiled at the grandmother, and said: 'The takeaway looks great now. When do you think you'll reopen?'

She gave me a sharp look and shook her head. *'Ne comprends pas.'*

I made an expansive gesture, indicating the takeaway, the alley, the chocolaterie. 'Everything's coming together,' I said.

'Soon, we'll be one of the most chichi parts of the Panier Quarter. Neon signs, arcades, a line of customers *this* long—'

I thought I saw a flicker of something like humour cross her face. Her French might not be perfect, but I thought perhaps she understood me better than she would have me believe. I smiled and drew a finger-sign across the palm of my left hand, sending a little carousel of lights tumbling against the wall. *A pretty.* More than a pretty, in fact. A glimpse of things as they might be; a taste of possibility.

Madame Li seemed to pause, a ladder of colours climbing her face.

Imagine a neon sign, right there, a bowl of noodles in flashing red. Imagine the scent of roasted pork, and garlic, and sizzling vegetables. Imagine the customers crowding the street; faces rosy in the glow of many lights. Imagine the money coming in; the luck of the family turning.

Madame Li's face opened up like a flower in a glass of tea. 'Luck,' she said.

I nodded. 'Here. I made these for you.'

I pulled out one of my little sample boxes from my bag. Green tea truffles, with darkest chocolate and *fleur de sel*: a flavour that reminds me somewhat of the rising tide in Normandy, where Maman and I spent a summer once, and where I ate *crêpes* wrapped in paper, with butter and fried sausages, while the waves crept closer and the gulls circled hopefully overhead.

Slowly, Madame Li took the box.

'Try one,' I said.

She took one, sniffed. *'Cha,'* she said.

I nodded. *'Cha.'*

She nibbled the edge of a truffle. I thought of the sea, and my mother, and the taste of crispy-edged *crêpes*, and the scent of the rising tide over the salt flats. Madame Li closed her eyes. I waited. Finally, she opened them again, and looked at me directly for the first time.

'What do you think?' I said.

She smiled. I thought she might have said something then, but just at that moment I saw Mahmed at the end of the alleyway. His long hair had fallen loose over his face, and I thought he looked unsteady, as if he had been drinking. That surprised me – I've never seen Mahmed drink more than a glass of wine with a meal. A trail of colours flamed in his wake; lurid orange; garish green; angry, complicated red. Madame Li vanished into the back of her shop as if she'd seen a hungry wolf. I saw her peering out at us through a tiny window.

I said: 'Mahmed, Guy was looking for you.'

Mahmed gave a kind of growl. 'Something wrong?'

I explained about the spoilt batch.

'*Heh.* That figures,' said Mahmed. 'Something needs fixing. Ask Mahmed. Job needs doing. Ask Mahmed. Fair enough. I have to earn my keep somehow.'

'You know it's more than that.'

He shrugged. 'If you say so.'

He walked by, hard-faced, towards the chocolaterie. I started to go after him, but something by the bins caught my eye: it was Pomponette, who had been missing since before Hallowe'en, looking as well-groomed, well-fed and content as if she'd never been lost at all.

'*Pomponette!* Where have you been?'

Pomponette sauntered up to me and nudged my ankle with her nose. I picked her up and stroked her. 'Let's get you back inside, shall we? Stéphane has been looking everywhere for you.'

The cat began to purr as I carried her back into the shop. Closing the door behind me, I thought I could still see Grandmother Li, watching from her window, her face as grey and crumpled as a tea ball out of water.

9

It has been over a week now since that fraught conversation at dinner. The broken window has been repaired, the conching machine is working again, and Guy is back to his usual self; making plans, talking non-stop; telling stories of what will be when Xocolatl is open.

Mahmed blames the Chinese family for the broken window. 'Who else could it be?' he tells us. 'They've always blamed us for everything.'

Guy, unsurprisingly, disagrees. 'It could have been anyone,' he says. 'Teenagers. Vandals.' He tries to make Mahmed understand that Happy Noodles isn't a threat. We are all part of the same community, trying to make a living. We should make friends with our neighbours. And November, he says, should be all about making stock for Christmas: bars and boxes of chocolate; Christmas decorations; gifts. This is our time to impress, he says; to make an impact on the community. The shop is fully fitted now; there is a counter, an old-fashioned till, a couple of little tables and chairs, and a glass display cabinet on the wall, where boxes of chocolates and gifts of all kinds will gleam like buried treasure. There will be a display window, too, with a Christmas scene in chocolate, and Stéphane's handmade sign outside, with the single word: *Xocolatl*.

The local newspaper has been informed, which hopefully will bring us some free publicity. There is even a telephone, which means that Mahmed will not need to go to the public phone box down the road whenever he needs to order stock. And Pomponette is back at last, which means that Stéphane is happy again. He has also finished his work on the van: there is now a customized counter inside, with a stack of paper cups, some jars of marshmallow toppings, and a large urn with a spigot with which to serve the freshly made hot chocolate.

But it is the bodywork of the van that represents the real transformation. Stéphane has painted it orange, with a design of cacao pods in brown, and gold, and scarlet, and pink, and the word *Xocolatl* flying across the side in a looping, cursive script. It is both cheery and eye-catching, and Guy has been fulsome in thanks and praise.

Mahmed has said nothing. Since last week he has been unusually withdrawn; his normally expressive face now immobile and unresponsive. 'He'll come round in the end,' says Guy with his usual optimism. 'You'll see. He always does.'

I wonder. I have never seen Mahmed like this. No comment, no complaint, even when he saw what Stéphane had done to his van. He simply gets on with his work, eats his meals with the rest of us, sleeps in his usual place. But something is missing. A layer of skin. Even Guy's gentle mockery fails to provoke a reaction. Tomorrow, I plan to go out in the van with Stéphane and try some outreach; Guy will work on his designs, and Mahmed will lay the new floor tiles – ochre and gold, like the wall paintings – in the public part of the shop. We should be celebrating. Everything is on time, and in place. And yet, in spite of all this, it feels as if something is about to fall; as if the power I summoned last week is working somehow against us. My mother's voice inside me says: *The wind does not come at your beck and call.* And yet I feel it in me; that power. *Try me. Taste me. Test me.*

I made a big bowl of ganache from the chocolate batch that was ruined. Where chocolate has seized, it can be brought back to a soft consistency by adding warm water and mixing. It's a method Guy disdains; the chocolate cannot be made solid again, so is good only for sauces or drinks. But we can use it for ganache, so it is not all wasted; and the rest will go into a cake to go with my hot chocolate.

I used one of Margot's recipes – *Gâteau Liégois* – made with rich vanilla cream and alternating layers of ganache. Tomorrow it will help us bring a little good into the world. I wonder what Margot would think of that. My mother used to tell me that no one ever dies if even one person remembers them. In these recipes, Margot lives on, gives comfort to strangers; feeds the world. If she had lived to bring up Edmond, she would have taught him this recipe; given him the spoon to lick; showed him how to spread the ganache using a round-bladed palette knife. The vision of Margot and Edmond is very vivid in my mind; their faces warm in the sunlight reflected from the window; their heads almost touching as they peer together into the bowl of ganache. And Louis is there, too, a Louis I have never seen before, his face alight with amusement.

What a difference it would have made, I thought, if Edmond had stayed at La Bonne Mère. A child is the future; a promise that the world will not forget us. I think of my little Anouk, no larger than a mango, and of Molfetta, and the harbour in New York, and of the bundle of clippings among my mother's papers.

And even though the kitchen is warm, I feel a sudden chill, the kind my mother used to call *someone walking over my grave*. And I reach for the half-finished bowl of ganache, and spoon some softly into my mouth, and feel it melting against my tongue, releasing its flavours like silent prayers towards the vault of my mouth, and I think; *Who were you, Maman? Who were you really? And if I don't know that, then how on earth can I know who I really am – Annie or Anne, Sylviane or Vianne – among all the possible lives I have had, the glimpses of possible futures?*

IO

9 November 1993

This morning, Stéphane and I went out in the newly refurbished van, with my chocolate ganache cake in its box and a stack of three hundred fliers. We parked by the market near Rue du Panier, where there were several other vans, selling coffee, and doughnuts, and pizza, and cheese, and spicy merguez cooked on a hot plate and wrapped in *galette* to eat by the road. People are always wary at first, when faced with goods given out for free. I left the van, and stood in the street with a tray of tiny paper cups.

Hot chocolate! Food of the gods!

People passed with barely a glance, carrying their shopping, eyes averted in that way we know well, Maman and I — that way that says; *I don't know you. I don't want to know you.* It was raining; a soft, thin rain that did nothing to encourage trade. My feet were getting wet; my hair was dripping under my headscarf.

Hot chocolate! Food of the gods!

No one takes my fliers. One man tries a sip from a cup; I try to hand him a flier, but he pushes past impatiently. People are not always friendly here; the unusual is not welcome. A seeming gift may be a trick, designed to lure the unwary

300

towards making an expensive purchase. A child holds out an inquisitive hand; its mother gathers it back into her skirts with a sharp word of warning.

What is wrong with these people?

An old woman looks at me, smiling. 'Hard work, isn't it? People are so wrapped up in themselves that they sometimes forget to be happy.'

She took a cup of chocolate from the tray, and tasted it. Closed her eyes. Savoured the moment. I thought she looked somewhat familiar, and tried to remember where I'd seen her – in La Bonne Mère, perhaps, or in the queue at the bakery? – and then she turned, and the sunlight broke for a moment through the rain-soft clouds, and shone summer-silver in her eyes, and then I saw that once again, I'd failed to recognize Khamaseen. She was wearing a yellow scarf on her head and holding a basket of vegetables, but there was no mistaking the clever brown hands, or the humour in her eyes.

'Wonderful.' She finished the cup, and put it back onto the tray. 'It tastes like happiness.'

I saw a man standing behind her glance in her direction. 'Excuse me, but – are those free samples?'

I smiled. 'Help yourself.'

Shyly at first, he stepped forward. 'Oh, this is amazing. Here—' To the man beside him, whom I took to be his partner, he turned and said, 'Hey, try some. It's really good.'

Khamaseen gave them a sideways smile. 'Isn't it? I could drink it all day.' A ladder of light shone up her face.

'Can I try some?' A young woman with a baby in a sling approached and took a leaflet. 'Is this your shop? Xocolatl?'

'Not mine, but a friend's. We're opening soon.'

'Selling hot chocolate?'

'And other things.'

'This is delicious. Oh, wow. Is that *cake*?'

People with shopping baskets; people with babies in strollers; people walking their dogs; tourists buying souvenirs. I recognized some of my regulars from La Bonne Mère: Monsieur Georges; Marinette; Rodolphe. A man with a battered rucksack and a face that had seen many nights outdoors shyly took a paper cup.

'I can't afford fancy chocolates.'

'That's fine. Here, have a piece of cake.'

Behind me, I could see Stéphane filling more cups. 'We make all this ourselves, you know. We make it right from the cacao beans. Did you know chocolate is older than Christianity?'

Marinette gave me a look. 'So this is what you're doing now?' Did you make the cake yourself?'

I nodded. 'Try some.'

'I shouldn't.' I noticed she took a piece anyway.

'I thought only coffee came from beans.' That was from a girl aged about nine; curly hair over berry-bright eyes.

'Chocolate comes from beans too. Want to see some?' I indicated a bowl of roasted beans on the counter. 'This is what they look like at first. Smell them. They smell of chocolate.'

Before long, all my ganache cake was gone, and there was a small crowd around the van, drinking hot chocolate from the urn, listening to me repeat some of the things Guy had taught me.

Did you know that cacao beans like these were once used as currency?

Did you know that the Aztec emperor Montezuma drank fifty cups of chocolate a day?

Did you know that the scent of chocolate helps lift your mood and relieve stress?

And so with every customer, we send out the gift of happiness. Small pleasures, small indulgences; a taste of something sweet and strange. Magic comes in so many forms. Sometimes it's a word, a smile; a candle in the darkness. And sometimes it takes a simpler form; perhaps a cup of chocolate.

Of course, I know there are risks to all of this. I am not used to being so visible. But if Khamaseen can hide in plain sight, changing to suit the circumstance, then so can I. The chocolate van; the business; the shop – all provides a kind of camouflage. And I feel safe in Allée du Pieu. We have walls. A place of our own. The promise of a future. *We could stay here*, I tell myself, daring for the first time to believe. *I could stay here and be Vianne. I could be a part of this.*

Inside me, my little Anouk agrees. I feel her inside me, exploring her world. And I am changing; I have changed. My belly is visibly rounder. My muscles have grown softer, more elastic. My sense of smell is keener; my sense of taste heightened even further. I dream in colour. I dream in scent. I dream of *you* at six years old, with eyes like the edge of a summer storm. I dream of you by a river, barefoot, paddling in the shallows. I dream of you in a bright-red coat, blowing a plastic trumpet. I dream of you in a little group of children, laughing and running. And I dream of Edmond Martin, sitting in a kitchen somewhere, waiting for me to find him. Where is he now? Is he here in Marseille? Does he know I am calling him? Does he hear my voice in his dreams? And if so, will he answer?

Cha

I

16 *November 1993*

I made another ganache cake today, and another fresh batch of hot chocolate. We parked down by the old harbourside and, as well as offering samples, this time, we also offered larger cups of spiced hot chocolate at ten francs a cup, with a piece of ganache cake on the side, and toppings of whipped cream and sprinkles.

And stories. Always stories. Over the past few weeks, I have learnt that chocolate is steeped in stories. Stories of the Americas, the ancient civilizations of the Aztec and the Maya; stories of conquistadores and treasure ships loaded with looted gold; stories of the Spanish court, and intrigues in the Vatican; stories of conquest and industry, stories of colonial power.

Did you know that chocolate was banned by two popes? That Casanova attributed his sexual prowess to drinking it? That the Aztecs believed that it was a gift from the gods themselves?

'We'll have to print more leaflets,' Guy remarked, when I mentioned it. 'Perhaps we can print something on the cups, too: chocolate facts from around the world. What do you think, Mahmed?'

Mahmed shrugged. 'I think we've spent more than enough money on printing.'

'Then *write* them on the cups,' said Guy. 'Write them on in marker pen. You could do that, couldn't you? It wouldn't take long.'

'Let me do it,' I volunteered, seeing Mahmed's expression darken. 'I can easily do that, and Mahmed has so much else to do.'

Mahmed gave me a sideways look. 'You don't have to do that,' he said.

'I'd like to,' I said. 'I want to help.'

'Thanks.' He made it sound like a curse.

For a moment I thought of Emile; the angry flame that seems to burn perpetually inside him. Mahmed reminds me more and more of him nowadays. He has always been the darker shadow to Guy's bright light; but now he is different; sullen; morose; the shadow of a shadow. *Love will do that*, my mother says. *Too much love will drag you down.* But why has the love between Guy and Mahmed shifted in this sudden way? What misunderstanding could have caused them to be disunited?

'I'm sick of the stuff,' he told me today as I offered him a chilli-chocolate triangle from my new batch. 'To tell you the truth, I wouldn't care if I never tasted it again.'

'You'll feel differently when the orders start coming in,' said Guy.

Mahmed made a dismissive noise. 'Tell me when that happens,' he said. 'Right now, all we have is bills.'

Just over two weeks remain now before the shop's grand opening. We have built a kind of routine: out with the van three times a week; building stock the rest of the time. We need as much stock as we can make if we are to ride the Christmas rush; this means processing thousands of beans, including removing the embryos by hand to ensure maximum sweetness. It takes up to six hundred beans to make one kilo of chocolate. So far we have stockpiled over eighty kilos – but as Mahmed likes to point out, we need to sell far more than this if we are to break even. And we will make far more money from elegant boxes of chocolates than from plain slabs of couverture, or sachets of chocolate powder, which is why we must concentrate on building up our stock of Christmas boxes. Guy still works faster than I do, but likes the freshness of my ideas, and so leaves me free to experiment, and to share my creations with customers on our outings with the van.

I also share my new ideas with the crew at Happy Noodles: Grandmother Li has acquired a taste for my sea salt and green tea truffles, and the two girls enjoy my red rose creams, as well as the chilli triangles. It has taken a long time to build even this degree of trust; but I am hopeful that this may mean the start of a more cordial relationship.

There have been workmen in the back of the takeaway for weeks. Now they are gone and the family is getting ready to start trading again as soon as they pass the inspection. It's not as easy as it seems. The kitchen has been refurbished and the working area is spotless, but the alley itself is unsightly, dark, half-blocked with litter, and lined with blind and boarded-up façades. To make this street appealing, we would need to clean it up, make the other shops presentable, fill potholes, plant window-boxes, hang signs. Months of work between us, assuming we worked together. I have already suggested this to Stéphane, who seems willing to help, if wary of Mahmed's reaction. And Madame Li and her family are equally wary of Mahmed, who Grandmother Li calls *Huodou*, the Black Dog. *Huodou. Bad luck*, she tells me as she watches him go by. I try to placate her with green tea truffles, but I can see she is not convinced.

I have also taken an assortment of my work to La Bonne Mère, where Emile and the regulars have tested three kinds of truffles, my cherry mendiants, as well as the rose and violet creams and, of course, the *Santons de Margot*. Building bridges always takes time, but I think that with this and the chocolate van, we are finally starting to make a dent in this close community. Louis has even accepted to let me leave a small pile of promotional fliers by the bistrot door – 'Not to hand out or anything, but people can take one if they like –' and someone from the local paper has asked to come round next week and take photographs for an article.

It's starting to happen, I tell myself. My little working on All Hallows' Eve is starting to bring what I asked for. Nothing too ambitious; just a little something to help us along. Of course, even this has its dangers. *We need to stay one step ahead. Take what you need, but always move on as soon as there's blood in the water.*

Except that this time is different, Maman. This time, we *need* to be visible. The Tower, with its neon sign, serves as a beacon to call them. Prospective customers; tourists, the press; all we are doing serves to make Xocolatl more attractive. I do what I can through the vapours; a gilding of light on the sooty stone; a promise of something in the air.

And, of course, someone else needs to find us. By law, there's no way to find an adopted child unless he chooses to be found. But that beacon shines for everyone. Since Hallowe'en, I have called Edmond every night, like a mother calling her child in after dark. The table at my bedside has become a little altar, of the kind my mother used to build in hotel rooms around the world. There I have my mother's cards, and the river stone inscribed with his name. The rest I have taken straight from Margot – as my mother always said, it isn't the ritual that matters, only what it means to you, and it seems right to use her words, and this, her final recipe.

We call our children. Sometimes, they come.

This is not my child, but I owe it to Margot to try. The moon is in the right house. My mother called it Oak Moon. Margot may have another name for it, but I know from her book that she burns sandalwood incense to welcome it in, just the way my mother did.

Burn a white candle with sandalwood; holy water; cup of wine. Broken bread at the threshold of the home and the bedroom. Scatter salt around the house to ward off evil spirits. Sing a gentle lullaby to make the child feel welcome.

I have no holy water, but I do have wine, and salt, and bread. And I know the lullaby that calls the wind, and other things too; the old, old song that sounds just as it did when I was a child:

V'là l'bon vent, v'là l'joli vent—

I light a pinch of sandalwood. The smoke is surprisingly acrid and dense. It smells of charred fields, burnt bridges; the scent of a herbalist's shop aflame. But in the smoke I see a boy – a teenager, almost a young man – and his face is almost familiar, and I already know his name.

Edmond.

That's not the name he goes under now, and yet he responds immediately. Names are things of power. I feel his gaze turn towards me, searching for me through the smoke. He must be asleep. Images of his life slip by like cards. He likes to cook. His parents are proud. He makes intricately decorated cakes; iced biscuits; sky-high soufflés. He hides his restlessness beneath a sleek dark suit of obedience. He has no idea where he belongs, but he knows it's somewhere else.

I send him the smell of Margot's kitchen; her herb garden, her bouillabaisse; the golden gleam of the Virgin as she watches from her eyrie, and the answering gleam of the ocean; the sound of the bar on a busy day. I send him the sign of La Bonne Mère; the bistrot where he should have been raised; the handmade cradle and rocking-horse; the guest room clean and ready. And I send him my mother's lullaby; the coaxing call of the turning wind; the welcome cry of distant shores; the creaking of a weathervane.

When it is finished, I cut the cards. The Tower, the Lovers, the Chariot, the Hermit, the Six of Swords – even Death – all are gone. For the first time in months I have a clean spread; the Two of Wands, the High Priestess, the Seven of Cups, the Ace of Swords, the Fool; the Star. I need to consider what this means. A change of course; a release from constraint; an intervention of the stars. But it still feels like a roll of the dice; a challenge to the universe. I fall asleep, still wondering, and dream of picking up hagstones on a beach; the sound of waves and sea birds, and Anouk playing there on the tide line, and my mother sitting on the sand. Except that it isn't my mother, it's Khamaseen, in a scarlet dress, with her long dark hair loose down her back, and jingling bracelets on her arms.

A change of air works wonders, she says. *It's putting good into the world*. And then she turns to me and smiles, and I see that the child by the shore is Edmond, and that my little Anouk has disappeared, like the story of the mermaid who vanished into sea foam.

2

20 *November 1993*

Today, someone came from *Le Petit Marseillais*, the local bi-weekly paper, to report on the new chocolate shop. Two people; a man and a woman, both bored; both on their way to something else. Mahmed had been up since dawn mocking up the window display with bright explosions of cellophane and great jewelled mountains of chocolates. Guy was wearing his favourite shirt, the one with the luminous palm trees.

'We've been preparing for this day for almost two years,' Guy told the reporter, while I served them cups of hot chocolate, and his colleague took photographs. 'It's wonderful, finally, to be able to share everything we've done with the public.'

'And what *have* you done?' The young man's voice is lightly accented, as if from a different region; his face is touched with the light of the north. He looks vaguely resentful at being called to this part of town. 'It's not as if Marseille doesn't have confectioners. Why is this one different?'

'Well, for a start, we're making our chocolate from bean to bar. Every stage is carried out here. That means the highest quality. Did you know that most chocolate farmers have never tasted their product? That's because they're paid so little, and yet cacao is one of the most lucrative crops in the world. It's—'

'Great. Let's have a photo. Maybe next to your wife?'

'Oh. *No!* She's not my—'

'Here.' I found myself being shepherded into position by the counter. 'Little smile? That's lovely. And your name?'

'Vianne.'

'With two *ns*?' He wrote it down.

In the corner, I saw Mahmed give a smile that was all in shadow. Guy gestured for him to come over, but Mahmed simply shrugged: *Why bother? There's still work to do* – and vanished into the back room.

'And what do the neighbours think of this place?' That was the young reporter again, glancing into the alleyway, which we have cleared of litter, but which still seems dark and disreputable. 'I heard the previous owner was the victim of an arson attack. And that recently you were the victims of vandalism yourselves. A broken window, wasn't it?'

Guy shook his head. 'Everyone's great. We've had nothing but support.'

'So, there's no feud? No curse?'

He laughed. 'Everyone likes chocolate.'

A flurry of photographs later, and the pair were gone, leaving their two cups of chocolate untouched on the marble counter. Stéphane, who had disappeared during the interview, came back to clear away the cups and to replace the newspaper over the shop window. I noticed Grandmother Li outside, watching the procedure. I took her a cup of hot chocolate, and explained about the journalists.

Grandmother Li drank her chocolate and handed back the china cup. 'They were here before,' she said. 'Asking questions.'

'Of you? When?'

She shrugged. 'Were here a week ago. They see the broken window. They ask about previous owner.'

I thought of the broken window, which Guy had replaced immediately. Broken windows attract more stones. Damage calls to damage. For a moment I felt unease, and wished the journalist had not come: but Guy is overjoyed at the publicity it will bring us.

Later, in the afternoon, I dropped by at La Bonne Mère, partly to take in a new supply of leaflets, and partly to check in on Emile, who has been increasingly scornful since my reconciliation with Louis. I sense that he is jealous; that he likes being Louis' only friend. I have made him insecure; I pay him in free chocolates. There were a number of regulars still drinking coffee after lunch, but most of the lunchtime crowd had gone, and the bar smelt of cigarettes and beer. Louis was in the back room; I brought out my newest experiment.

Coconut clusters, dipped in dark chocolate and a little sea salt. A woman seated by the bar looked up and smiled. 'My favourite.'

Khamaseen has changed again. This time she was fifty or so; dressed in jeans and a pullover; greying hair tied back in a ponytail. I handed her a chocolate.

'Very nice,' she said, with a smile. 'I always did like coconut. I think that little shop of yours should be having its grand opening soon.'

'It's not my shop,' I said. 'But yes.'

'Of course. It belongs to Guy Lacarrière. But the *heart* of it – that's all you. You knew that, of course. You have a knack for guessing people's favourites.'

'I do?'

Khamaseen took another of my coconut clusters. 'These are very good,' she said. 'You ought to make a career of this. It's easier than the other thing, and comes with much less personal risk.'

'What do you mean?'

'You *know* what I mean.' Her eyes had a curious, silvery shine, like coins at the bottom of a well. 'Granting wishes comes at a cost. Your mother knew that. So did Margot. There's only so much happiness anyone can have in a life. You can keep it for yourself, or you can give it to others. Not both.'

I realized that Emile, who had been sitting at a table nearby, had shown no reaction to any of this, even though he should have heard every word of the conversation.

'Don't worry. He hasn't heard a thing.' Khamaseen's voice was crisp and amused. 'He won't, unless I want him to, and believe me, I never do.'

I looked at her again. She was real: I could see the lights behind the bar reflected in her silvery eyes. And she smelt of something familiar; a kind of patchouli-tobacco scent I associate with my mother. She took my hand in both of hers. Her skin was warm as honey, and smooth.

'Don't worry. I'm not a ghost,' she said. 'I'm just good at passing unnoticed. It's easy to do that at my age, especially when you're a woman.' She grinned, and I wondered just how old she was, because suddenly she seemed very young, and filled with childish mischief. 'Want to see something funny?' she said, and without awaiting my reply, she forked a little sign with her hand. As if in response, I saw Emile jump as if he'd been woken from deep sleep.

'You know I don't like coconut, Vianne,' he said in a cross, bewildered voice. 'You should have brought more of those rose creams.'

'I did. I know they're your favourites,' I said, and from the tail of my eye, I saw Khamaseen slip away through the door, back into the streets of the Butte.

3

Today, the article came out in *Le Petit Marseillais*. I awoke to
the sound of the telephone ringing from the front of the shop. I
got up and ran to answer it. The ringing stopped before I could
reach it, but a few seconds later, the phone rang again.

'Good morning. Xocolatl?'

'This is Chloë from Le Vert Galant. I'd like to place an order.'

'Er, yes. Of course. How did you hear about us?'

'I saw the piece in the paper.'

'Just one moment, *madame*.' I took down her details on the
pad and promised Guy would get back to her. Le Vert Galant
is a hotel and golf club ten minutes' drive from the Vieux Port.
They often host corporate gatherings, and wanted some gifts for
their special guests. In this case, twenty gift boxes and an assortment of chocolates and *petits fours* for a dinner on 22 December.
An excellent start to the season, and just what Guy was hoping
for. I couldn't wait to tell him, and to read the article. The fact
that orders are coming in on the back of the newspaper piece –
less than two weeks before our grand opening – seems to him
almost too good to be true. But all we needed to succeed was
a little more visibility. Now we have that, things will change.

I washed and dressed, then went downstairs, where Guy was making coffee. There was a pile of fresh croissants on the table, along with some fruit, and a silver pot of hot chocolate. Stéphane was outside, feeding the cat, and Mahmed was feeding boxes of beans into the mechanical grinder.

'Hear that, o ye of little faith?' called Guy to Mahmed, when I told him the news. 'We have our first order! Le Vert Galant wants our chocolates!'

'Great,' said Mahmed from the back room. 'Believe it when we see the cash.'

Guy laughed. 'Come in, and have some coffee. I'll get the paper. Let's read what it says.'

Le Petit Marseillais is a free tabloid, consisting mostly of local news, adverts and human interest stories. Our story is there on the lower front page, under the appointment of a new mayor and a stabbing down by the docks:

New Chocolaterie in Le Panier

Did anyone say chocolate? Ghislain Lacarrière and his partner Sylviane are passionate about the stuff. All kinds of delicious confections from cacao beans from the forests of West Africa and Peru. Why is their process different? Lacarrière says: 'We make all our chocolate from bean to bar, which ensures its quality. And we'll be opening to the public on 4 December, with a preview of our Christmas stock, and the chance to sample creations like Nipples of Venus, Sea Salt Truffles and Montezuma's Revenge.' As a gesture of goodwill, Lacarrière is offering 40 per cent off every order he receives before then. And the opening of a new boutique should create a welcome boost for the community, which has suffered a decline in recent years.

But can a chichi chocolate shop survive alongside the old bistrots of the Vieux Quartier? And will the curse of Allée du Pieu – a curse that locals believe caused the fire that ended the previous business – turn out to be a blessing?

The piece is flanked by the shop's name and contact details, plus a photograph of Guy and me, taken inside the shop. I am wearing a sweater and jeans, my hair loose over my shoulders. Guy has his arm around me, smiling at the camera.

'You look like a couple,' said Stéphane, reading over my shoulder. '*And* they got your names wrong.'

'And what's this about the forty per cent?' said Mahmed. 'You never mentioned that to me.'

Guy shrugged. 'It's just for a week, man. And look at our first order. It's Le Vert Galant, Mahmed. If they like what we do, they could end up being a regular customer. Hotels serve chocolates all the time. After dinner; special guests; on the pillow every night. Think of it as an investment in the future.'

Mahmed seemed about to say something else, but was interrupted by the ringing of the phone. 'Let me get that,' said Guy. 'Might be another order.'

Mahmed said nothing. His colours were bleak as a winter sky. I poured a cup of chocolate and took a croissant from the pile. 'It's only a week.' I echoed Guy's words. 'And the orders are a good sign. It means the campaign is working.'

He gave me a sideways look. 'You think? I think it means forty per cent less money than we were expecting. And I know that when you start off by giving discounts, it makes it much harder to persuade customers to pay full price.'

'You could just try being happy for him,' said Stéphane unexpectedly. 'I mean, you could just try, for a change.'

Mahmed looked at him, surprised. 'I'm sorry?'

Stéphane put down his coffee cup. His mild face looked surprisingly harsh. 'I mean that he's happy. He's doing what he really loves, for the first time in his life. Let's all just support him, instead of questioning everything.'

I braced myself for an outburst. Mahmed's patience with Stéphane has never been especially great. And recently he has been so withdrawn, sullen as a thundercloud. But this time he simply shrugged and said: 'Perhaps you're right. Let's get the grand opening over with, and then we can think about the accounts.'

And at that, he sat down at the table and poured himself some chocolate. 'This is good,' he told me, and smiled. *At last*, I thought. *It's working.*

4

27 November 1993

Three more orders have come in since then. None are as
large as the Vert Galant, but every order is welcome. Guy
has bought an answering machine, to ensure that we do not
miss calls. Everything is working just as we'd hoped. And
yet, there's something troubling him. Perhaps it's only the
build up to the shop's grand opening; perhaps he's started to
realize just how much there is at stake. And he looks tired;
I wonder if he is sleeping properly. Of course, we are all
working harder in preparation for the big day; Guy with
a nervous energy, Mahmed with quiet, methodical, tireless
attention to detail. As for myself, I do what I can, although
Mahmed has banned me from heavy work, in view of my
condition.

This morning I got up early to write chocolate facts onto
paper cups. *Did you know that Napoleon loved chocolate? That
the Mayans prized it more highly than gold? That chocolate liquor
is not brown, but blood-red? That a bishop of Chiapas, in Mexico,
banned the consumption of chocolate during his services, and was
subsequently poisoned by his congregation? That Pope Clement XIV
was also allegedly poisoned with a cup of bitter chocolate?*

'This time, you can drive the van,' said Guy, as we prepared to leave. 'I could use Stéphane today, if you can manage without him.'

I shook my head. 'I'm sorry. I can't.'

'You can't *drive*?'

I know it sounds ridiculous, but when would I have learnt to drive? Maman and I never owned a car. We walked. We rode on buses; hitched lifts in battered vans that smelt of sweat, and smoke, and engine oil. We stole rides on freight-trains; crept in and out of stations. Sometimes we bought passage on a ferry or a fishing boat; once or twice we even flew. But driving? That costs money. Vehicles – even second-hand – cost more than we could ever afford. And of course, they leave a trail. They're easy to identify. My mother must have known that. And yet—

'I'd like to learn,' I said quickly.

'Okay, we'll have to teach you,' said Guy. 'You're a fast learner. It shouldn't take long. Mahmed can do it, can't you, Mahmed?'

I tried to protest, but Guy was already moving on to his plans for our Grand Opening; the chocolate fountain we will hire, with strawberries to dip into it; the Christmas display in the window; spiced drinks in jewelled goblets. 'Vianne can make her hot chocolate, and serve it by the counter. And there'll be dancing in the street, and music, and a neon sign, and maybe some Christmas lights, and a tree with little gifts for everyone—'

The old Mahmed would have commented on this obvious provocation. His shadow simply shrugged and, addressing me, said: 'We'll both go out in the van today. We'll find some-where quiet. I'll show you the ropes.'

'Thank you.' I was a little surprised.

'It's fine. I could do with an outing.'

We took out the van to the place that has become our usual parking spot. We follow the markets, day by day; the fish, the fruit and vegetable markets, the flower markets, the *marché aux puces* on Sundays. I had, along with the chocolate urn, a spiced Morello chocolate cake as well as some of Margot's madeleines. We parked up at nine; by twelve-thirty, every piece of cake and cup of chocolate had been sold. I did the talking; Mahmed dealt with the money and the service.

Did you know that chocolate was once bitterly controversial? That clerics debated for centuries whether or not it broke the fast? That the first utensils for preparing it date from four thousand years ago? That my Nipples of Venus recipe dates back to the eighteenth century? That we'll be serving them – and more – on the day of our Grand Opening?

'You're good at this,' observed Mahmed, when we were finally ready to leave.

'People like stories,' I said with a smile.

'Guy's good at telling stories. He likes to make people happy.' He nudged the van out of gear and set off slowly through the end of the market, where stallholders were already packing up their wares. But instead of heading back into the Panier district, he turned along the seafront, and was soon heading away from the old town and into the industrial zone and the docklands.

'We'll start with just the basics,' he said, stopping the van by a silent quay. 'Just the pedals, and the gears. She's a temperamental old girl, and needs a sympathetic approach.'

He was right; the van was old, the gears were stiff, and the clutch was spongy. I stalled it for the sixth time, trying to make the soft clutch bite, and flooded the engine completely.

Mahmed shrugged. 'You'll get there,' he said. 'I think that's enough for today. We'll try some more driving tomorrow.'

Heading back, I watched his face as he steered the van through the traffic. 'Who taught *you* to drive?'

'No one. I taught myself when I was twelve. I was so small I could hardly even see over the steering wheel.'

I tried to imagine Mahmed as a child, and found it surprisingly easy. There's something oddly vulnerable behind his forbidding manner. And he is less guarded around me now; perhaps because I am a woman. I forked a sign in the palm of my hand. Reflected a shard of light on his face, as if from a wristwatch in the sun. Saw his features soften, as if at a distant memory. Around us, the van smelt of fresh paint, and diesel fumes, and chocolate. *I'm sick of the smell of it*, he'd said. And yet I don't believe it. I *do* believe he's sick, though; I see it in his colours unfurling like smoke on the water.

'How did you and Guy meet?' I said.

'What did he tell you?'

'Nothing much. He said he met you in a bar.'

Mahmed gave a short laugh. 'In fact, I was *outside* the bar. I was drunk. I'd been in a fight. I was always getting into fights in those days. I was trouble.' That laugh again, coloured with bitterness. 'He had this smile. This *slow* smile. Most people smile automatically, before they even know who you are. But Guy—' He smiled, suddenly wistful. 'He looks at you for a moment, as if he really *sees* you, and *then* he smiles. It makes you feel—' He paused again. 'It's just the way he is, I guess. He never could resist a stray. He's the king of hopeless causes.'

'You said that once before.'

'It's true. Some people just need to fix things. You should know; you're one yourself.' I looked at him, taken-aback. First, at his directness; second, at his insight. 'Don't tell me I'm wrong,' he said. 'I've seen you, trying to fix them. That angry old bastard from the bistrot. That Chinese family next door. Yesterday it was Stéphane. Today, it's me.'

'Mahmed, I—'

'Don't waste your time denying it. Guy knows it, and you know it too. It's an addiction. You're both the same. Addicted to hopeless cases.'

Is that true? Surely not. And yet it feels as if he has glimpsed a little piece of my soul. Little pieces of broken glass, reflecting scenes from another life. My mother's voice, saying: *There's only so much happiness anyone can have in a life. You can keep it for yourself, or you can give it to others. Not both.*

'I don't think that's true,' I said.

The shadow was back; I could see it unfurl. 'You don't? So tell me. Maybe you know. This game of his – this chocolate shop, this cute little van selling hot chocolate and cake – how long do you think it will really last, once his father – who pays the bills – finds out he's been lying all this time?'

'How long have you known?'

'Long enough. Stéphane heard you talking.'

I thought again of my talk with Guy; to the sound from the passageway. 'He told you?'

'I persuaded him to co-operate. I hid his cat in the cellar.'

Now I remembered Hallowe'en – Stéphane's fruitless searching for Pomponette; his late-night discussions with Mahmed – and saw how things must have developed. Poor Stéphane, who tries so hard to be accepted. Poor Mahmed, who, even now, thinks of himself as a hopeless case. I thought of that broken window, and the way Mahmed had been afterwards; a shadow of himself, a cloud of anger and betrayal.

'*You* broke the window,' I said at last. 'And you put water in the conching machine.'

He shrugged. 'Are you going to tell him?'

I shook my head. 'You don't think he'll stay.'

'And you think he will?' His voice was bleak. 'I'm a project, like this business. A little fantasy. A game. But in the end, when the money runs out, he won't have any choice. He'll go home, and tell himself he tried, that it isn't his fault it all fell apart.'

I shook my head. 'That won't happen,' I said. 'We're already getting orders.'

His smile was like the dark face of the moon. 'Oh, Vianne. It's happened before. Guy feels things very passionately – until he suddenly doesn't. When I first met him, he was convinced he was going to be a chef. He lasted three months in his first job, less than a month in the second. After that, he spent six months moving from one idea to the next, before he finally settled on this; to open a chocolaterie. It's a fantasy, that's all. A little holiday romance.'

I said: 'It's his dream. You know it is. And Mahmed, he *loves* you. You must know that. Whatever else may need fixing.'

But we had arrived at Allée du Pieu; there was no time to pursue the topic. Mahmed drove the van around the back of the shop, but as he did I saw someone standing by the door, face pressed against the glass to peer into the window.

I felt a sudden luminous certainty. My heart began to pound. *Edmond!*

For a moment I even *saw* him there, standing by the door of the shop; a boy about my own age, shadowed profile turned away. Then I saw that it was a man, an old man in a black winter coat, with the collar turned up against the cold, and I felt a sudden chill, as if of recognition. But when I ran back to the front of the shop, the man in black had already gone – that is, if he'd been there at all.

5

Of course, it means nothing. A man in black, trying to see through the window. There is no reason to believe in anything more sinister. People are curious in Le Panier; a new shop is always intriguing. And Allée du Pieu has been transformed since I first arrived here. Gone are the piles of litter, the bins, the drums of used cooking oil to be collected. Gone too are the rats and mice – since Pomponette's arrival, they have vacated the alleyway. The boarded-up windows have been concealed behind some wooden panels, which can be painted with Christmas designs, or hung with Chinese lanterns. The crew at Happy Noodles are in some part to thank for this – it was Madame Li's idea to put up the wooden panels – and the takeaway now has a new neon sign, which, once the place is open again, will illuminate the street.

And there is increasing interest about the shop from the family. Grandmother Li is openly so; Madame Li and her daughters are more discreet. But this morning, curiosity won out over discretion, and I opened up to find the Li girls peering in through the cracks in the newspaper. They both jumped back when I appeared, but I gave them a reassuring smile.

'There's nothing much in there for now,' I said. 'But I'll be dressing the window on Friday night. Would you like to help me?'

The two girls looked at each other. I could see caution there, and desire. All girls like chocolate, of course, and yet they are still wary.

'Help you?'

'You could be my testers.' Another pause, during which I see their colours reflected in their eyes. 'But first, I need to know your names,' I said. 'How else can I thank you?'

A fraction's hesitation. Names are things of power. 'Françoise,' says the eldest. 'Karine,' says the younger. Of course, these are not their Chinese names. These have been adopted in order to fit in more readily at school, and in the neighbourhood. True names are for family, kept secret from strangers.

'I'm happy to meet you, Françoise, Karine. Come to the front door on Friday, at five. I'll look forward to seeing you.'

No, it means nothing. A man in black. Simply my mother's fears given shape at this, my final coming of age, this claiming of my power. She cannot change me now; cannot bind me to her path. I have my own path now; I have my own name. Who I was – who I may have been – is part of a different story.

In those final weeks in New York, I asked her about my father. Before that, she had always avoided talking about him, or had told me extravagant stories – at times he had been a pirate, an astronaut, an explorer. Sometimes he had black hair, sometimes he was bearded; sometimes he was mixed-race; sometimes fair and clean-shaven. And as I grew, I secretly wondered if *he* was the man she fled – the Man in Black of her stories, with his eyes that saw through walls, and his voice that summoned the wind.

He's here. I know. I can feel him, she would say in her delirium. *He'll find us, 'Viane, he'll follow us all the way across the world.*

'But what does he want?' I would ask her, hoping she would go to sleep; hoping the wind would stop blowing; that the luck would finally turn.

My mother would laugh. 'What does he want? What do any of them want? They think I'm crazy. They think I can't be trusted to look after a child. They want to lock me away, to take you and make you forget me. You won't go with them, will you, 'Viane? You won't let them put me away?'

'Of course not. Of *course* not. Please, Maman. Close your eyes and try to rest.'

But long after that, when she was asleep, my mind was still racing. Could my mother have suffered from some kind of mental illness? Was that why we ran away – because she was afraid I might be taken away from her? Had she spent my childhood hiding from my father?

I looked for answers among her things. I thought I knew everything she had. But among her papers, her passport, her few photographs, I found some newspaper clippings – Maman, who never kept *anything* – eighteen-year-old clippings from *Le Parisien*, *Le Figaro*, *Ouest-France*, even *Le Monde*, recounting the disappearance of a child, Sylviane Caillou, stolen from her mother's car while the woman stopped by the chemist's. The papers were faded and brown as dead leaves. The story was lacking in detail, and yet I remembered parts of it: the toys that were taken along with the child – a red plush elephant, a bear, a pink plush rabbit – along with the little girl's changing-bag. Why had she kept those clippings? I thought. How could that little girl with my name be more than just a coincidence?

It explains so much. My mother's fear. Her perpetual dread of losing me. Her lifelong flight from the Man in Black. That burning need to go unseen. And the rabbit. Always the rabbit. *Your invisible friend*, she used to say. But Molfetta was *real*; I remembered her; the scrap of ribbon around her neck; the silky feel of her well-worn fur; the bud of silk on the tip of her nose. And somehow – *always* – the memory was linked to that night in the confessional; to the Virgin standing over us with her baby in her arms, and the music sweeping over the crowd, and the Man in White with his crucifix, and the scent of polish and incense-smoke and the voice of my mother calling me, and my own voice rising furiously:

You're not my mother! Get away! You're not my real mother!

When she was herself again, I tried to ask the question. But she refused to answer, or to speak of Sylviane Caillou, or that bundle of newspaper clippings, or the fact that I still *remembered* the toys in those newspaper articles. *We choose our family*, she said. *We choose our fellow-travellers.* And later, when the pain was worse, and the morphine was taking hold, she said; *Don't worry. I fixed it, Viannou. I fixed it, for a pretty. I won't lose you. You'll lose me. That's how it always works for our kind. Everything must be paid for.*

She died three months later, not of cancer after all, but in a hit-and-run accident. At the time, I wondered if this was her way of avoiding that conversation: the one in which we could have discussed that little girl in Paris, and the woman who stole her. But it was just an accident; a busy road in Chinatown; a blare of horns; a flag of a cry unfurled against the summer air. We never got to see Florida. But she never lost me. Perhaps that was what she meant, after all; payment, for a pretty.

After that, there was no point in asking questions any more. Whatever her reasons, whatever her sins, there was no doubt she loved me. Love goes deeper than the bonds of blood, or genes, or family. And she was my mother. I loved her. Even knowing what I know; that somewhere, in another life, I had another mother. But to claim this other life, I would have had to deny Maman. To deny who I have become. To unravel the threads of my past; to go back to the beginning. How can I do that? How can I erase myself for the sake of a woman I don't even know? No, this is my life now. This is my path. I can only move forward. Whoever I was – who I *might* have been – that story died with my mother. I am an adult. I choose my path. And even if they found me now, what could they expect from me?

6

Three days to go, and everyone knows about Saturday's grand opening. Word has gone round the Old Quarter, partly because of the article, and partly because of the chocolate van, and the fliers we have distributed. People have started wandering by to glance at the papered window, the wooden *Xocolatl* sign, the neat little planters of fir trees that line the side of the alleyway. If we seem to notice them, they pretend that they are lost, or looking for another street, or simply going for a walk. But the air is charged with their desire – to know, to taste, to see, to tell – and their colours light up the alleyway like a string of Christmas lights.

Guy remains oddly subdued for a man whose dream is ready to come to fruition. Mahmed keeps his distance, working outside, or sorting boxes in the cellar. I followed him there, and found him picking up empty tins from the floor; tuna, sardines and *pâté Hénaff*. Whatever his motives, Pomponette fed well during her time there.

'Guy seems under the weather,' I said. 'Any idea what's wrong?'

He shrugged. 'Probably just nerves,' he said. 'There's a lot riding on Saturday. We've done everything we can. Now, we learn if it was enough.'

332

There has been no further sign of the man in the black coat. Khamaseen, too, has been absent, nor is there any sign of Edmond. And yet, the beacon has been lit. Others have already seen it. I hope Edmond will want to come, but I cannot force him to do so. And as Khamaseen says, why should he seek out a man who didn't want him?

Last night, in the hissing silence that comes in the wake of a thunderstorm, I got out of bed and looked out of my window into the alleyway. A small fine rain was falling, filling the air with a street-lamp haze. The cobbles gleamed with the neon red of the new sign over the takeaway: a stylized pagoda or tower, topped with Chinese lettering. At last, after weeks of refurbishment, Happy Noodles is back in business.

As I watched, I saw a man in black emerge from the shadows. I couldn't see him clearly; foreshortened by the perspective, I couldn't even make out his height, but I thought there was something furtive about the way in which he moved, following the line of the wall. I expected to see him come closer, but as I watched I saw that he was making for the noodle shop. It is an eccentric building, L-shaped, with the living space at the back, and a flat roof over the shop front, over which the neon sign stands. Positioned about six feet from the ground, it dominates the front of the shop; I could just see it in profile, though here, in the alley, its scarlet glow was scattered over the cobbles.

I watched as the man moved purposefully towards the back of the neon sign; saw him reach up towards the cables that supplied it. I saw that he was carrying something – maybe a bolt-cutter of some kind. Did he mean to disable the sign? I couldn't see his face, although his figure was clearly visible now, outlined in red from the neon sign. The man readjusted the bolt-cutters, reaching for a cable. And now I recognized who he was; the hair, torched red by the neon glow; the shapeless dark jacket and knitted cap; the familiar set of the shoulders.

It was Stéphane.

I opened the window and called his name. My voice seemed very loud in the night. Stéphane froze at the sound of my voice; then ducked back into the shadows. I heard the sounds of his boots on the road; the clang of something hitting the ground. Then he vanished, and I heard the sound of the back door opening, then softly closing again.

I stood, barefoot on the cold tiled floor, uncertain. Should I confront him? Go back to bed? Pretend I mistook him for someone else? My feet were getting cold; my head was filled with contradictions. *Stéphane?* Why would gentle, sweet, Stéphane want to damage Happy Noodles?

Mahmed, of course. The answer came as clearly as if he'd spoken aloud. I remembered how hard Stéphane had tried to get Mahmed to like him; how often Mahmed had complained about the cooking smells from the noodle bar. Had Stéphane also reported them to the health inspector? I picked up Pomponette, who had been sleeping on the end of my bed, and carried her into Stéphane's room. He was sitting on the bed, fully dressed, with the light on. He seemed unsurprised to see me, but stroked Pomponette as I put her down, and handed me a blanket.

'Here. You'll catch your death, Vianne.'

I sat on the bed beside him. I noticed he had oil on his hands; the kind you get from handling tools. We sat there in silence for a time, and Pomponette curled up and purred. Finally, without looking at me, he said:

'I didn't go ahead with it. I was going to, but I didn't.'

I said nothing, but nodded.

334

'I just wanted the noodle bar to be closed for the big day on Saturday. I wouldn't have done it otherwise. But everyone's worked so hard, and—'

'The Lis are part of that,' I said. 'They've helped us fix up the alleyway. If you wanted the takeaway closed, you could just have asked them.'

He shook his head. 'That wouldn't work. After the broken window—'

'That wasn't them, Stéphane,' I said. 'Besides, I thought you *liked* that place.'

He looked at me. 'I did. But—' He gave his Hallowe'en-pumpkin smile. 'I like it *here*. I *love* it here. For the first time in years, I have a home. I can work. I can help other people. I can't afford to lose all that.'

'But you told Mahmed about Guy.'

Stéphane looked stricken. 'I had to,' he said.

'Yes, I know. Pomponette.'

He shrugged. 'I suppose you think I'm ridiculous, making a fool of myself over a cat. But Pomponette—' His pumpkin smile was both wistful and self-mocking. 'For all those years, she was all I had. I couldn't bear it if something happened to her.'

I thought of all those empty tins of tuna in the basement. 'Mahmed would never have hurt her, you know.'

'I know that. But I couldn't be sure.' He gave his sad, cartoonish smile. 'I never told you why I ended up on the streets, did I, Vianne?'

I shook my head. He'd told me certain things – that he'd been an alcoholic, that he had had issues with depression and unemployment – but there was always something more; a kind of cheerful bleakness. 'Stéphane, you don't need to tell me,' I said.

'Perhaps I want to,' said Stéphane. 'Perhaps you need to know who I am.'

'People are a lot of things. You don't have to always be who you were.'

'But I have to carry it,' said Stéphane. 'I have to carry what I did. Some days it's like a pile of stones waiting to fall on my head. Some days it feels like I'm buried alive. Some days it feels like I'm already dead.' He looked at me again, and with a kind of desperation. 'Vianne, you deserve to know the truth. And I deserve to tell it to you.' He spat out the words and sentences like bitter little cherry-stones. 'I'd been drinking. I drank a lot in those days. I wanted to drive out to buy some beer. Elise didn't want me to go. We argued. I got angry. I jumped in the car, backed out onto the drive. I didn't see my son, Matou, playing with his tricycle.'

It's a sorry little tale. Maman and I saw so many of those during our time on the road. Everyday tragedies, accidents that can divert the path of a life. Most people are not inherently bad. But people make bad decisions, mistakes that tumble a life like dominoes, taking plans and loves and dreams with the same inevitability.

The boy survived. He says it as if that, too, is a kind of tragedy. Survived, but with an injury that left him paralysed from the waist down. No more playing with tricycles. No more running in the park. No chance of grandchildren for Elise; instead, a round of hospitals and surgeons and operations, and finally the terrible truth. There was no hope of recovery. Stéphane had stopped drinking. But it was too late. His marriage was broken beyond repair. His wife took their son to her parents' in Rouen. The police asked Stéphane to stay in Marseille while they looked into the crime.

'And so I ran,' Stéphane went on. 'I ducked under the radar. I ended up in a *bidonville* on the outskirts of Marseille, doing whatever I could to survive. I went back to drinking. I wanted to die. I wanted to see Elise and Matou. I wanted the life I'd thrown under the bus. I wanted a second chance. But life doesn't give second chances. And so I drifted from place to place, waiting for the inevitable. And then, one day, by the river, I decided it was time to go.' He sighed. 'It's funny, isn't it? The first decision I'd made in years. And all it took to derail it was a bag of abandoned kittens.' He stroked Pomponette, who stretched lazily, showing a sudden spread of claws. 'And here we both are.' He looked away. 'Eight lives down, and one to go.'

I put my hand on his arm and said: 'Everybody makes mistakes. And every day is a new start. Every day you have the chance to make a difference to the world.'

He nodded. 'Yes, I know. And yet—'

'One little thing at a time,' I said. 'Little things make a difference. Come downstairs. I'll make you some chocolate. It'll help us both to sleep.'

'You and your hot chocolate,' he said, but this time, he was smiling. 'Can I have a cognac instead?'

'Absolutely not,' I said.

He followed me down to the kitchen.

7

2 December 1993

Today was our last day in the van before the start of our opening celebrations. Guy was subdued, but hard at work, packing boxes of chocolates and tying coloured ribbons, while Stéphane worked out in the street, painting the wooden panels that hid the disused properties in red and yellow swirling designs of cacao pods and lanterns. Meanwhile, Mahmed and I took the van to the top of the Butte, selling cups of hot chocolate and spiced madeleines, and giving out invitations.

Grand opening on Saturday! 10 a.m. to 7 p.m.!

Taste our specialities! Bring your friends and family!

Then at noon, I went to La Bonne Mère to remind everyone about Saturday. But when I arrived, I found only Emile, drinking coffee laced with cognac and holding a half-smoked *Gitane*. The kitchen was closed, the bar empty. Louis was nowhere to be seen.

'Where's Louis?'

Emile gave a listless shrug. 'He left me in charge yesterday. Said he'd be back in the morning. But there's no news from the hospital yet, and I don't know what to do.'

'The hospital?'

338

I looked through the smoke of his cigarette for answers, but saw nothing there. Normally his colours show a mixture of rage and chaotic energy; but here I saw a dullness that I'd never seen in him before. 'Heart attack; yesterday lunchtime. At least, that's what I'm assuming. No one tells me anything. It was the shock. I know it was. I found him in the kitchen—'

'What happened, Emile? What shock do you mean?'

'The boy.' Emile seemed half in shock himself. 'Walked in yesterday lunchtime. Asked for Louis, bold as can be. Said Louis was his father.'

'What did he look like? What was his name?' My heart was beating wildly now, like a shutter in the wind. *You came, Edmond. You really came.*

'What the hell does it matter?' he said. 'He was a half-wit. A chancer. People like Louis attract his kind. People who think they can take advantage of a man with money.' He took a drink of his coffee. 'He must have heard about us somewhere. Thought he'd try his chances. Heard Margot's child was born a—' I saw the ugly word in his thoughts, his mixture of pity and disgust. I thought of what Khamaseen had said. *The child was a child, who deserved to be loved.* What else really matters?

'You knew her child was alive?' I said.

He pulled a face, and I realized that there was far more cognac in the cup than I'd thought. 'Some sort of genetic condition, Louis said. Probably wouldn't survive. And besides, who would have looked after it? Knowing what it had done to Margot? Knowing it had cost her life?'

I thought of the baby album, and what Margot had written there. *He's afraid: he doesn't know how we would cope with a damaged child. But Edmond is already perfect. Already he's a miracle. I wish Louis could see it that way. I wish he could let himself love our son without being afraid to lose him.*

I said: 'Let me show you something, Emile.'

The baby album was still in the chest in the guest room, with the linen. I went upstairs and retrieved it, then handed it silently to Emile. I waited as he looked through the book, turning the pages one by one. Outside, I heard the van start up, and knew that Mahmed was leaving.

'Where did you get this?' said Emile at last.

'From Khamaseen.'

'Of course you did.' He lingered on the final page; the footprint; the inscription. 'This is where you got the idea.'

Silently, I nodded.

There are times when I do not look. I could already feel his distress. To reach into his memories would have been an intrusion. Instead I took his coffee cup. 'I'll make you something better than this.'

Emile said nothing as I took my copper pan down from the wall. I don't think it has been touched since I left. Whole milk; grated chocolate; a pinch of Guy's xocolatl spice. The scent was safe and comforting, like the childhood I never had. Poor Emile, I thought suddenly; living his life on the edges of the life he would have wanted. Poor Emile; so much anger, and with nowhere for it to go. I set the cup in front of him; I'd made it sweet, to help with the shock. He drank it without comment, still looking at the album. Then he said in a gentler voice than I'd ever heard him use:

'You know, she would have adopted a child. But Louis didn't like the idea. He thought he wouldn't be able to love a child that belonged to someone else.'

I said nothing, but let the soft vapour from the chocolate spice rise into the smoky air, teasing out its secrets.

'He always blamed that foreign woman for encouraging Margot to keep trying. But really, she was doing it for him.

Margot would have loved *any* child. Wherever they'd come from. Whatever they were.' He reached out to touch the album; traced the words with his fingertips. *'Edmond Loïc Bien-Aimé Martin.* That boy said his name was Loïc. D'you really think he was the one?'

'I think so, yes.'

'He's gone now. I told him never to come back.'

'It's okay,' I said. 'I'll find him.'

8

The Hôpital Saint-Marguerite is in the 9th arrondissement. I found Louis there, in a private room, but not accepting visitors. 'Are you a relative?' said the nurse.

I nodded. 'I'm his daughter.'

'Then maybe come back in the morning? And could you persuade your brother to leave? He's been waiting here for hours.'

I looked across from the desk, and saw a young man of about my own age sitting in the passageway. Dark-haired, round-faced, absurdly youthful for twenty. Warm brown eyes and a wide mouth that broadened into a sunny smile as soon as I approached him.

'Can I go in now?'

I shook my head. 'Not yet, I'm afraid.'

The big smile wavered mournfully. 'I've been waiting ages.'

I smiled and came to sit next to him. 'I'm Vianne. I'm a friend of Louis'. I've been waiting for you, too.'

'Oh?' The smile was back, like the sun from the clouds, and I thought for a moment of Margot. Sometimes we inherit our parents' features; their hair, their eyes. But sometimes a piece of the soul shines through, like fragments of mica caught in stone.

342

I convinced him to leave the hospital on the understanding that we would return the next day. Then I found a café nearby and bought us both a coffee. Loïc drinks his very sweet, with milk and lots of sugar. He likes pastries, too; the small, round, sugared brioches that Stéphane would probably call pomponettes. As we drank coffee and made our way through a pile of the pastries, he told me how he had come to be here, and why he had come in search of Louis.

'It was my birthday this month,' he said. 'Maman and Papa threw a party. We all had champagne and chocolate cake. They said it's because I was all grown up.' He smiled. He has a winning smile, which seemed to fill the whole of the room, as well as the kind of enthusiasm that seems not to care who is watching. He went on: 'And then they said there was something that they had to tell me. A secret they'd kept for me since I was born. My other parents didn't die. My *mother* died, but my father's alive, and living in Marseille.' He paused and took a *pomponette*. 'I like these,' he said. 'You should have one. I'm not supposed to eat them all.'

'Thank you,' I said, and took a brioche. There was something appealing about this young man, an exuberance and a sincerity that was just as profound as wisdom. 'Do your parents know you're here?'

He shook his head. 'They're in Cassis for their wedding anniversary.'

'For how long?'

'Just for the weekend.' He smiled, a little ruefully. 'I took the bus into Marseille. I guess I'm lucky it was so close.'

'So you've always known you were adopted?'

He nodded. '*Chosen*. That's what they said. The families we choose are the best.'

'My mother used to say that, too.' As always, grief catches me unawares. When will that stop happening? The families we choose are the ones we carry always in our hearts. Loïc understands that, and yet, he was the one who went looking for Louis.

The big smile wavered a little. 'Used to?'

'She died.'

'Mine did, too. She died and I never knew her.'

I thought about Margot's cookery book on the shelf at La Bonne Mère; and her photographs of Bergerac, and the baby album, and the river stone. 'I think there's a way to fix that,' I said. 'Where are you staying?'

He looked mournful. 'I thought I might stay with my father. But he's sick. Is that my fault? The man in the bistrot said so.'

I said: 'It's not your fault, Loïc.' And because he still looked uncertain, I scrawled a sign against my palm; a little shard of lightning. 'Come and stay at La Bonne Mère. I'll show you your mother's kitchen. Her photographs. Her cookery book. Her poetry.'

That smile again. 'She liked cooking?'

'Yes. Louis taught me her recipes.'

'Could he teach *me*? Could *you*?' said Loïc. The light was back in his face again. 'I love to cook. I cook all the time. That's because I love to eat. I want to be a chef one day, but Maman says for that I'd need to go back to school and study.'

I smiled. 'I think there are other ways. Would you like to come with me?'

He nodded. 'Can we take the last of the pomponettes? In case we get hungry on the way?'

I smiled again. 'Of course we can.'

9

2 December 1993

It was dark by the time we got back. Looking up at the clock on the wall, I realized with a jolt that it was already past five o'clock. In the bar, the lights were off, except for the one in the kitchen. The door sign read *Closed.* The keys to the *bistrot* were by the till, a bunch of rusty, headless blooms. Emile was sitting in the dark, only discernible by the red tip of his lit *Gitane*, and the nimbus of smoke that surrounded him. He looked at me.

'You found him, then.'

'I did. Emile, this is Loïc Poirier. Loïc, this is your father's friend. He knew your mother, too, Margot.'

Loïc gave a smile like a mirrorball. 'You did? I'm so glad. That makes you sort of my uncle, or something!'

Emile gave him a wary look. I could see him, reading Loïc's face, trying to find a trace of Margot in those open features. Loïc stepped forward and flung his arms around Emile in a great hug.

Emile protested. 'Let me go!'

I should perhaps have warned Loïc that Emile avoids physical contact. Where others kiss, he is content with a simple handshake. But Loïc was too excited to care. He kissed Emile on both cheeks with what I am starting to understand is his usual exuberance. Emile pulled away, looking shaken, but there was no anger in his face. Instead he looked almost awed, as if he too had recognized Margot in the young man's features.

'I told Loïc he could stay here,' I said. 'There's a guest room he can use. Maybe you could stay here, too? Mind the place till Louis gets back?'

Loïc looked uncertain. 'Vianne, don't go. You were going to show me my mother's kitchen.'

Emile made an explosive sound. 'If you think Louis will stand for that—'

'Louis isn't here,' I said. 'And Loïc needs somewhere to stay. Would you stay with him tonight? I'm needed at the chocolaterie, but I'll be back in the morning.' I saw him hesitate. 'Emile. Please. I'm trying to help. I know it may not seem that way, but—'

I thought I saw his colours shift back to their usual gas-jet blue. But then Loïc put a hand on his arm and said: 'Please, monsieur. I don't want to stay here all night, all on my own.' And then I was sure I saw him fork a little sign against his palm, casting a brightness onto the wall. Maybe Margot's son has inherited more than just her smile.

I saw Emile's discomfort, but there was no anger in him now, and the permanent scowl that seemed to be so much a part of his natural expression was gone. 'All right,' he said at last. 'But you'd better come back in the morning. I'm not cooking lunch.'

I smiled. 'Loïc and I can cook lunch,' I said. 'We'll make your favourite. Pissaladière.'

After that I went back home, where Allée du Pieu was lit up for the night. The Happy Noodles sign was casting scarlet shadows. Strings of paper lanterns hang between the buildings, and there are tiny Christmas lights twisted around shutters and doors. More Christmas lights in the front of the shop; and although the display window remains hidden behind sheets of paper, the window has been lit from inside, giving it a lantern shine.

But when I looked for Guy and Mahmed, neither of them were home. Instead I found Stéphane in the back, looking drawn and anxious. 'Where's Guy?'

Stéphane shrugged. 'I don't know. He went out this morning.'

'Where?'

'He didn't say.'

That was odd. But then, Guy has been odd over the past few days. I said: 'Did anything happen? Did he quarrel with Mahmed?'

Stéphane shook his head. 'But there was a man. He talked with Guy for a long time.'

'What kind of a man? Did you see him?'

'Not really. He was an older man. Wearing a long black winter coat.'

I thought of the man I'd seen last week, and felt the hairs on my arms rise. 'Do you know what they talked about?'

He shrugged. 'I don't know. I stayed out of the way. But I heard them go out soon after that, and Guy hasn't been back since. And as for Mahmed —' He shrugged again. 'Who the hell knows where he goes?'

This was worrying, I thought. Stéphane's description of the man in black was too close to the man I'd seen looking in through the window. And Guy has been so quiet and strange — I should have noticed something was wrong. But my mind has been so full of other things, and now that I have found Edmond—

347

The world demands its balance, 'Viane. There is no gift without a loss. My mother's voice, so clear in the night, is like the wind from the rooftops. *There is no gift without a loss.* Does that mean, that by calling one friend, I have lost another?

10

3 December 1993

One more day to go until Saturday, our grand opening. Tonight, Françoise and Karine Li will come round and help with the display window. The panels on the street are bright with murals, painted by Stéphane and the Li family, with cacao pods and Christmas scenes and lucky Chinese dragons. The front of the shop is spotless; display cabinets filled with jars that gleam like sunken treasure. Everything is perfect, except—

Guy did not come back last night. No one has seen him since yesterday. A brief note on the back of an envelope, then stuck to the side of the fridge, says: *Called away in a hurry. Back soon. G.* There is no explanation, no further sign of disturbance. The van is still at the back of the shop. On inquiry, Grandmother Li says she thinks she saw him get in a car with a man. 'Expensive car. Maybe Mercedes.' No one else saw anything. Mahmed alone seemed unsurprised, drinking his coffee at breakfast as if nothing unusual had happened.

'I don't understand. Aren't you worried?'

He shrugged. 'No, why? It wouldn't be the first time he's gone running off to Toulouse when he's suffered a crisis of confidence.'

It's not always easy to read Mahmed. His colours are often troubled. This morning, they were muted; grey as morning mist on the harbour. But I saw no anxiety there; he knows exactly where Guy has gone, and why.

'You think he's gone to Toulouse? Why?'

Mahmed took a croissant and dipped it into his coffee. 'Maybe he needs to explain things – *this* place – to his father.'

'Why now? Did he say something?'

That shrug again. 'Why would he?'

I thought of Guy, and the Liars' Chair, and the secret he has been hiding. Two different lives in two cities; both divided by a single lie. How long did he hope to keep it up? *Just till the chocolaterie breaks even.* So why would he tell his father now, when everything hangs on this crucial week?

Mahmed continued to eat his croissant, dipping it slowly, piece by piece. I thought about the day we first met, and the warmth I'd seen in both of them. Guy's passion tempered with Mahmed's common sense; the closeness of their relationship.

'*You* told him, didn't you?' I said. 'You sent him the newspaper article.'

Mahmed gave a humourless smile. 'That would explain it, wouldn't it? It's almost as if I expected him to take responsibility. To make a choice. Well, I guess he has.' He finished his croissant and stood up. 'Things to do, Vianne. Things to do. It's the big day tomorrow.'

I watched him go, feeling helpless. How could things be going so wrong? I did it right, didn't I? I cast the circle. I called the wind. I spoke the words of power. So why isn't it working, Maman? Why are things falling apart like this?

You need to be gone. Her voice is stark. *This is what happens when you try to interfere with people's lives. Things get broken. People, too.* And yet, I called Edmond. He came. Surely that means something?

But what does it mean to Louis, 'Viane? Is Louis in a better place? Or have you simply given him another cause for grief?

I shook aside the troubling thought. I will not run away from this. I cannot − will not − abandon my friends. I have to finish what I began. And besides, I'd promised Loïc I'd make his mother's pissaladière.

Rosemary

I

3 December 1993

It's such an easy dish to make. All you need is onions, flour, olive oil, anchovies, olives, butter and fresh rosemary – the kind you find growing in every back yard. Even in Louis' absence, and with no time to run to the market, these ingredients could be found among his depleted supplies.

Loïc was excited to see me. I found him in the bar with Emile, along with a couple of regulars who had called in for breakfast and to ask after Louis. There was a coffee pot on the bar, along with some bread, and a plate of croissants. Marinette said: 'We missed you. Emile won't set foot in the kitchen.'

'I said I could help,' protested Loïc, 'but Emile said to wait for Vianne. Said I'd only make a mess if I did anything on my own. I don't think that's fair, do you, Vianne? Besides, it's already a mess in there. Does Louis really use all those things? Did they belong to my mother?'

Emile saw me coming and stubbed out his *Gitane*. 'Thank God you're here,' he said fervently. 'I've never known anyone talk so much. People keep coming in to ask if we have any news of Louis. I tell them I phoned the hospital. It sounds like he's doing better.'

355

'Good,' I said, and smiled. 'I'm glad.'

Emile gave a short laugh. 'So am I. The boy kept pestering till I called. Why don't you take him somewhere else? It's exhausting. Like having a dog.'

'He likes me,' said Loïc.

'I know.'

'But maybe you'd like to get to know your mother's kitchen with me?' I said. 'Cook with me from her cookery book? Use the instruments she used?'

The brown eyes shone with excitement. 'Yes! Oh, please. Let's make—'

I looked around at the regulars. They were watching both of us with that combination of wariness and curiosity I know well. I said: 'We'll be serving lunch today for anyone who wants to come. Loïc and I will be helping Emile, at least until Louis gets back. So spread the word: we're still open. Today we'll be making—'

'Pissaladière.'

While I began to make the dough, Loïc began to peel and chop and caramelize the onions, using a small copper-bottomed pan and one of Margot's hand-carved spoons, scarred and burnt with years of long use. The boy has a knack. I can see that from the way he handles the chopping-block, the kitchen knives, the copper pan. He does not read the recipe, but he does read his mother's side notes; following the words on the page with a blunt and earnest finger.

'*Better a heartache than a bellyache.* What does that mean?'

'A quotation,' I said. 'From *Cyrano*.' I told him about his mother's love of Edmond Rostand, and the story of the man who thought himself too ugly to love.

'Too ugly to love?' repeated Loïc. He worked in silence for a while. Then he said: 'A boy at school once told me that's why my parents gave me away. Because I was too different for normal people to love.'

I looked at him. 'That isn't true. That boy was just being mean to you.'

Loïc nodded uncertainly. 'But I *am* different, aren't I? My parents say I'm *special*. Other people say that too, but not like it's a good thing.'

I bit my lip. There are so many things that I would like to tell him. Instead I showed him the album; the name written under his footprint. *Edmond Loïc Bien-Aimé Martin.*

'That's what your mother called you,' I said. 'Bien-Aimé. *Beloved.*'

Loïc looked at the page for a while. 'I wish I could have known her,' he said, a forlorn note in his voice.

'What do you think you're doing now?' I said. 'You're getting to know her. She's here, in her books and her recipes. She's here in the pots and pans she used. She's outside, in her garden.' I showed him a handful of rosemary I'd picked outside the back door; the scent was sweet and nostalgic. 'She planted this,' I told him. 'Now you're using it to make one of her recipes.' I had a sudden memory of Khamaseen, and her scented sachet. 'You should put some among the clothes in your wardrobe,' I told him. 'It will help you remember.'

By now, the onions were caramelized, and the dough had rested and risen. Emile was dozing by the bar in a square of winter sunlight. Loïc took the onions off the heat. The scent was complex, rich and sweet. 'Now for the olives and anchovies.'

While he was busy with topping the dough with olives, anchovy fillets, sea salt and pieces of rosemary, I reached in my bag for the chocolate spice I'd brought with me from Allée du Pieu. It works on almost any dish; its influence can be subtle or strong, savoury or bittersweet, depending on its companions. In this dish it would be smoky, I thought; woodsmoke and paprika. Herbs to heal a troubled heart. A welcoming smile from Marguerite.

'What's that?' said Loïc, whose sense of smell seems almost as well-developed as mine.

'A spice mix,' I said, handing him the jar. 'It's—'

'*Chocolate,*' said Loïc in delight. 'Chocolate, and some other things. Chilli, cardamom, er – cumin?'

'Nearly. Star anise,' I said. 'It works in nearly everything. Go on. Try it.'

He shook out some of the mixture into his palm and sprinkled it on the laden dough. 'I like it,' he said. 'Did my mother use this?'

I nodded. 'Yes, I think she did.'

The big smile was open, unabashed. I wondered what Louis had made of it. Had the shock of seeing his son provoked his collapse? I slid the finished pissaladière into the oven, while Loïc sliced ripe tomatoes into a wooden salad bowl.

'Are you a chef?' he asked me.

'No, I work in a chocolaterie.'

'Wow!' The brown eyes widened. 'That's cool. Can I see it?'

'Tomorrow.'

2

At midday, the *bistrot* started to fill up as usual. All our regulars were there – Amadou and Monsieur Georges, Marinette, Rodolphe, Tonton and his dog, Galipette. Curious glances at Loïc from those who had not seen him at breakfast. But Loïc seems impervious to judgemental looks and whispers. Instead he is openly curious, asking questions all the time:

'Did you like the pissaladière? I helped make it, you know. Vianne and I baked the madeleines. And we're going to have hot chocolate.'

Tonton gave him a quelling look. 'You're supposed to serve the food, not talk about it.'

'Sorry,' said Loïc. 'Is that your dog?' He knelt to stroke Galipette, who growled, unused to attention.

'He doesn't like me,' said Loïc.

'He doesn't like anyone,' said Tonton.

Loïc stroked the dog again. 'You're a good dog,' he told Galipette. 'You just needed someone to tell you.' Galipette tried another growl, but it didn't sound convincing. Rolling over, he licked Loïc's hand. 'I *knew* you were a good dog!'

There's something about Loïc that makes it hard to be annoyed with him. In some ways, he reminds me of Guy; his openness; his exuberance. Emile was eating pissaladière, watching Loïc all the time, his colours a perplexing swirl of troubled greens, anxious yellows. I sense that he is discovering something new in himself – a strange and hitherto unexpected capacity for affection.

'You made this?' he said to Loïc.

Loïc nodded.

'It's not bad. But it's an easy dish to make. Vianne started off with bouillabaisse.'

'That infernal *mouli*,' I said, laughing at the memory. 'I wouldn't wish it on anyone. How on earth did the new man cope?'

He shrugged. 'The new man didn't work out.'

'Is that why you stayed here?'

The shrug again. 'Where else would I go?'

Loïc went into the kitchen to make a start on the chocolate. He knows exactly what to do; whole milk, sugar, chocolate. I have shown him which pan to use; which wooden spoon is best for the task. And of course, a generous pinch from the jar of chocolate spice. *Herbs to heal a restless heart. Try me. Taste me. Test me.*

The scent of chocolate begins to fret the smoky air of the bistrot. It smells of winter nights by the fire; of marshmallow sunsets; of snowball fights. Loïc has his own way of making this simplest of recipes; but this is Margot's kitchen, and here her presence lingers. And now it almost seems to me as if the light has shifted; the colours have merged; the cards are falling into place. Fragments of light rise up from the floor like bubbles in an aquarium.

'Here, I made hot chocolate.'

There comes a kind of collective sigh, barely audible in the room. *Mmmm.* 'I've missed it,' said Marinette. 'I've tried to make it your way, Vianne, but it never seems to taste the same.'

'Maybe I'll have a cup,' said Tonton, who was feeding sugar to his dog. 'It's cold. I need the energy.'

One by one, the regulars held out their cups. In the eerie light, they looked like children at a firework display, faces keen and luminous. Loïc poured out the hot chocolate, his round face rosy with pleasure. He had just gone into the kitchen to fetch the dish of madeleines, when the bistrot door opened, letting in the scent of the sea, and engine oil, and woodsmoke. A man came in, and for a second I saw him outlined against the door; a figure in a dark coat.

'Louis!'

Heads turned as he walked to the bar, and I saw him react to the atmosphere, the comforting scent of chocolate.

'It's good to see you back,' I said. 'How are you?'

'Fine.' His voice was cool. 'They're telling me it was stress, or something. They kept me in to run some tests.' He looked at me sardonically. 'I suppose you assumed I was at death's door?'

'We all care about you, Louis.'

'Well, as you see, I'm fine.'

'Emile has been looking after the place. And—' I saw his face darken. A silence fell. Loïc was at the kitchen door, holding a plate of madeleines.

'Who let *him* into my kitchen?'

I said: 'Loïc's been helping here, Louis. We couldn't have opened without him.'

'We made pissaladière,' said Loïc, with his big and open smile. 'Vianne makes it with chocolate. And there are chocolate madeleines, and—'

Louis turned to look at me, his face alight with anger. 'You did this. You planned this, somehow. You found out where he was and you thought you'd ambush me.'

'Louis.' I put a hand on his arm. 'He's your son. He deserves to know you.'

He shook me away. 'I don't have a son. Whoever that boy is, I want him gone. I don't want you befriending him, or giving him ideas. Understand?'

I understand. I see you, Louis. I see your anger and self-doubt, all snarled into a banner of flame. Most of all, though, I see fear; the fear of a man who is afraid to feel anything that may not be returned.

'I understand,' I said. 'You're afraid. Don't be. People love you here.'

Louis made an inarticulate sound. 'What the hell do you care?' he said. 'Things were fine before you came along. I was managing just fine. I had my café, my routine. Why did you come and change all that?'

I said: 'Change is the only way we survive.'

'And what if I don't *want* it? What if I just want to stay here, in the place we were happy?'

I thought of the anniversary plate, with the piece knocked out of the rim. *Good Lord bless this happy home.* 'But you weren't happy, were you?' I said. 'She wasn't happy. She wanted a child. She wanted him so badly that she was willing to risk her life. And now he's here, it reminds you of everything she sacrificed.'

'No more from you!' Louis' voice was harsh. 'You should look after your own affairs. I hear things about people too. I've heard about you, and your mother—'

Now all eyes were fixed on me. Marinette's mouth was half-open; Emile's face was blank with distress. Under that harsh exterior, his heart is as tender as Loïc's.

'My mother?' I said softly.

'That's right.' His voice was almost a sob. 'I guess you don't know everything, Vianne — if that's your real name. Because

362

that man who came looking for you the day you ran off to Toulouse seemed to think it was something else. Sylviane, perhaps? Sylviane Caillou?'

I suddenly felt as if the ground beneath me had been pulled away. That name – the name from the papers Maman had kept for all those years – was like a sudden gust of wind, blowing me off-course towards a dark and rocky coastline.

'I don't know what you mean,' I said.

He grinned like his ancient *mouli*. 'I mean you're not the only one with a secret or two to hide. The day you left, I was worried. I reported you missing. The police wouldn't help, but I did get a call. A man, a private detective, working for someone in Paris. He was looking for Jeanne Rochas, a person of no fixed abode, who might be travelling alone, or with a younger woman. He even had a photograph. Do you want to see it, Vianne?' And he pulled out from his wallet a black-and-white picture of a child – a little girl of two or three – wearing a sundress and sandals, and carrying a stuffed rabbit that I would have recognized anywhere.

Molfetta.

'So you see, Sylviane. You're not the only one with a past. Maybe you should be thinking of that instead of meddling with mine.'

3

There are some assaults for which not even the strongest spell can prepare. This was one of them; an attack that sent my house of cards flying. I felt my vision darken; my breath caught in my throat like a fishbone. Suddenly I couldn't breathe, and my little Anouk inside me was struggling for deliverance. Once more I was in the confessional, with the choir like birds in the eaves, and the scent of smoke and candle wax, and my voice in the trembling darkness:

You're not my mother! Get away!

Louis watched me with a look that combined hurt and satisfaction. I could feel his bitter triumph behind the shades of his misery. Behind him, I could see Emile, Marinette, Monsieur Georges watching in confused distress. Loïc, too, was watching me, his eyes as dark as the future. I felt my throat tighten, my vision blur. The room was spinning and sparkling like a Christmas bauble. I took a step away from the bar, and found myself falling – down, down – into the vacuum of memory. And it smells like Christmas; like gingerbread and sugar cakes and galette des rois; and it feels like the first gasp of winter, when the sky is only a moment from snow; and it sounds like

364

a distant carillon, and the hush of a crowded cathedral, and I am still in the confessional, eight years old and already making the choices that lead me to this, this moment of discovery.

You're not my mother! Get away!

No, I'm not your mother.

I look up from my place at the back of the church. The wood, dark oak, the cushions sewn from panels of midnight-blue velvet. It might be a box at the opera, except for the scent of incense smoke; and here she is in her red dress, her hair as white as Santa Claus.

'Khamaseen.'

The sense of relief is powerful. All this must be a dream. I must have passed out at La Bonne Mère; somewhere in the church vaulting, I seem to hear their voices, like bats' wings in the darkness.

'If you like.' Her voice is dry. 'Names are a distraction. Your mother was *Mother* because of what she *did*, not because of who she *was*. The question is, who will *you* be? Will you be the woman who rides the wind, picks up hagstones, turns lives with a fork of the fingers? Or will you be the one who pays for your mother's actions? Will you be Vianne, or Mother?'

And now, in the confessional, I understand the choice I must make. Security, or the call of the wind. The chocolaterie, or the highway. My little Anouk in a railway station, late at night, in some nameless town, or a kitchen with knives of my own, and polished copper pans on the wall? And each decision comes at a price; freedom, or discovery.

'Why must I choose?' My voice is small, and I know that this is because I am eight years old; eight years old, and poised between two choices no eight-year-old should have to make.

'Because we choose our family,' she says, and I realize that

365

she is not Khamaseen after all, but Maman, my own beloved Maman, with her curly hair bound in a scarf, and her eyes pinned with golden light. 'We choose them, just as I chose you, and you must make your own choice.'

Choose?

Vianne or Mother. Mother, or Vianne.

'It isn't fair,' I whisper, and now I can smell the paint fumes, see the blur of faces far above mine on the dusty floor. 'It isn't fair. This wasn't my choice.'

And yet I realize, it was. I chose to be here, just as I chose to follow in the path of the wind. *Jeanne Rochas, of no fixed abode, who might be travelling with a child.* I chose to follow that path, that life. I chose to love her as she loved me. And I chose to leave behind the things that had been dearest to me: Molfetta; my home; the people who were my family. Why had I left them behind? Why had I chosen to follow the wind?

'Vianne.' The voice is not Khamaseen's. It is a young voice, cracked with anxiety, and it comes from a long way away, from a place of paint fumes and plaster dust. 'Vianne! Wake up!'

'Loïc.'

His round face was sleek with distress. Louis was standing behind him, and for the first time I saw the similarity between them both; the young face and the old juxtaposed, like phases of the same moon. For a moment I thought of Maman, her strong features which were so different to mine; although we'd come to look alike in travelling together. *You're not my real mother*, I'd said: and yet, I'd never believed it. We choose our family, she'd said. We lay our claim on those we love.

Anouk. I put my hands to the place where she slept, so soft and silent. *Jeanne Rochas, of no fixed abode.* They must have been tracking us for years. They must have had money. They wanted me. To know, to love, to claim me. But to accept my new family, I must reject the old one. And what then? How much scrutiny? How much attention from the press? How many questions to answer; how many broken dreams to mend? How much of me would be left, once they had all taken their piece? And what if they found out I had a child? How soon would they claim her, too?

I tried to sit up.

'Don't move.' It was Louis. His colours had shifted again, and he was no longer angry now; his face a miserable map of all the barren places. 'Don't move, Vianne.'

'I have to go.'

'I'm calling an ambulance,' said Louis. His face was ashen now.

'No ambulance. No doctor.' A hospital leaves a paper trail: a written proof of existence. So much harder to vanish then. My mother always understood. I struggled dumbly to my feet. My throat was as tight as a clenched fist. I could see the faces of my friends in a circle around me, smell hot blood and chocolate.

'I don't need help. I'm fine,' I said. 'I just need to get back home.'

4

3 December 1993

Blindly, I pushed my way outside, where the sunlight was already fading. A garland of lights around the Butte, a corresponding string of lights around the misty harbour. I took a deep breath of the salty air, and almost ran into Khamaseen, who was waiting outside La Bonne Mère, her hair a candyfloss tangle beneath the hood of her winter cloak.

She said: 'I tried to warn you, Vianne. Change is a door that swings both ways. There's a price for what we do. For being who we are.'

I know. It's what my mother believed. But I thought I could be different. I—

'You thought you could escape who you are? You can, but there's a choice to make. The open sky or the warm hearth. The wind that rocks the cradle, or the four walls of domesticity.' She sighed. 'It's going to be hard for you, travelling with a baby. Always living hand to mouth; always staying one step ahead. Always castles in the sand instead of building a permanent home. Handing out dreams to others without ever achieving one of your own. Changing your name at every town; always, forever on the alert. Is that really what you want?'

'*Why* do I have to choose?' I said. 'Why can't I have what other people have?'

'Because you're *not* other people. You can decide who you want to be. The question is, will you be Vianne, or will you be that *other* girl, the one who was taken in Paris?'

I took a deep breath of the winter air. It smelt of incense, and pine wood, and well-lit homes seen from the street, and Christmastime, warm blankets and the magic of an early snow. *Small comforts. Little dreams.* Are we not allowed these things?

'Of course you are,' said Khamaseen. 'But there's a balance. Upset it, and everything goes flying.'

'What balance did my mother upset? Why did she have to pay a price?'

She smiled. 'Because she wanted you. It's the price every mother pays.'

I said: 'My mother had demons. My childhood was infested with them. My child will be different. *I* will be different.'

She gave a sad little smile. 'You want your child to be safe. That's good. But there's a restlessness in you, just like there was in your mother.'

'You never knew my mother,' I said.

'Of course I knew her,' said Khamaseen. 'Just as I know you. Our kind always know one another, Vianne, even when we're in disguise.'

'*Our kind?* What does that mean?'

That smile again. 'You know what it means. We've always been here. We're everywhere. The outsiders. The ones that don't fit. The ones who see beyond the edges of the painting. The ones who are different from the rest. Sometimes, that difference is visible. Sometimes, it's barely perceptible. But they feel it. The knowledge. The *shine.*'

'I don't have any knowledge,' I said.

'You see things in other people. And you hear the voice of the wind. The wind knows who you are, Vianne. She recognizes her children. She's been calling you for months, asking you to make a choice. Will you be Vianne, or that *other* girl? Will you claim your child as your own, or pay the price your mother could not?'

A glimpse of something in the sky; two intersecting vapour trails, scratched against the faded blue. It looks like a rune – Gebo, a gift – and it reminds me of Guy and Mahmed, and all the friends I have made here. I can't abandon them today. I have to finish what I began. I have to help them, one more time.

'I'm doing this for my daughter,' I said. 'So that her life will be different.'

Once more, that gentle, troubling smile. 'You named her, Vianne. You named yourself. In doing so, you made a choice. Power, and the way of the wind. It calls. You answered. It's yours now. To refuse it is to deny yourself, and the person you chose to be.'

'I don't believe that's true,' I said.

'The wind doesn't care what you believe,' she said. 'She only does what she has to do.'

5

I managed to get back home somehow. *Home.* That word again, so barbed with dangerous promises. I'd forgotten my coat in my haste to be gone, and the wind was suddenly biting cold, and the garlands of Christmas lights on the streets looked small and lost against the dark. But when I reached Xocolatl, my heart beating ferociously, I found the display window brightly lit, with fairy lights on the window-ledge and along the shelves of chocolates. Cellophane-wrapped and gleaming like a pirate's buried treasure, they seemed to glow with a precious light, those gilded piles of mendiants, and truffles, rose creams and *santons de Margot*, while above them rose the centrepiece; a statuette of the *Bonne Mère*, much larger than the ones in the shop, one hand raised in benediction, the other holding the infant Christ, and robed in darkest chocolate. And all around the dishes and jars were origami animals; little angular butterflies and cranes and fish and rabbits in multicoloured paper. I detected the hand of Grandmother Li: imagined those clever old hands at work, folding the pretty papers.

I opened the door. Stéphane was there, putting the finishing touches to a glass display case of smaller chocolate figures,

371

each one wrapped in cellophane and tied with a flourish of ribbon. He looked up as I entered, and smiled.

'The girls from Happy Noodles came by to help with the decorations. The paper things were their idea. What do you think? Is it okay?'

I felt a sudden sense of loss, as if something small but very much beloved had been taken away. Then I smiled.

'It's perfect,' I said. 'You didn't really need me at all.'

He looked at me. 'Are you okay? You look a little—'

'Fine, thanks. Any word of Guy?'

He shook his head. 'If he doesn't show, we'll just have to manage together. It'll be fine; we have all the stock. The chocolate fountain's arriving at ten. The sax player at twelve-thirty. The heaters are in place, in case we need to give folk an incentive. Everything's ready. You'll front the shop; Mahmed and I can take turns in the back. Mrs Li and her daughters volunteered to help out, too. We can do this. I promise.'

Stéphane so wants it to be true. I can see it in his face, his good-natured, hopeful smile. He has fought for his place here even more than the rest of us; and he so wants it to succeed. But for me, my time has run out. The Man in Black is at the door. I think of the man who spoke with Guy. Is this the same man who spoke to Louis? And what does he want of Sylviane Caillou, after so many years in the shadows?

My little Anouk, so silent now, clings tight as a promise to my heart. I have done nothing wrong here. I have to keep reminding myself of that. But if I let him talk to me, who knows what we will discover? For the moment, Sylviane Caillou is nothing but a story from a bundle of clippings. Even the photo Louis showed me may be nothing more than coincidence. One stuffed rabbit, one small child looks very like another. But open this box of secrets, and anything could escape. *Jeanne Rochas, of no fixed abode. Who might be travelling with a child.* Imagine the pain of losing a child. Imagine the terrible loneliness. Imagine waking up every day, knowing that someone had taken her. But to acknowledge one family is to reject another. How could I do that to Maman, after all she did for me?

Of course, I said nothing of this to Stéphane. I cannot leave in Guy's absence. I cannot abandon my friends at this, their time of reckoning. In the shop, everything's ready. The checklist of things for the morning – chocolate fountain, gift bags, cards, a trio of cakes and some madeleines to go with the day's hot chocolate – has been checked for the third time. Dinner was a little cold quiche; a simple salad; olives; cheese. Mahmed ate with us, but silently; Guy's absence weighs upon us all. I went to my room and read the cards with a kind of desperation: but nothing made sense, and every hand was the same combination of Change and Death. Finally I fell asleep with the cards on the bedspread beside me, and when I awoke, with a headful of dreams, to the sound of the bells from Notre-Dame, I could hardly remember where I was, or even what I was doing here.

6

Traditionally, the feast of Sainte Barbe marks the start of the Christmas season. Lights along the Canebière; Christmas markets selling *santons*; Christmas trees in the town squares, and every shop window in Marseille displaying the best of their merchandise. And by Notre-Dame, there will be a crèche, and bakeries all the way down the Panier will sell the traditional sachets of wheat, to be germinated and planted in time for the great celebration on Christmas Eve. We've worked so hard to reach this point. So many hours of labour, from sorting piles of cacao beans to making the different chocolates. Now it is ready, and what I feel most is a terrible sense of foreboding. So much depends on what happens today. So many opportunities. And yet the visibility that we have worked so hard to build is also the spotlight that pins me.

Tsk-tsk, begone. This has to work. It has to.

I got up and dressed with unusual care – summer dress, winter boots, hair in a practical ponytail – and washed my face in cold water. Outside, the sky was growing light. A sharp wind came from the ocean. A thrill in the air, like the promise of snow. A rosy pallor in the sky; reflections from the

374

Christmas lights that hang like fruit along Le Panier. Feeling a little better, I went downstairs to make breakfast, and found Stéphane already there, with coffee on the table.

'I couldn't sleep. I got croissants.'

I smiled and took a pastry. I don't have morning sickness any more, but I do need to eat at breakfast. 'Are you ready?' said Stéphane.

'We're all ready,' I told him.

There came the sound of the door opening, and Mahmed came in, wearing an apron, his hair caught up in a topknot. 'Less than two hours to opening time. Everything's ready. Machines are on. Now all we need is the magic.'

At any other time, his words could have been a joke, but today his face was unreadable. The magic, if it was ever there, was part of Guy's belief in us; in his passion for chocolate and in his conviction that we could succeed.

'My mother used to tell me that we have to make our own magic,' I said. 'Here.' I added a pinch of chocolate spice to the pot of coffee; poured a bowl for each of us. Mahmed drank his slowly, eyes half closed through the rising steam. I tried a little finger-sign, to coax a spark from chilly air, but there were no glamours to be found, no colours but the Christmas lights.

'No sign of Guy, then.'

Mahmed shrugged. 'We're on our own. It'll have to do.'

I nodded. 'Of course. And when he comes back—' I hesitated, thinking of Guy in his Toulouse apparel; well-cut suit, slicked-back hair, as comfortable in this guise as in his Hawaiian shirts and straw hat. Which Guy will come back to us? The *chocolatier*, or the stranger?

If he comes back. The words stayed unsaid, but I could feel them in the air, like tiny stinging insects. I poured more coffee and ate my croissant, and wished it could be over.

Stéphane reached into his pocket and brought out a little muslin sachet. 'Wheat seeds,' he said shyly. 'We're supposed to plant these today.'

'Why?' said Mahmed.

'For luck, I suppose. We always did when —' he paused — 'when I lived with my family.' He reached for a saucer. 'Look, like this.' He opened the little bag carefully, then, holding the seeds in one hand, added a little water to the absorbent muslin. 'Now we scatter the seeds on here in three little piles, for the Trinity, and leave them here to germinate.' He took a glass bowl from a cupboard and placed it over the saucer.

'What's that for?'

'It keeps them warm. And stops Pomponette from eating them.' He reached down and stroked the cat, who had been sniffing around under the table. Pomponette gave a rusty purr, and Mahmed almost smiled. 'Oh.'

I like this tradition. It's hopeful, somehow. A dream of something better. On Christmas Eve, the shoots will be there to remind us that nothing starts fully formed, and that with love and hard work, we can grow. I think of the rose in Khamaseen's garden, *Vianne*, the rose that has my name. I too can grow. With hard work, and love, I can grow and flourish.

7

At ten o'clock, the bells of Bonne Mère ring for the end of the
service. They announced our opening. Stéphane went to put
the signs in place at the end of the alleyway: *New chocolaterie
opening today! Everyone welcome!* After a dull start, the sun was
out; the air was crisp and sparkling. We waited; Mahmed in
the back, Stéphane in the alleyway, I in the shop, almost trembling with hope and indecision.

At ten fifteen, I wedged open the door, to make sure
prospective customers knew that we were open. At ten twenty-
five I thought I heard a sound outside, but it was only
Stéphane, lighting the patio heaters on either side of the shop
front. Now they are lit, it looks welcoming. *Everything* looks
welcoming. Bar stools by the counter, to encourage people
to sit. A viewing gallery at the back, for people to watch the
chocolates being made. Behind the counter, on the bar, a
pot of hot chocolate stands ready to be served; three cakes,
under their glass *cloches*; a pile of chocolate madeleines. Still,
there are no customers. Why do they not come? There has
been so much curiosity about the new chocolaterie. Why are
there no customers? What have I done wrong?

377

Ten thirty-five, and a woman wanders into the alleyway. Maybe fifty or older; grey-haired; overcoat the colour of rain. I saw her look into the window; cross the street to come closer. I saw the lights of the window display reflected in her hungry eyes.

'Feel free to come in,' I said. 'Have a cup of chocolate.'

She looked at me suspiciously. I recognized her now as one of the people who came to the van; one of those people Mahmed says will never be our customers. She never talks to us, but takes her little paper cup and dashes away into the crowd, as if she fears that someone will accuse her of stealing. Now she came closer; I saw her face shining with indecision. This woman doesn't buy chocolates. Her home is a women's shelter; her job, cleaning rooms in a cheap hotel. And yet I know that she will love my violet creams, blanketed in dark chocolate: that they will remind her of something she had thought forgotten.

'On the house,' I told her. 'Please, come in. You're welcome.'

She entered, with the cautious look of a wild thing, fearing a trap. I smiled and poured her a cup of spiced hot chocolate from the pot. She took it almost fearfully, handling the china cup with exaggerated care.

'Pretty, isn't it?' I said. 'None of the cups or the saucers match, which is why Stéphane picked them up for almost nothing at the Marché aux Puces. This is how people used to drink chocolate three hundred years ago; sweet, spiced with vanilla, nutmeg, cloves.'

The woman drank her chocolate, and I thought she looked less troubled. 'You're the ones from the chocolate van,' she said. 'I wasn't sure at first. This place is so—' She looked around. I saw her looking at the figures of the Virgin, in dark chocolate, features picked out in a lighter grade; the glass

display cases, with trays of Nipples of Venus, gilded mendiants, coconut clusters, hazelnut swirls. And the dishes filled
with *santons de Margot*; those little chocolate babies in three
different grades of chocolate. 'This place is too fancy for me,'
she said, putting down her chocolate cup. 'I wouldn't even
know what to choose.'

'You don't have to choose,' I told her. 'I bet I know your
favourite.' With the silver sugar tongs, I reached into the
display case and brought out a violet cream.

'Trust me,' I said. 'I have a knack.'

Reluctantly, she accepted it. I watched her eat the chocolate;
wary at first, then tasting, testing every moment. She closed
her eyes. I could see her trying to remember—

My grandmother's house, on Sundays. Her violet perfume. Her
stories. The scent of her wardrobe, filled with clothes that hadn't
been worn for a hundred years; silk scarves, sequinned dresses, and
dancing shoes and ostrich plumes, and it smelt of cedarwood, and
silk, and the ghosts of a thousand matinees—

'Oh, yes,' she said in a soft voice.

'You're my first visitor. On the house.' I made up her gift
– four violet creams, in a box, tied with a pink ribbon – and
gave it to her to take away. She left as if she were walking
on air; her face alight with memories.

From the back, I heard Mahmed say: 'Did she buy anything?'

I shook my head. He went back to work. His silence was
somehow more damning than words.

8

4 December 1993

By eleven, we'd had three more visitors, all of them chocolate van regulars. Two of them in their sixties, with a look I associate with Stéphane; that look of having to try too hard to get what others are given for free. The third was a young man I'd seen before, with a woman and a child; this time he came alone, and bought an assorted gift box, some mendiants and a chocolate Virgin. I gave out cups of hot chocolate to all three of my visitors, with slices of ganache cake, and *santons de Margot* on the house. Mahmed was dismissive; one box doesn't make for a profit, he says, especially given the samples we're handing out for free, but it made me feel better, somehow; as if putting good into the world could make the world a better place.

At ten past eleven, Grandmother Li came in with Françoise and Karine; sighed at the display window with its origami birds, and stayed to drink hot chocolate, while the girls watched Mahmed through the window.

'This is *so* cool,' said Françoise. 'I like to watch how he dips the shapes into the melted chocolate.'

'I like watching the machine go round and round. It's like magic,' said Karine.

Grandmother Li chose four boxes: one of her green tea truffles; assortment boxes for the rest. I told her: 'These are on the house. To thank you all, for your help here.' Behind the glass, Mahmed shook his head, but did not comment further.

At twelve, the chocolate fountain arrived. I set it up on the counter. We should have more people by now. Now, they *must* start coming. Three more chocolate van regulars; two young men and a woman carrying three shopping bags. All of them wide-eyed, hesitant; wondering if they'd be turned away.

I said: 'I know your favourites. 'Here, come try them. On the house.'

Funny, how easy I find this game. I barely even have to look. A hint of colours through the steam that rises from the chocolate pot; a memory of happiness, glimpsed through the gleaming shadows. This man's rough exterior comes with a secret tenderness: he will love my apricot hearts, topped with crushed pistachio. His friend will love my mendiants; the woman will prefer pralines. One by one, I send them away with the sense of something accomplished; I don't know what it is yet, but seeds must take their time to grow.

At last, there's someone from La Bonne Mère. Sweet-toothed Marinette, then Rodolphe, whose favourites are my chilli squares, and finally, in a commotion, there's Tonton, with Galipette, who has discovered Pomponette sitting by the counter. Pomponette hisses; seeks shelter on the top of one of the cabinets. I coax Galipette into silence with a piece of leftover croissant, and pour hot chocolate for my guests, and cut slices of ganache cake.

'How's Louis?' I try to make the question as neutral as possible.

Tonton and Rodolphe exchange glances. '*Bof.* You know Louis. Serving lunch. I don't think he'll be here today.'

'And Loïc?'

Once again, that look. 'He stayed in the bistrot overnight. But Louis says that's it. No more nonsense. The boy goes home today, he says, or there'll be serious trouble.'

That means Loïc stayed all morning. I hid a smile behind my hand. 'What was for lunch?'

'Bouillabaisse. And tiramisù for dessert.'

Bouillabaisse. I smiled again. That *mouli*. I wondered how Loïc had coped with it; if he'd been allowed in the kitchen at all. Somehow I imagined he had; Loïc has a certain way of getting through defences.

'I'll take a box of truffles, please. And a chocolate Virgin.' Marinette's voice was determined. 'A gift to myself this Christmas.'

'Maybe some lemon slices. And a *florentine* for the dog.'

'And for me, a big box of those.' Rodolphe indicated the truffles. 'Maybe I have a lady friend,' he said, when Tonton seemed surprised. 'Maybe I want to impress her with my sophistication.'

I wrapped up their various purchases and tied them with coloured ribbon. The air was starting to shimmer once more with rising steam and coloured lights. I felt my heart lift – *it's working*, I thought – and then I caught sight of a man in black standing in the alleyway. A man of maybe eighty or so; stern-faced, white-haired under a wide-brimmed hat. I expected him to come in, but he stayed where he was, under the heater, watching people come and go. Four more regulars from La Bonne Mère: Amadou, Hélène from the flower shop, Henriot, André from the bakery – plus a handful of tourists, instantly recognizable; accents from London, Paris, Bruges. Five boxes of truffles, three Virgins, a couple of packets of *santons*, and now the saxophone player Guy hired has settled himself on the corner, and has drawn a little crowd, to whom we bring cups of chocolate.

'Grand opening today! Come in! Watch our chocolates being made!' Stéphane is eager to help draw people in, but Françoise and Karine have more success, with their bright eyes and smiling faces.

'Did you know that chocolate has been used for five thousand years?'

'Did you know Montezuma drank fifty cups of chocolate a day?'

Outside the shop, we have installed a handful of little tables and chairs; it's warm there, under the heaters, encouraging people to linger. Stéphane offers the man in black a cup of chocolate; he takes it and sits at a table, still watching the shop. Through the open door comes the scent of freshly prepared hot chocolate; a scent like a dark caress over the little alleyway. The sign from Happy Noodles lights the murals in orange and scarlet; more people come to see the shop, exclaiming over the window display.

There were so many that at first, I hardly noticed Khamaseen, waiting at the edge of the group, eyes like polished hagstones under a moth-coloured headscarf. I glanced at the other customers, but none of them seemed to have noticed her.

I said: 'Have you come to warn me again?'

She shook her head. 'You've made your choice. But I wouldn't say no to some chocolate.'

I poured her a cup. 'On the house.'

She drank it, eyes closed. 'Wonderful. You know, I've missed it here, Vianne. I've missed the sense of community. *You* did that, of course,' she said. 'Made this place visible. Made it *shine*.'

I smiled. 'It's only chocolate.'

She laughed, a surprisingly youthful sound. 'You don't really believe that. You've found a new kind of magic. Not the kind your mother used, but a gentler, sweeter kind. Look.' And she indicated the door, where a trio of people was standing.

'*Vianne!*' A round ungainly shape hurled itself towards me. Loïc flung his arms around me. 'This place is amazing! Is it yours? What are these? Can I try some?' Suddenly the little shop seemed very full of Loïc, as he ran around the display cases, exclaiming at the window display, then stopped at the viewing window, awed into sudden silence.

'*Wow!*'

Behind him, Louis and Emile, both of them looking warily at the piled gift boxes; little sachets of nougatines and mendiants; the chocolate Virgins all in white; the gleaming bouquets of Cellophane.

'Emile! Louis!' I felt a tug of happiness that almost felt like tears. 'You came!'

Emile gave a shrug. 'You said it was free.'

I laughed. 'Of course!' I poured him a cup of hot chocolate, with a rose cream on the side. 'And you, Louis—'

A dry, disapproving sound. 'The boy insisted on coming. He wouldn't give me any peace. He said he'd finally go home as long as we came here first.'

I tried not to smile, but poured him a cup. He made no attempt to take it. He said in a low voice: 'I understand what you tried to do, Vianne. I'm not saying it was *right*, mind you, but I understand.'

I nodded and waited. Some people need time. Louis picked up his cup of chocolate and tasted it reluctantly. I caught the scent of cardamom and star anise, and allspice. This chocolate blend is confessional; teasing out transgressions and fears; promising the solace of change; the peace of absolution.

Emile had said nothing so far, but I knew he was listening. The flame that burns almost constantly around him had intensified; but this time, its colour had shifted to something warmer, more intimate. His friendship with Louis has always been coloured with resentment: a friendship of shared experience rather than genuine liking. Today, though, he is different. Perhaps Loïc has changed him. Or maybe he senses this change in Louis, this reluctant letting-go.

'You think you know me,' said Louis. 'You think you know about Margot. But Margot was never mine. We married because she was pregnant. And when she lost the child at three months—' He lowered his voice. 'I was *happy*. Because I knew it wasn't mine. Because I knew she loved someone else.'

Once more I thought of my mother's cards, and the ones I had drawn when I first arrived. The Two of Coins. Change. The Lovers, the Fool, the Hermit, the Six of Sorrows. And finally, I saw the thread that bound them all together, not in the vapours, not in the cards, but in his colours, and in Louis'. A tale of one woman and two men, bound together by friendship, and love, and sorrow, and hope, and jealousy. A woman disillusioned by the men who claimed to love her, seeking unconditional love, and finding it in motherhood—

'You idiot, Louis,' said Emile. Both of us turned to look at him. 'Is *that* what you thought for all those years?'

Louis stared at him, uncomprehending.

'It was a stupid mistake, that's all. A one-night stand, that meant nothing to her. She loved you. She'd always loved you.'

For a long time Louis was silent. Then he said: 'She told you that?'

'She didn't have to,' said Emile. 'Louis, I was there. I know.'

The group of customers had gone. Only Loïc remained inside, staring through the display-window glass, fascinated by Mahmed and his chocolate-making. Khamaseen, too, had faded away, although I thought I saw her outside, standing in the scarlet light from the Happy Noodles sign. Night was falling: I could see Stéphane had placed tea-lights on the tables. The sound of saxophone music came plaintively from the alleyway. And the Man in Black was still sitting at his table, a cup of hot chocolate by his side, his face consumed in shadow.

'So it was you,' Louis said at last. His colours were close to breaking. 'You were the father. I never knew. Margot never told me.'

'Because it didn't matter,' said Emile. 'She loved you, Louis, even when you tried to push her away. And now you're doing the same to the boy Vianne took so much trouble to find.'

Louis turned to face me again. 'Why did you come here?' he said. 'We were happy before you came.'

'No, you weren't,' said Emile. 'You were dead before she came. Now you're alive, and sometimes it hurts.'

Louis watched us both in silence for what seemed like forever. The distress in his colours was gone, replaced by something more than grief; maybe even more than love. 'I told him you'd already moved away.' His voice was almost a whisper. 'That man from Paris. The private eye. I didn't tell him anything.'

'I never thought you had,' I said. I handed Louis a little box of *santons de Margot*. To Emile, a sachet of rose creams. To Loïc, a white chocolate mouse, wrapped in crinkly Cellophane and tied with a long, curly ribbon. 'Go ahead. They're on the house. I happen to know they're your favourites.'

9

By the time they left, it was dark. The cakes and madeleines were gone, and we were down to the last cup of chocolate. Outside, the saxophone player packed up his things and went home, although the customers still came and went, buying Christmas chocolates. At my count, we have already sold forty-two chocolate Virgins, five dozen Christmas assortments, eighty sachets of *santons*, and many more of chocolate mice, Nipples of Venus, mendiants, and the thirteen desserts of Christmas, re-imagined in chocolate. Louis almost has to drag Loïc away from the viewing area, only coaxing him to leave by promising to teach him how to make his mother's tapenade. As they leave, I hand Loïc the river stone with the footprint.

'This is yours,' I tell him. 'To remind you that we all make our mark. Even in the smallest ways, we can put good into the world.'

Six forty-five, and it's time to close. The man in black is still there, sitting at his table: now, in the lull at the end of the day, he finally gets up and enters. I've known this moment was coming, of course. I've played it back and forth in my mind. His questions, and my answers. The moment of confrontation.

He came in; an elderly man in a suit and an expensive-looking coat. Now that he is closer, I see his clever, mobile face; his eyes a surprisingly sunny blue beneath the dark fedora hat. He looks about eighty, but hale and alert; the suit under the winter coat is not black, but charcoal-grey.

'Welcome to Xocolatl,' I said. 'Please, let me pour you some chocolate.'

The man in black gave a quizzical smile, but accepted a cup of hot chocolate, and drank it as he inspected the shop. I saw him linger over the trays of Seville orange slices, mendiants, black and white nougat, chocolate dates, chilli truffles, apricot creams, navettes, quince jellies, *calissons*; those sweet temptations, candied dreams, tiny fragments of history, kept under glass like butterflies, awaiting their moment to unfold.

Finally he turned and said: 'You can't be turning a profit, giving out so many samples.'

I smiled again, feeling suddenly cold. 'We had to make a name for ourselves. We can't take goodwill for granted.'

'Why not? Don't people like chocolate in Marseille?'

I tried to explain; the challenge of starting a business in the Panier; the initial resistance; the outreach; the chocolate van; the hours of preparation, and now, the hope that today would mark the turn of a new page for Guy and Mahmed.

'The owners?' said the man in black. 'And who are you?'

'A friend,' I said. 'They gave me a job when I needed one. Taught me all about chocolate. Did you know that chocolate was used by .the—'

'Mayans and Aztecs,' he said. 'And before them, the Olmecs and the Mayo-Chinchipe. Its use goes back many thousands of years, long before the birth of Christ. Columbus was a parvenu. Like so many of his kind.' He smiled. 'Forgive me. I happen to know quite a lot about chocolate.'

I smiled again, feeling stiff and forced. 'I'm sorry. I didn't catch your name?'

'That's because I didn't tell you. I'm Ghislain Ducasse. And you?'

'Vianne Rocher.'

'How apt.' He gave a smile. 'I seem to remember something different in *Le Petit Marseillais*.'

'The paper got both our names wrong,' I said. 'They thought I was Guy's partner.'

He has a surprisingly sunny smile, illuminating his features. 'Local papers. What do they know? I'm very pleased to meet you, Vianne. This place is something special.'

Now he'll start asking questions, I thought. *Where were you born? Are you from Marseille? Have you ever heard the name Jeanne Rochas? Sylviane Caillou?*

Instead, he said: 'What's your favourite?'

I must have looked confused. That's *my* trick; no one ever asks me which chocolate I prefer.

'Let me guess,' said the man in black, and, looking over the display, seemed to consider the chocolates, the candied fruits, the *nougatines*. Lingered for a moment over the green tea truffles; the salted pralines. Then he looked up, and his sea-blue eyes were filled with crazed reflections.

'You didn't like chocolate at first,' he said. 'You never used to eat it. But now, you're starting to understand. Its power to awaken the past; its dark and troubled history. The stories it tells about itself. Its many re-inventions. Ah. Here we are.' He paused at a tray of chocolate-dipped cherries, still with the stalks attached, and said. 'These, I think, Vianne Rocher. Dark chocolate, not always your favourite, but here, with cherries, it evokes something almost magical. Bite through the bitter chocolate shell to the brandied fruit inside. Hold the little

stone on the tongue. Roll it gently around your mouth, like
a long-kept secret.' He smiled, and I found myself liking him
in spite of the coldness in my heart: the Man in Black has a
kind of charm that I would never have suspected.

I said: 'You may be right, *monsieur*. Yours is—' *A gilded thread
in the air. A little bastide on the Garonne. Not Vianne, but somewhere
close; light, like the bloom on an apricot, a sky like the edge of forever—*

I said, in a slightly trembling voice: 'Apricot hearts. They're
your favourite.' I reached into the display case, using the silver
sugar tongs. 'Here, try one. On the house.'

He smiled again; took the chocolate. 'I don't think I've
ever tasted these. My local man doesn't make them.'

'Your local man?' I took a deep breath, feeling suddenly dizzy
and disoriented. Sat on the stool behind the bar. Caught the scent
of incense smoke and Christmas on the salty air. *He knows me,*
I thought. *He's toying with me. Somehow he sees who I really am—*

The Man in Black finished his chocolate. 'You may be
right,' he said at last. 'What do you call these?'

'Apricot hearts.'

'I'll take a box. Here, keep the change.'

My heart was still beating furiously as I wrapped his choco-
lates and tied them with a ribbon. *Is he playing games with me?
Will he turn at the door and say: 'I know who you are, Sylviane
Caillou. You'll never escape who you once were?'*

He took the box and smiled at me. 'Thanks again, Vianne
Rocher. Give my regards to my grandson. I'm always happy
to invest in a thriving business. After all, we graduates of the
Liars' Academy should always stick together.'

And then I saw someone at the door, a figure in a Hawaiian
shirt under a battered overcoat, and felt my heart fly like a
rocket. 'I'm sorry I missed the opening,' said Guy. 'I see
you've already met my pépé?'

10

4 December 1993

'Guy!' My cry alerted Stéphane. We both went to embrace him. He smelt of old wool stored in mothballs, and of the chocolaterie. 'But where have you been? We all wondered if you were ever coming back!'

He grinned. 'You don't get rid of me as easily as that,' he said. 'But I had business in Toulouse. My father phoned the other day. Made it clear that if I didn't go to see him immediately, then any financial assistance I hoped to get from the family – including my allowance, plus any inheritance to come – would be cut off without delay.' He paused, and his gaze moved beyond me, to where Mahmed had left his place in the preparation area, and was standing, stone-faced, hair in his eyes, round the back of the counter.

'Turns out somebody sent him a copy of the article.'

Mahmed shrugged, but I sensed his apprehension. 'And what did you say?'

'I told him it was nonsense.'

Mahmed stiffened imperceptibly.

'I said Vianne wasn't my partner,' said Guy, 'but that I'd been living with a man who was much more than just a friend.'

391

Still Mahmed seemed not to react, but I saw his colours shifting. 'And what did he say to that?'

Guy shrugged. 'Cut off my allowance immediately, and told me to get back to Marseille.' He gave his old familiar smile. 'I'm done with being someone I'm not,' he said. 'I'm done with expectations.' He looked at Mahmed. 'And I'm done with living half a life. I want to do this on my own terms—whatever *this* turns out to be.'

I looked for distress in his colours, but saw nothing but liberation. 'So – how will you manage?' I said at last.

'We'll manage,' said Guy. 'My grandfather says he'll invest in our business. Says he believes in what we do. Wanted to meet you, and see for himself. And it wouldn't be a gift, but a business loan, to be repaid.' He grinned at Mahmed. 'What do you say?'

Mahmed shrugged.

'I mean, we'll be bankrupt by Easter,' he said. 'Probably sooner at this rate.' Then he smiled, and his face transformed. For the first time in weeks, I could see him again; the warmth, the mischief, the friendship, the love.

'Magic beans,' he said. 'I'm in.'

Vianne

Epilogue

The first of January, and the wind has finally decided to change. A strange, warm wind from the south-west, bringing with it the scent of salt, and the glamour of other places. For a moment I remember New York, and the fireworks on that Fourth of July, and the smell of diesel on the wind, and the blush of fried, sugared dough on the air. But then I think of the village called Vianne; the little *bastide*, with its massive walls and tiny lancet windows; and the riverboats on the brown Baïse, with the smoke rising from the chimneys. And the thought is like a little voice, an echo of the future, repeating softly:

Which will it be? Will it be Vianne, or Mother?

I have not seen Khamaseen since the day of the opening of the chocolaterie. Perhaps she has already moved on, like the desert wind of her name that blows for fifty days at a time over Egypt and North Africa. Besides, I know what I must do: the wind has its own way of speaking.

Christmas Eve at Xocolatl was both poignant and celebratory. We invited some friends for dinner, and I made Margot's *soupe à l'oignon*, and her herb-roasted chicken with pastis and green grapes, served on a bed of fennel. Loïc has gained confidence during his time at La Bonne Mère. His parents have come over to stay for a couple of weeks in Marseille, and have cautiously approved their son's urge to find his father. And Louis' gruff demeanour has veered to a kind of tolerance, punctuated from time to time by a bark of unwilling laughter. Yes, Louis Martin *laughs* now. It is a miracle Emile assumes to be a sign of senility. And yet he too has been known to display signs – not quite of hilarity, but certainly of improved good cheer, in spite of his avowed hatred of Christmas, and church, and festivals, and the clergy.

My mother's cards are back in their box. I have not looked at them since the eve of Xocolatl's Grand Opening. My clothes, too, have been put away in boxes to give to charity. The one pair of boots that still fit me – my feet have swollen in pregnancy – are well-worn, seam-stretched, comfortable. My clothes, too, are good for travelling. A pair of oversized cargo pants; a knitted sweater; a pea coat. And I have taken to carrying my bag – with my papers, my mother's cards, the pink bootees, the map book – with me every time I go out, in case of sudden developments.

Ten o'clock; and the sound of the bells strikes me like a crosswind. The Good Mother is almost raucous today; clashing against the hard blue sky like a call to battle. And there's a wind from the top of the Butte; a cold, dry wind, like the Mistral, bringing with it the scent of sage and spices from the hills. Two winds; one warm, one icy; each with its own set of stories.

Which one? Vianne or Mother? The cold clash of the bells on the Butte, or the whisper of the water? Either way seems hard today, and yet it will be no easier tomorrow, or the next day. And my Anouk is ready to go, scenting out the trail of the wind like an eager puppy. I turn towards the top of the Butte, where Bonne Mère looks down from her golden perch, her infant in her arms. Whose was the toy rabbit I found that day? Did it find its way back to the child who left it by the confessional? Was it a sign for me to hold on, or to leave behind my past?

'So, have you decided yet?'

I turn, expecting Khamaseen. But turning, all I see is Stéphane, wearing his coat and woolly hat, and carrying his duffel bag, and his wicker basket. Inside the basket, Pomponette gives a low, impatient yowl.

'Decided what?' I look at him. 'Stéphane, where are you going?'

He gives his sweet and damaged smile. 'I might ask you the same thing. Don't think I haven't noticed you, hanging around the station, the docks? You're trying out ways to leave. I know. I've done that often enough myself.'

'But there's no reason for *you* to leave! You've earned your place. You *love* it here!'

'I'm not letting you go alone.' His expression is gentle, and adamant. 'I know people in Toulouse. People on the river. River-rats, they call them. They're a good community. Working, helping each other get by. I travelled with them once, for a time, before the booze got hold of me. But if you want to go that way, I can help you get there.'

I smile. 'You're already helping, Stéphane.'

Looking into his colours, I see the deep division in his heart. The need to do something to pay for the things he did when he was first in Marseille; his years of alcoholism; his failed and abusive marriage. I see his love for Allée du Pieu; for the crew at Happy Noodles; for Mahmed and Guy; for the Li family; for all the little community we have built with nothing but hope and chocolate. And yet he is willing to give that away, to go back to a life of uncertainty.

I smile at him, and make the sign that I have watched Khamaseen use so many times. A tiny scrawl of light in the air; almost a benediction. I see it mirrored in his eyes; a glow that could be a reflection of the Virgin on the Butte; or a memory of home, or the promise of new beginnings.

I whisper: 'Go home, and be happy, Stéphane. Only daughters follow the wind.'

And I leave him there by the water's edge, with a dreaming smile on his face. In a few minutes' time, he will hear Pomponette yowling from her basket, and return to the here and now, but a few minutes is all I need.

The soft wind from the south-west calls in a voice like my mother's. *Italy*, it whispers. *Greece. Corsica, Sardinia.* Its name is *Sirocco, Levante, Ostrale*, and sometimes even *Khamaseen*, and it promises magic, and freedom, and love. But that cold, clean wind from the north-north-east has a chilly charm of its own: its name is Mistral, and it calls to me in a voice I think I know; a voice I first heard when I opened the map and saw the village with my name. The voice of an unknown future.

Vianne or Mother? Which will it be?

The bells have stopped their carillon, and everything is silent again. But for the whisper of the wind, and the sounds of waves on the pier. I reach into my travelling bag and pull out my mother's map book. The road to Vianne is marked in blue; the river Garonne, and its tributaries, branching all across the page. I think of Stéphane's river-rats. *Working, helping each other get by.* Follow the river, and the Man in Black will not know how to find me. And there will be a community; travelling people just like me; following the river's call, moving with the seasons. Will this be the place, Anouk? Or will it be just another place on a road that never ends? In any case, the choice is mine. Not my mother's. Not this time.

I close the map book and replace it in the bag's inside pocket. Behind me, the cries of the gulls on the wind are scratches of silver in the sky. And it smells of smoke, and the carnival, and of the river in the sun, and sugared dough fried on the hot plate, and herbs to heal a troubled heart. I walk from the harbour and do not look back.

Vianne, or Mother?

Vianne it is.

Acknowledgements

It takes a community to make a book; just as it takes a family to bring a recipe to life. Heartfelt thanks to my own family, especially to Kevin and Fred, without whom none of this story would ever have been written. Thanks too to my agent, Jon Wood, and to all my adopted family at Orion: Charlotte Mursell, my editor; copy-editor, Marian Reid, jacket designer Charlotte Abrams-Simpson, publicist Francesca Pearce and Yadira de Trinidade in Comms. My thanks to Notre-Dame de la Garde, and all the city of Marseille: I hope she will forgive me the liberties I have taken with her. Thanks to all the book-sellers, bloggers, Tik-tokkers, and social media friends who always help to spread the word. And thanks, most especially, to you; to the readers who have followed Vianne throughout this twenty-five year journey. Without your affection and loyalty we could never have come this far. Finally, my thanks to Vianne, wherever, whoever she may be: her story isn't over yet, but at least, I know how it begins.

Credits

Joanne Harris and Orion Fiction would like to thank everyone at Orion who worked on the publication of *Vianne* in the UK.

Editorial
Charlotte Mursell
Snigdha Koirala

Copyeditor
Marian Reid

Proofreader
Linda Joyce

Audio
Paul Stark
Louise Richardson

Contracts
Rachel Monte
Ellie Bowker

Design
Charlotte Abrams-Simpson

Editorial Management
Charlie Panayiotou
Jane Hughes
Bartley Shaw

Finance
Jasdip Nandra
Nick Gibson
Sue Baker

Marketing
Yadira Da Trindade

Publicity
Francesca Pearce

Production
Ruth Sharvell

Operations
Jo Jacobs

Sales
David Murphy
Esther Waters
Victoria Laws
Rachael Hum
Ellie Kyrke-Smith
Frances Doyle
Georgina Cutler